World Birds

Brian P. Martin

GUINNESS BOOKS

EDITOR: Honor Head
DESIGN AND LAYOUT: Michael Morey

© Brian P. Martin and Guinness Superlatives Ltd, 1987

Published in Great Britain by Guinness Superlatives Ltd, 33 London Road,
Enfield, Middlesex

Phototypeset in 10/11pt Linotron Palatino by
Input Typesetting Ltd, London SW19 8DR
Printed and bound in Great Britain by
Butler and Tanner, Somerset.

'Guinness' is a registered trade mark of Guinness Superlatives Ltd

British Library Cataloguing in Publication Data

Martin, Brian P.
  Guinness world birds.
  1. Birds
  I. Title
  598 QL673
  ISBN 0–85112–891–2

Contents

Introduction   4

Extinct Birds   5

Bird Populations & Distribution   19

The Bird Machine   77

Endurance & Performance   99

Breeding   137

The Search For A Meal   159

Birds & Man   165

Glossary   188

Acknowledgements   189

Index   191

Introduction

Birds are at once the most beautiful, most widely admired, most entertaining and most studied group of animals on earth. In capturing our imagination they reign supreme and thus have done more to promote wildlife conservation and care of the environment than all other creatures put together.

Their variety is enormous. Some 9,000 species – more than twice the number of mammals – survive in every habitat in every continent. No country is too hot for them and none too cold. No mountain bars their way and even the smallest among them can cross the world's oceans.

Many flourish through great adaptability and are extremely widespread, but others are so specialized in form and behaviour they remain localized and then often endangered. Some have been living in our backyards for centuries, but others have always gone unnoticed in deep, distant jungles and are only now coming to the attention of science. Within this great diversity of life, the specialist, unique and record-holding species are specially deserving of our attention.

Despite their most enviable mobility, birds remain threatened by all the environmental evils of the day. Pollution and human population growth are serious enough, but the major battle is against continuing worldwide habitat destruction. Whether it's nibbling away at the green belt in suburban England or America, or wholesale destruction of tropical forests, the erosion goes on day in day out, year after year. And as a result we have almost certainly lost many species before they could even be recorded by science.

Fortunately, such headway has been made in recent years the way is open for a rethink of the conservation ethic. And this is where record birds can play their part. Instead of putting all their energies into setting up reserves and saving endangered species, conservationists are now striving to get a better deal for all wildlife. The green revolution is certainly underway, but in order to achieve success conservation must be emphasized more in our education systems. Then the effort will be more positive, thinking of the future and not always fighting that clichéd rearguard action.

And what better way to win more friends or gain the attention of young people than by stimulating their interest in these spectacular, fascinating and remarkable creatures and all that stands to be lost if we do not safeguard their future? Therefore it is my earnest hope that the wonderful birds I have described in this book will arouse that special excitement which can so easily lead to a lifetime's devotion to birds.

Increasingly we are all concerned with birds and conservation on an international scale, for all the good done in caring countries can be rapidly undone when migratory species fly to less sympathetic climes. *World Birds* should help to focus on critical areas. And all the time we are getting more and more feedback as birdwatchers with increasing mobility are just as likely to spend several weeks birding abroad as they are to make trips to the local reserve. Now they are even visiting Antarctica, where the greatest bird record holder of all – the emperor penguin – resides.

I have made every effort to be as accurate as possible, but there is obviously far less research and recording done in the less-developed parts of the world, where there is often more interest in putting a bird in the pot than ringing it. But one day more observations and statistics will emerge from the isolated corners of this planet and then my facts will need revising. At the same time all bird populations will continue to expand or contract and no figures will ever be static. Thus I will always be pleased to receive more up-to-date information from any source whatsoever.

Brian P. Martin

Extinct Birds

Unfortunately birds do not fossilize at all well. Most specimens are broken up and scattered by scavengers and weather, and in many instances data such as weight and shape must be estimated from incomplete specimens. Rarity of bird fossils is also thought to be due to the fact that the majority of species have always lived on the land, where preservation is far less likely. But where birds have died in water or have been carried off by streams or wave-action after death, skeletons have often been buried in muds and silts where the prospects of fossilization are much greater. Therefore there are great gaps in our knowledge of extinct birdlife, especially of species whose habitats were away from standing water or marsh.

Furthermore, there has been a distinct lack of interest in fossil birds among researchers. So far fewer than 2,000 fossil species of bird have been described, including over 900 extinct fossil species. A mere 15 or so research paleontologists have been involved in the identification of over three-quarters of extinct-bird fossils, against the hundreds of researchers who have been attracted to and closely involved with the often spectacularly large fossil reptiles and mammals.

What we can say for sure is that birds have a far greater ancestry than ours, and their variety, while still enormous, is much less than it once was. It has been estimated that there were most bird species – some 10,600 compared with the 8,650 or so today – during the Pleistocene epoch of between 2–3 million and 10,000 years ago. None is thought to have evolved during the last 25,000 years or so and it has been estimated that (based on known fossil species and our present avifauna) the total number of species which have ever lived is about 154,000.

Sadly, the number of extinctions has grown rapidly throughout recent history as habitat destruction, pollution and competition with introduced species have intensified. Even in today's increasingly conservation-conscious society bird species continue to become extinct, especially in the so-called developing countries where economic survival is the main spur, and many species are thought to have faded away over the last few hundred years without science ever recording or describing them properly.

Over 80 full species and 50 subspecies have ceased to exist since the beginning of the 18th century. About 35% of these went between 1850 and 1900 (21 between 1885 and 1907 – eight from the Hawaiian Islands alone). Most of the 10 extinct continental species disappeared in the early years of this century. Island forms have been particularly vulnerable as they evolved in the absence of human and other predators and therefore succumbed quickly when man arrived with his attendant rats, domesticated animals and guns.

AD 1600 is the boundary date for historic extinctions accepted by the International Union for the Conservation of Nature Species Survival Commission. Some of the fossil evidence they consider is only a few hundred years old and includes all avian remains which are not accompanied by written historical documentation. The most important and most common avian fossil is bone, both mineralized and unmineralized, but mummified skins, eggshells, feathers, feather impressions, gizzard stones and footprints have all added to our knowledge. In just a few cases, for example moas, rock drawings have been accurate enough to build up a good picture of a species' external appearance.

THE EARLIEST BIRD IN THE WORLD
ARCHAEOPTERYX – over 140 million years ago

Until further research is done on recently discovered fossils, the first known bird is *Archaeopteryx lithographica von Meyer* from the late Jurassic period of over 140 million years ago. These remains do not represent the so-called missing link between reptiles and birds, but they do confirm the reptilian ancestry of birdlife. First described by von Meyer in Germany in 1861, the remains consist of five partial skeletons and one isolated feather and provide the best evidence of bird evolution that we have accepted so far. About the size of a raven and with an estimated mass of 270 g (9.52 oz), it is thought to have been a weak flyer, the relatively small brain indicating a poor quality of sensory-motor co-ordination for flight.

Archaeopteryx is maintained in a

Archaeopteryx, the world's earliest known bird, may now be dethroned by recent fossil finds. (Suzanne Alexander)

sub-class of its own – the Sauriurae – and its features suggest that it was not a direct ancestor of modern birds. It differs from every other known bird in lacking an ossified sternum, but it has been demonstrated that the arrangement of the shoulder girdle with a sort of surrogate sternum could have supported flight muscles. The wing feathers were at least long enough to facilitate lengthy gliding, and feather impressions reveal that the feathers were of a modern type.

Controversy continues over whether Archaeopteryx was arboreal (tree-dwelling) or terrestrial (ground-dwelling). Clawed digits on the wings might have been used for clambering about trees, but they might have served equally well in manipulating food or prey capture. It probably caught insects and small vertebrates such as lizards, the skull having a pointed snout with teeth resembling those of crocodilians. The long tail was not flexible and tended to move as a unit so that flight manoeuvres would have been difficult compared with those of modern birds. But the claws resemble those of modern birds, and are long, sharp and curved back. One other feature which would have made sustained flight awkward is the non-pneumatic bone structure. Development of air spaces within the bones to reduce weight occurred late in avian evolution and did not feature in the skeletons of Archaeopteryx, nor in the extinct Hesperornis and Icthyornis which came after Archaeopteryx.

As interest in paleontology develops it is quite likely that fossil birds older than Archaeopteryx will be found. Indeed, there are already two serious claimants which are gradually being evaluated by the scientific establishment. For over ten years now Dr James Jensen, of Brigham Young University in the USA, has contended that in Jurassic times there was a bird far more advanced in flight than Archaeopteryx. His theory is based on fragmentary remains he found in

the Western Colorado Dry Mesa Quarry and he named his type specimen *Paleopteryx thomsoni*. He was the first to claim in scientific print (1981) that birds capable of 'powered flight' (which Archaeopteryx was probably not) were evolved earlier than Archaeopteryx. The British Museum comments that some of the Jensen elements appear bird-like, but are no more bird-like than Archaeopteryx, while others contend that Paleopteryx does not have avian affinities.

Then, in August 1986, Texas Tech University paleontologist Sankar Chatterjee pronounced that Archaeopteryx had been dethroned by his *Protoavis* ('first bird'), which is said to have lived 75 million years before Archaeopteryx. His contention was based on two fragmentary fossil skeletons found in the arid 'badlands' of western Texas in 1984. Protoavis is said to have been contemporaneous with the earliest dinosaurs and crow-sized, being even more bird-like than its younger cousin. Chatterjee points out that while both species have wishbones and forelimbs elongated into wings, the older fossil has a bird's wide eye sockets, a large braincase and a breastbone designed to anchor muscles used in flight. And tiny bumps along the forelimbs of Protoavis indicate where feathers could have been attached.

Found in 225-million-year-old rocks near Post in Texas, Protoavis had four teeth in the upper part of its jaw but had lost the teeth in the back part of its jaw, indicating that it was more advanced than Archaeopteryx with its full set of teeth. Protoavis also had hollow (and therefore lightweight) bones. Its skull in particular suggests that it was a bridge between the dinosaur and the bird. The ears of the Texas fossil are well developed, indicating that the birds communicated through sound whereas most dinosaurs were mute. Moreover, dinosaurs, like modern crocodiles, had two holes in the temple behind the eyes to accommodate muscle bulges. In both modern birds and Protoavis these holes have merged with the eye socket (which is why birds' eyes are large in relation to body size).

The powerful hind legs also indicate probable dinosaur heritage, as do the clawed fingers. Thus Protoavis seems to have been far more advanced than Archaeopteryx, which is likely to have been a side-branch of avian evolution. This makes evolutionary sense of the proliferation and diversity of bird species that began about 100 million years ago. The similarity of some fossil birds to modern families has long suggested that they shared an ancestor far older than Archaeopteryx.

Whatever the world's paleontologists make of Protoavis and Paleopteryx, it is virtually certain that other bird remains will one day be found to help piece together this gigantic jigsaw. At the time of going to press, Dr Chatterjee had not yet published his findings in a scientific paper and doubtless will have a great struggle in convincing the world that Archaeopteryx is no longer the world's earliest known bird.

THE EARLIEST BIRD IN BRITAIN
ENALIORNIS – 100–108 million years ago

Little is known about this bird, which appears to have been little larger than a pigeon, as there have been no further finds since those of the 1850s and 60s. In 1858 Lucas Barrett of the then Woodwardian Museum in Cambridge discovered the remains in the Cambridge Greensand at Coldham Common between Grantchester and Cambridge. Later there were further finds, the material consisting of several unassociated fragments, including a cranium and several limb fragments which are thought to represent the remains of a diver/grebe-like bird which Professor H. G. Seeley attempted to describe in 1864. For various reasons the original names were not acceptable and it was not until 1869

that Seeley provided a valid description of the material, which included the creation of a single genus, Enaliornis, and two species, barretti and sedgwicki. There was subsequent disagreement as to the exact age of the specimens, but they are now regarded as being Lower Cretaceous (Albian), for they are thought to have been derived from a slightly older deposit than the Cambridge Greensand.

Enaliornis is one of a small number of fossil birds from the Cretaceous period and so far no other species have been found to represent the 30 or so million years between them and Archaeopteryx. They are all obviously similar to modern birds, and thus many 'missing' links remain to be found.

In 1973 C. A. Walker and C. Harrison of the British Museum (Natural History) described a fragmentary humerus from the Wealden of Sussex, which is somewhat older than Enaliornis. They named the specimen Wyleyia valdensis, but as there is some considerable argument about its avian affinities it is being disregarded at present.

There are numerous fossil birds from Britain, which have been found in sediments of various ages. Possibly the most extensive avifauna known from 60 million years ago has been collected from the Lower Eocene deposits of south-east England.

THE HEAVIEST BIRD THAT EVER LIVED
DROMORNIS STIRTONI – over 500 kg (1,100 lb)

Weighing half a ton, Dromornis was one form of a group of giant birds (family Dromornithidae), unique to Australia, which lived between some 15 million and 26,000 years ago, perhaps even much more recently. Though emu-like, they certainly were not emus and have come to be called the Mihirung birds. Some were only slightly larger than the modern emu, but stirtoni was over 3 m, almost 10 ft high.

Remains from a site near Alice Springs in the Northern Territory show that stirtoni lived alongside two much smaller forms of Dromornis and Aboriginal man. This was in the Pliocene and Miocene epochs, between 2.5 and nine million years ago. Yet fossil birds of up to 130 million years ago are known from Australia.

During the Miocene period central Australia must have been decidedly wetter and had a more predictable climate. It was inhabited by some very familiar forms, such as emus, ducks, pelicans, cormorants and rails, as well as some very unfamiliar and unpredictable forms such as dromornithids and modern flamingoes. Pollen collected from sediments of similar age in the area indicate much higher rainfall with forests of southern beech and many lakes surrounded by lush vegetation.

In such an environment there was a clear niche for grazing animals, which is what the dromornithids were. Plant material is generally of low nutritive value and needs to be ingested in bulk to yield viable energy levels. Thus generally herbivorous mammals and birds tend to be large to maximize feeding efficiency.

Dromornis and the other Mihirungs had very deep lower jaws, hoof-like toe bones and a distinctly shaped bone called the quadrate connecting the upper and lower jaws. Their lack of down-curving claws and a hook on the beak also suggests that they were plant eaters rather than carnivores. Their jaws were capable of withstanding large forces and were very unlike the slender jaws of emus and cassowaries, but their precise diet remains a mystery.

These great birds appear to have been most successful in the forest environments which characterized

The Australian Dromornis stirtoni grew to half a ton on a diet of plants. (Suzanne Alexander)

much of Australia for much of the Cainozoic period. But as the climate changed, the forests contracted and the grasslands expanded, the dromornithids were increasingly unable to cope with the rise and diversification of the kangaroo, which adapted superbly to new openings for grazing animals. What dealt the final blow to the dromornithids is unknown, though man might have had a hand in causing the eventual extinction.

Five genera and eight species of dromornithids are currently recognized.

THE TALLEST BIRD THAT EVER LIVED
DINORNIS MAXIMUS –
3.7 m (12 ft)

The giant moa Dinornis maximus was less than half the weight of Dromornis stirtoni, at about 227 kg (500 lb), but it was significantly taller, the largest of many skeletons found measuring 3.7 m (12 ft). The 12 species of moa so far identified were wingless, cursorial (limbs adapted for running) ratites endemic to New Zealand and they are all extinct. However, some became extinct only within the last few centuries and they were certainly hunted by Maoris.

The name moa was taken from the widespread Polynesian word for chicken after European settlers had found bones of giant extinct birds. Remains were first exhibited in 1839 and gradually a great mass of material has been discovered, enabling us to construct a fairly accurate picture of these remarkable birds. For example, between 1937 and 1949 44 fairly complete skeletons of Dinornis maximus, ranging from 3 m (10 ft), were found in Pyramid Valley, Moa Swamp, North Canterbury on South Island. There have been many other Dinornis bones, eggshell, a few unbroken eggs, a few feathers and pieces of skin, some gizzard contents, occasional footprints and associated plant and animal remains to provide clues.

Most moas were strong and generally slow-moving birds, but capable of bursts of reasonable speed, and they probably had the loop-necked stance of emus rather than the erect carriage of the ostrich. Their great height and long, flexible necks would have been a great asset in reaching food and they appear to have been entirely herbivorous, seeds, berries and shoots of a wide variety of shrubs and forest trees having been found in gizzard contents. As with all browsing animals, their bulk would accommodate efficient digestion of food with relatively low energy value.

There are accounts of white settlers seeing moas after Cook's first visit of 1769, but radiocarbon dating suggests that the birds were never common after the 15th century. Although man seems to be responsible for the extinction of all the moas by about 1800, some large areas of suitable habitat did remain and were never disturbed. Thus it is possible that at least one of the smaller moas survived beyond 1900.

OTHER EXTINCT HEAVYWEIGHTS

Apart from dietary adaptation, great size has been of benefit to terrestrial flightless birds in compensating for their inability to escape into the air. This has been more pronounced in continental species which had to offer significant defence against a wide range of predators, but less marked in island endemics where few predators existed before man came along.

AEPYORNIS MAXIMUS
(The Elephant Bird)

For a long time this was thought to be the heaviest bird ever but it is now thought to have tipped the scales at 'only' about 450 kg (almost 1,000 lb), and stood 3 m (10 ft) high. The three genera of these flightless ratites (Aepyornis) appear to have been confined to Madagascar and were primitive members of the ostrich-rhea-emu lineage. These giants had strong, conical bills and only vestigial wings. The four *Aepyornis* species (there are also three of *Mullerornis* in the *Aepyornithidae*) had very stout legs with relatively short leg/foot bones, suggesting that they were rather ponderous forest-dwellers. Their feet appear to have been three-toed.

Radio-carbon dating of eggshell fragments suggests that elephant birds, on which Marco Polo's legendary roc appears to have been founded, survived well into this millennium. Extinction probably came about through a combination of habitat destruction (deforestation), with ensuing drought, and hunting pressure. Aepyornis laid the largest known egg.

This reconstruction shows how Dinornis maximus, the tallest bird that ever lived, was once hunted by Maoris. (New Zealand Wildlife Service)

DIATRYMA STEINI

The huge, flightless Diatryma steini stood 2.2 m (7.15 ft) tall and with its large head (as big as that of a modern horse) and very powerful beak must have posed a serious threat to the mammals of North America and Europe some 38–54 million years ago. With its very strong and heavy legs it would have been one of the largest predatory birds which ever existed, taking over the niche for a bipedal carnivore left vacant by the extinction of the flesh-eating dinosaurs.

THE LARGEST SWIMMING BIRDS EVER KNOWN

One species of the recently discovered Plotopterids was over 2 m (6.5 ft) long. These huge, flightless *Pelecaniformes* of the northern hemisphere occurred in the late Oligocene and early Miocene periods of Japan, Washington and California some 20–25 million years ago. Like the giant penguins, these were wing-propelled divers, but differed in having teeth.

The largest penguins were somewhat smaller, but nonetheless some stood as tall as many men, Pachydyptes and Anthropornis being 1.64 m (5.33 ft) and 1.54 m (5 ft) respectively.

THE LARGEST SWIMMING BIRD IN BRITAIN

GASTORNIS KLAASSENI

This very large, ratite-like bird from the late Paleocene/early Eocene period (50–55 million years ago) reached up to 2.15 m (7 ft) and is the largest bird known to have lived in Britain. It was originally compared with geese but is now said to have had rail-like affinities. It is also suggested that it was closely related to Diatryma.

Known from a number of European sites, Gastornis was first described by E. T. Newton in 1886 from remains found in the lower Eocene beds near Croydon by Mr H. M. Klaassen. They were exposed during excavation of the Park-Hill railway-cutting in 1883.

Newton suggested that Gastornis was 'at least as large as, and far heavier in build than, any recent ostrich', but subsequent study found that the proportions were very hard to determine and the height of 2.15 m (7 ft) is the best recent estimate.

As the six specimens of bone from the Park-Hill cutting represented at least four individuals, and were from a comparatively small area, Newton concluded that these birds were locally very numerous.

THE LARGEST BIRD WHICH EVER FLEW

ARGENTAVIS MAGNIFICENS –

Wingspan 7–7.6 m (23–25 ft)

The bird world was turned upside down in 1979 when two well-known Argentinian paleontologists announced that they had unearthed the fossilized remains of a creature as large as a small glider. A bird which at rest could look a man in the eye and in flight cast a shadow as wide as four 2 m (6 ft) men lying end-to-end was almost too much to believe, for such a wingspan was far greater than any other represented in the fossil record. The boffins went dashing for their slide-rules and as a result had to re-examine their theory as to size limitations in flight. Even now, it is admitted that our understanding of avian flight is still very limited, but there was a great deal of concrete evidence to deduce from this new genus and species of teratorn. Assuming that it is reasonable to extrapolate directly from the size of other species, there is considerable confidence over A. magnificens' calculated standing height of 1.5 m (5 ft) and weight of 120 kg (265 lb), but it has been pointed out that the wingspan is just as likely to have been greater as smaller.

Stretching 3.35 m (11 ft) from the tip of its bill to the tip of its tail, A. magnificens dwarfed the previous record-holding teratorn – incredibilis with its 5.2 m (17 ft) wingspan. Its remains had been found several years prior to 1979 by Drs Eduardo Tonni and Rosendo Pascual

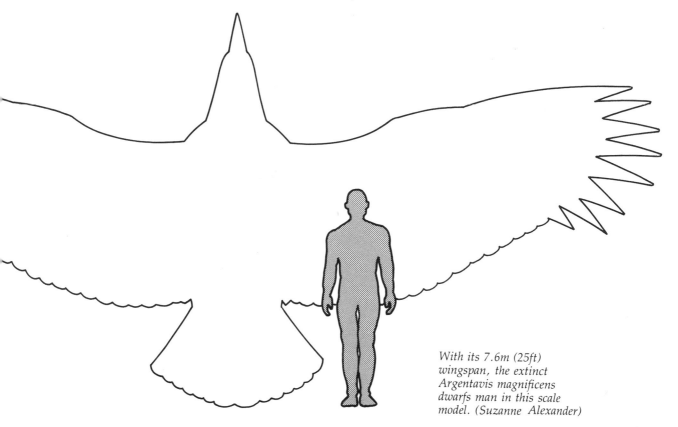

With its 7.6m (25ft) wingspan, the extinct Argentavis magnificens dwarfs man in this scale model. (Suzanne Alexander)

beneath the dry, dusty plains of central Argentina. There were a number of pieces of skull, wing bones and leg bones, all from a single bird. This was found to be the oldest known teratorn, dating from the late Miocene period of 5–8 million years ago.

There is no doubt that this great bird from a site 160 km (100 miles) west of Buenos Aires did fly as its discoverers found pieces of four different wing bones, and they are all of a size to be expected in a flying bird with such a wingspan. Living large birds which have lost the ability to fly, such as ostrich, rhea and emu, have only rudimentary wings and wing bones which are very reduced – some even missing. Also, one A. magnificens bone bears the marks where the secondary feathers were attached. The primary flight feathers might well have been as large as 18 cm (7 in) wide and 1.5 m (5 ft) long.

It is assumed that this bird relied on soaring and only flapped its wings briefly when absolutely

necessary because the physical limits of bone and muscle activity would have worked against sustained flapping. This is suggested by the similarity between the structure of the bones of teratorns and condors. To get airborne, it is thought that all A. magnificens had to do was spread its wings into the wind, as condors of today often do. And there is considerable evidence to suggest that strong winds were a permanent feature of the Argentine climate in the late Miocene era. But with such large wings, taking off among and flying between trees and bushes would have been difficult so it is assumed that A. magnificens would have been restricted to living in savannas or open grassland. Also walking in and around dense vegetation would have been avoided because of the increased danger of predators there.

Though similar to condors in flight, teratorns differed in being much more agile on the ground. Indeed, this seems to have been essential for the way in which they fed. They did not swoop from the air on large, unsuspecting animals, but used their huge wings to hunt over vast areas in search of places where the generally low-density game of suitable size was concentrated – possibly around lake edges. There they stalked their prey until they were close enough to seize it with a quick thrust of the bill.

The skull of A. magnificens was over 55 cm (22 in) long and 15 cm (6 in) wide and examination shows that it could have spread its mandibles wide enough to swallow prey larger than 15 cm (6 in) in diameter. Other animal remains from the same geological formation indicate that a hare-sized, rodent-like creature was particularly abundant at the time, but small armadillos may also have featured in the diet. Living forms of these animals are easily approached on foot, making them ideal prey for a stalking carnivore. Furthermore, the long, narrow, hooked beak of A. magnificens is indicative of a bird that grabs small animals and swallows them whole, and their feet were not of the type found in birds such as hawks, eagles and owls which use their claws to catch and kill prey. It is thought prey was swallowed whole because the jaw bones were too weak to kill large prey by biting or to tear large prey into pieces small enough for swallowing. And as they were probably hunters, their heads would have been feathered, as in almost all birds which are active predators.

The evolution of these gigantic birds seems to have proceeded in phase with the development of South American grasslands and semi-arid habitat, and the extinction of all the teratorns in North and South America may well have been linked to intolerable habitat alteration brought about by extreme dessication at the end of the Pleistocene era. Few other known birds had wingspans over 5 m (16.25 ft). Among the most impressive was the Pelecaniforme *Gigantornis eaglesomei* from the Eocene deposits of Nigeria, which had long, narrow wings spanning some 6.1 m (20 ft), but such calculations are based merely on a single breastbone similar to that of an albatross.

THE SMALLEST FLIGHTLESS BIRD EVER

This may well be the Inaccessible Island rail (see page 86) which is still alive today, but there is one extinct species known to have been smaller which is reputed to have been flightless. This was the 10 cm (3.93 in) Stephens Island wren (*Traversia (Xenicus) lyalli*), a New Zealand endemic of the family Xenicidae, which has three surviving members.

Unfortunately, hardly anything is known about this mysterious bird as it became extinct almost as soon as it was discovered in 1894. The only observations of it alive were by the lighthouse keeper, who saw it just twice in the evening, when, disturbed from holes in the rocks, it apparently scurried around on the ground like a mouse. It was never seen to fly. About a dozen specimens were collected, but the species was rapidly wiped out by the lighthouse keeper's cat as there had been no natural predators for the bird to adapt to.

Its bone structure and short, rounded wings suggest weak flight, as does its soft plumage, and if it was flightless then it would have been the only flightless passerine ever known. Sub-fossil bones found in the North Island and believed to be of Traversia indicate that the species was once more widespread.

THE LARGEST EGGS EVER LAID

Although the 'elephant' bird Aepyornis maximus is not quite the heaviest or tallest bird discovered in the fossil record so far, it did lay the largest eggs of which we are aware. However, it is pointed out that we do not know how many Aepyornis species there were and we can only assume that maximus laid the largest eggs found.

Pieces of Aepyornis eggshell and even whole eggs – some containing

The flightless Stephens Island wren was wiped out by a lighthouse keeper's cat in the year of its discovery. (New Zealand Wildlife Service)

This Aepyornis maximus egg – the largest specimen ever found – dwarfs a hen's egg in the Bristol Museum. (©Bristol Museum)

embryo bones – are quite often washed out of the sand on the beaches or near lakes in Madagascar, where the people use them for carrying water.

Many have found their way into museums and collections around the world. The British Museum has 11, the largest of which is 85.6 cm (33.7 in) around the long axis, with a circumference of 72.3 cm (28.5 in) giving a capacity of 8.88 litres (2.35 gallons), equalling that of 180 hens' eggs. But there is an even bigger one in the natural history collection at Bristol Museum. It came from the collection of Sir John Henry Greville Smyth in 1926 and its dimensions are: circumference around the long axis – 89 cm (35 in), circumference around the middle – 73.2 cm (28.8 in), length 34.5 cm (13.58 in), width 24.6 cm (9.68 in). Nothing is known of the egg's history.

Other large Aepyornis eggs include one collected in 1841 and now in the Academie des Sciences, Paris, France. It measures 39 cm (15.4 in) × 32.6 cm (12.8 in) and is said to have weighed about 12.2 kg (27 lb) with its contents. Another in the Western Foundation of Vertebrate Zoology in California, USA measures 32 cm (12.59 in) × 24.2 cm (9.52 in), with the respective circumferences being 88.8 cm (34.96 in) and 72.5 cm (28.54 in).

It has been suggested that such large eggs must have been close to the theoretical maximum size as the pressure of the internal fluid in an even larger cell might be so great that the containing shell would have to be excessively thick, and then the chick would find it very difficult to get out.

THE MOST NUMEROUS BIRD EVER
PASSENGER PIGEON

It is not possible to give an accurate estimate of the population of this North American bird (*Ectopistes migratorius*) as it became extinct in the wild in about 1900, and the position is complicated further through American definition of a billion – a thousand million, whereas in Britain it is a million million. Nonetheless, there are so many reports about this remarkable bird we are safe in suggesting that its population was in the region of 5–10,000 million in the first half of the 19th century before hunting with guns was very extensive. It might well have provided 45% of the total bird population of America, though a lower figure is more likely. Even the most conservative estimates talk of 'hundreds of millions', and 3,000 million are thought to have been alive at the time of Columbus so its great success cannot be attributed entirely to agriculture or other human interference with habitat.

The extinction of this prolific continental species in such a short time is probably the most dramatic decline of all time. The bird was hunted relentlessly in vast quantities for the table and no one could ever conceive that total extermination was possible. Yet the eventual disappearance remains puzzling as the last few millions went with such suddenness.

Some authorities suggest that a migratory disaster or even disease contributed to the demise over the last 20 or so years. Another theory is that the bird's breeding success might have been dependent on its gregarious habits. It has been suggested that the reproductive rate could have dropped with the size of the colonies, some of which were several square kilometres in extent with a hundred or more nests in a single tree. Physical and chemical damage to trees was great.

The species bred throughout the northern forests from Manitoba to Nova Scotia and south to Kansas and West Virginia. It wintered from Arkansas and North Carolina south to central Texas and northern Florida. Many reports tell of migrating flocks of 1–2,000 million birds. The famous author and artist Audubon (q.v.) estimated a flock near Louisville at 1,115,136,000. Fellow ornithologist Alexander Wilson estimated an even larger

flock in Kentucky to contain 2,230,272,000 birds, yet considered this to be far below the true number. He suggested that if each bird ate ½pt of acorns a day their daily consumption would be 17,424,000 bushels. This single massive flock would have outnumbered 10 to 1 *all* the birds in the British Isles as once estimated by James Fisher.

The last immense nesting took place in 1878 at a time when vast acreages of the bird's forest habitat were being converted to farmland. Quite apart from sport and some local subsistence shooting, market gunning took its toll. Countless barrels of birds were shipped to the big cities where they often rotted on the sidewalks for want of buyers. The last well-verified shooting took place in Wisconsin in 1899.

The last recorded passenger pigeon of all, 'Martha Washington', died in Cincinnati Zoo, Ohio, USA at 1 p.m. Eastern Standard Time on 1 September 1914. She had been hatched at the zoo and died aged 29. The mounted specimen is exhibited at the Smithsonian Institution, Washington.

Bird Populations & Distribution

Despite the fairly large number of professional ornithologists and ecologists now scattered around the world, and the ever-increasing army of amateurs who volunteer to help with organized counts and records, the study of bird numbers and distribution could never be highly accurate. With wild, mobile subjects and widely varying coverage of often remote and inaccessible areas, the ornithologist must be content with his best estimate. In addition, local populations often fluctuate greatly through migration, seasonal food supplies, breeding success, natural disasters, pollution and habitat destruction.

NUMBER OF SPECIES IN THE WORLD
There are thought to be between 8,600 and 9,016 species in the world. A precise figure could never be given for new species continue to be discovered in remote or little-known areas while the status of others is very vague, sometimes bordering on extinction. Some 265 species were listed as threatened by the ICBP (International Council for Bird Preservation) Red Data Book *Endangered Birds of the World* (2nd ed rev 1974–9) compiled by Warren B. King. But this is already very out of date and a third edition is being prepared. Added to this there is constant reappraisal of the classification of species by taxonomists and there has been a tendency for some widespread forms to be subdivided. During the years 1980–5 at least five checklists of the world's birds were published and a study of these reveals some of the disagreements encountered in determining species and sub-species.

NUMBER OF SPECIES IN BRITAIN
Of some 232 species recorded as breeding in Britain, 207 are regulars and 25 irregulars, but these are likely to be added to in the near future as an ever-increasing number of birdwatchers report further colonization from neighbouring countries. On the other hand, others may be lost through long-term climatic or habitat change.

Including all breeding species, regular visitors and vagrants or 'accidentals' (irregular visitors), the British list stands at about 540, with records of some five further species awaiting official acceptance.

TOTAL NUMBER OF BIRDS IN THE WORLD
The question of how many individual birds are alive on Earth at any one time is yet to be answered with any certainty. It is hard enough to census or estimate the populations of individual species, except those which are very restricted in range and sedentary in habits, and the smaller and more secretive a bird the harder it is to study. In addition, there is tremendous seasonal fluctuation, hitting a low before hatching and peaking at the end of the breeding season, which itself varies according to geographical position. At times of maximum numbers juveniles would outnumber adults several times, thus giving a false impression of population security as many of the young die in their first winter. The annual death rate of adult passerines is 40–60%, but the percentage of eggs which reach full adulthood averages only about 12%.

Yet man remains fascinated by such matters, and to be able to gauge population trends reasonably accurately is a good way to keep an eye on the health of the world's environment. Thus in 1951 Fisher made an educated estimate of 100,000 million birds, give or take a few hundred millions. However considering the suggested large populations of a small number of species alone, it is tempting to suggest that Fisher's estimate is extremely conservative. Since then mankind has made great inroads into bird populations through tremendous habitat destruction and pollution, and to a lesser extent through more efficient killing for food and sport. This has been balanced to a certain extent by our introduction of some very prolific species into favourable habitats around the world and incidental assistance for some species – e.g. provision of rubbish-dump food for gulls, lawns for blackbirds and road-casualty mammal carcasses for magpies and other scavengers. But it has to be suggested that the huge scale of habitat destruction must mean a steady overall decline for the world's bird population.

TOTAL NUMBER OF BIRDS IN BRITAIN

It would be hard to think of a country whose bird population is more variable than that of Britain for its geographical position brings huge numbers of passage migrants. And just as many come from most points of the compass to spend the winter in Britain because of its unusually mild coastal maritime climate, while many millions of Britain's predominantly insect-eating summer visitors must go south in winter. In addition, being an island with a long and intricate coastline, Britain is the base for innumerable sea-going birds, those which breed in Britain being relatively easy to monitor at their colonies.

Despite the problems, several attempts have been made to estimate the British summer landbird breeding population. In 1932 E. M. Nicholson suggested 80 million, and in 1939 James Fisher arrived at 100 million, upping it to 120 million in 1946. In 1974, using figures available from annual census returns and Ministry of Agriculture land-usage statistics, Fisher and James

PALEARCTIC   NEARCTIC   ORIE

The Neotropical of South America has more birds than any other zoogeographical region. (Suzanne Alexander)

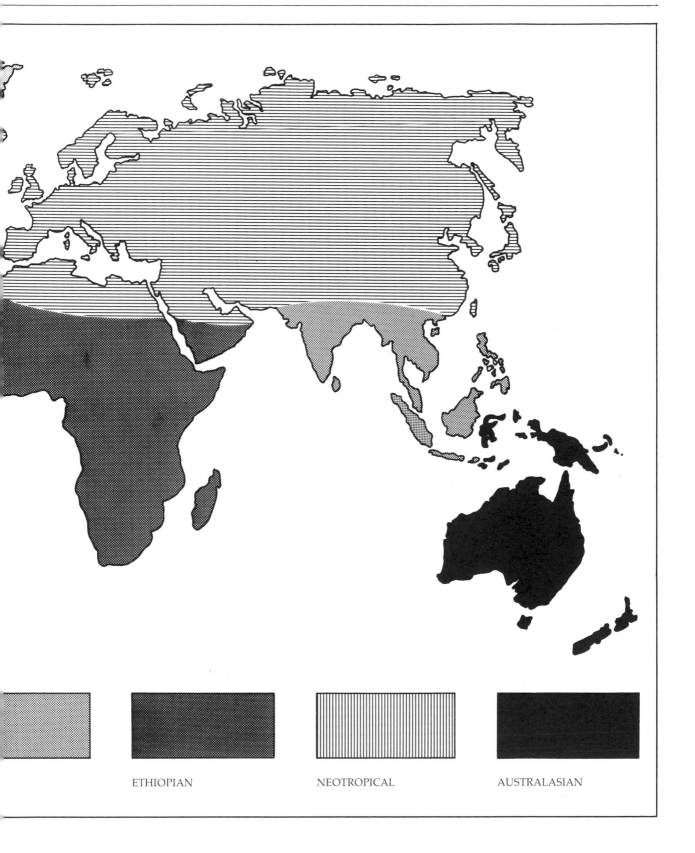

ETHIOPIAN   NEOTROPICAL   AUSTRALASIAN

Flegg arrived at a figure of about 134 millions for 1972.

In the last 10 years the army of amateur ornithologists has grown rapidly and through their co-ordination and enthusiasm future counts should become more and more accurate. Much of their work will revolve around the BTO's (British Trust for Ornithology) Common Birds Census, and it must be remembered that only 100 of our 500-plus listed species contribute significantly to numbers. Some 50 of these make up about 75% of the total population.

THE RICHEST AVIFAUNA IN THE WORLD
SOUTH AMERICA – over 2,500 breeding species
The Neotropical Region – South America, known as the 'bird continent', is already credited with over 2,500 breeding species and much of the area is still largely unexplored. There is, of course, overlap between regions, and seabirds are more easily grouped by ocean than landmass, but the number of breeding species of the other regions can be given approximately as: Palearctic (Europe, Africa north of the Sahara, and arctic, boreal and temperate Asia north of the Himalayas) about 950, Nearctic (North America north of the tropics) 750, Afrotropical (Africa south of the Sahara but excluding Madagascar and the Comoro Islands while including the islands of Zanzibar, Penbra, Mafia and the Gulf of Guinea) over 1,500 and Australasia (Australia, New Zealand, New Guinea and all island dependencies) about 1,100, seasonal migrants apart. Colombia is the country with the highest number of breeding species – over 1,700.

THE POOREST AVIFAUNA IN THE WORLD
THE ANTARCTIC 'MAINLAND' – 11 breeding species
Within the Antarctic Circle only 11 bird species breed regularly. These are the **Antarctic petrel** (*Thalassoica antarctica*), **adélie penguin** (*Pygo-scelis adeliae*), **snow petrel** (*Pagodroma nivea*), **Antarctic skua** (*Catharacta maccormicki*), **emperor penguin** (*Aptenodytes forsteri*), **chinstrap penguin** (*Pygoscelis antarctica*), **southern giant petrel** (*Macronectes giganteus*), **Antarctic fulmar** (*Fulmarus glacialoides*), **cape pigeon (Pintado petrel)** (*Daption capense*), **Antarctic prion** (*Pachyptila desolata*) and **Wilson's storm petrel** (*Oceanites oceanicus*). A wider variety of species breed within the strict geographical definition of Antarctica, including the entire Antarctic Peninsula, its off-lying islands, sea ice and surrounding ocean and islands northwards to the Antarctic Convergence.

The only terrestrial birds in Antarctica are the **snowy** or **yellow-billed sheathbill** (*Chionis alba*) and **black-faced** or **black-billed sheathbill** (*Chionis minor*), which are related to the pigeons. These peculiar birds are a possible evolutionary link between shorebirds and gulls. They have a rudimentary spur on the carpal joint of the wing (the 'wrist', forming the forward-pointing part of the folded wing) and a broad, strong bill with a horny sheath which partially covers the nostrils. Natural food includes stillborn seal pups and afterbirths, penguin eggs and droppings, and krill which they force penguins to regurgitate. But they are opportunist feeders with a varied diet and in winter scavenge the rubbish tips of whaling stations and Antarctic survey bases.

THE RICHEST BIRD HABITAT IN THE WORLD
There is no doubt that the tropical forests hold a greater number of birds of a wider variety than any other habitat. Although they occupy only 6–7% of the land surface of the globe, they hold 40% of all known animals and plants and many of the world's species occur exclusively there. For example, the lowland forests of eastern Brazil hold 940 species: 214 are endemic and of these 80% are of humid lowland forests. But sadly these

forests are among the most endangered habitats in the world as struggling 'emergent' nations seek to exploit their timber and minerals. This habitat is full of secretive species and there seems little doubt that some of the endemics there have become extinct without their ever having come to the notice of science.

Other great centres of endemism (having range restricted to specified areas) survive in remote or protected areas of East Africa, particularly in some of the isolated mountain ranges. Among the most productive are the Usambaru, Uzungwa and Uluguru Mountains in Tanzania and some of the coastal forests such as Arabuko-Sokoke in Kenya.

THE RICHEST BIRD HABITATS IN BRITAIN

Britain has a great variety of habitats and figures derived by Fisher and Flegg from the Common Birds Census suggest that scrub is generally the richest habitat with 17 birds per hectare (2.5 acres). Scrub is rich in birdlife because as an intermediate stage between heath or marsh and mature woodland it attracts birds from several habitats. True scrub includes species of shrub which will never grow tall enough to create a woodland and many birdwatchers prefer to wander among vegetation of varying height, such as gorse, hawthorn and elder, because the birds are generally easier to see than those in mature forest.

Scrubland is closely followed by deciduous woodland and suburban areas. Deciduous woodland is the natural habitat of much of Britain and holds both a large number of birds and a great variety of species, though the mix varies considerably according to how dense the wood is and the variety of trees present. The most productive woods are those 'untidy' ones with clearings and scrubby areas and fallen as well as standing timber.

At the other extreme is farmland with six birds per hectare; water areas with 2.5 birds per hectare and bare uplands and hill grasslands with just one bird per hectare.

In winter the pattern of British birdlife changes significantly with both international migration and local movements. The British Trust for Ornithology's *Atlas of Winter Birds Survey* 1981–4 has highlighted some of the best places to watch birds. The 10 km (6.2 miles) square with the highest number of species was that in east Kent including Stodmarsh and the North Kent Marshes where 166 species were located. Another in north-west Norfolk, including the RSPB reserve at Titchwell, returned 164 species. All the areas with the highest number of species were along the coast in the south-east quarter of England. The highest inland total was 148 from a square in Leicestershire including part of Rutland Water.

At the other extreme, the mountains of central Scotland were found to be nearly devoid of birds in winter, and even relatively small upland areas such as Exmoor and Dartmoor returned both few species and small numbers of birds.

Britain is particularly fortunate in having a wealth of coastal mudflats and saltmarshes which are unbelievably rich in animal life, providing a tremendous store of food for great concentrations of wildfowl and waders. Extensive counting and ringing programmes have shown that the British coastline holds about 1.5 million waders in winter – about 40% of the European total. Over a half of the waders winter at just 10 top sites: Morecambe Bay, the Wash, Dee, Solway, Severn, Thames, Humber, Strangford Lough, Firth of Forth and the Chichester/Langstone Harbours complex.

While the waders are attracted by marine worms, molluscs etc, many of the large numbers of ducks and geese are drawn to the salt-tolerant plants. For example, brent geese and wigeon are particularly abundant where eel grass is present, though in recent years this important food has been affected by pollution. Where these salt-tolerant plants colonize the mudflats naturally, the marsh created soon rises by deposition of silt trapped by the stems and these 'saltings' then become important high-tide roosts for waders.

THE LARGEST BIRD ORDER
PASSERIFORMES (perching birds)

The class Aves (birds), sometimes reduced to the rank of sub-class of the class Reptilia (reptiles), has a varying number of orders (groupings of families with common characteristics) according to the system of classification adopted. The popular method adopted by Ernst Mayr, and leading to what has become known as the Basel Sequence, recognizes 27 orders containing 159 families. Of these, by far the largest, and also the most advanced, is the order Passeriformes, containing some 5,100 species – almost 60% of the world list! The 'perching birds' always have four toes with the irreversible hallux ('first' toe) directed backwards to form a foot which is well adapted to gripping a slender perch such as a branch, twig, reed or grass-stem. Toes are never webbed. Song is another feature of the Passeriformes and, though the quality varies, the order certainly contains the world's best songsters and mimics.

These landbirds frequent a wide variety of habitats, hatch blind, naked and helpless young, and their parental care is mostly well developed. The order is cosmopolitan, absent only from polar latitudes and some inhospitable islands.

Current research into DNA-hybridization (a method which assesses the similarity between the chromosomes of different species) should help to settle many of the disagreements over classification which still occur.

Representatives of the Passeriformes (perching birds) – the world's largest bird order, containing some 60% of all species. (Suzanne Alexander)

TYRANT FLYCATCHER
NORTH AMERICA

SKYLARK
BRITAIN

HONEYCREEPER
HAWAII

MOCKING BIRD
MEXICO

ANTBIRD
SOUTH AMER

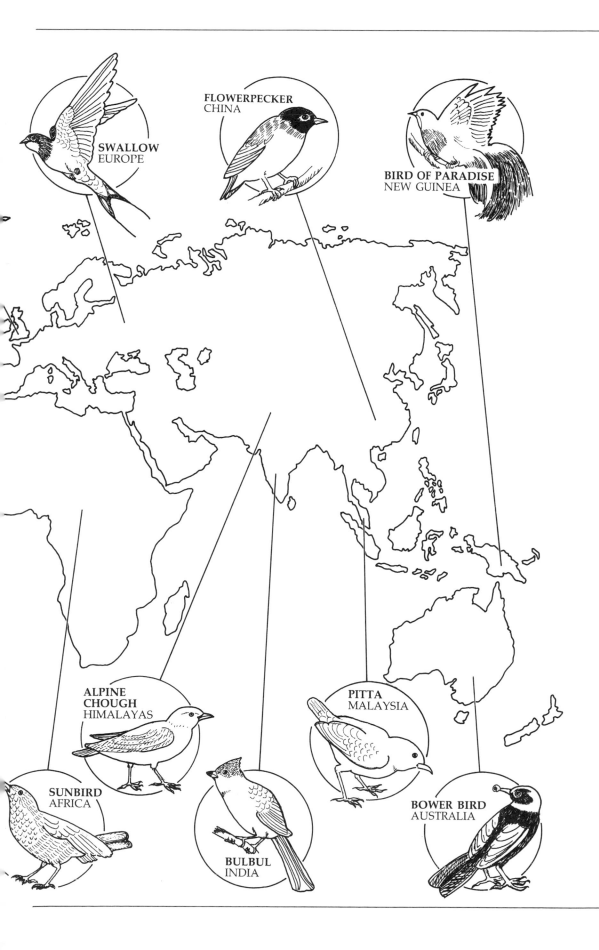

SWALLOW
EUROPE

FLOWERPECKER
CHINA

BIRD OF PARADISE
NEW GUINEA

ALPINE
CHOUGH
HIMALAYAS

PITTA
MALAYSIA

SUNBIRD
AFRICA

BULBUL
INDIA

BOWER BIRD
AUSTRALIA

THE LARGEST BIRD FAMILY IN THE WORLD
TYRANNIDAE ('TYRANT FLYCATCHERS')–376 species

This very diverse family of some 90 genera is entirely restricted to the New World, chiefly the Neotropical region, where numerically it is the dominant landbird family, and in South America more than one tenth of all landbird species are tyrant flycatchers. They are also found in the Galapagos Islands and West Indies.

No other family contains species which breed all the way from the cold, coniferous forests of northern Canada south to the treeless hills of rugged Tierra del Fuego, along the way utilizing all but the most inhospitable habitats. The 34 species breeding in North America are all at least partially migratory, moving south to Central or South America in winter.

Tyrant flycatchers tend to be active, often rather aggressive, birds, and most pursue insects rather than sit and wait for the prey to come to them, as the spotted flycatcher does in Britain. However they are not restricted to an insect diet – some regularly take fruit and a few are primarily frugivorous. Larger species may take small lizards and snakes, and sometimes fish or tadpoles, making good use of their strong, slightly hooked bills.

The tyrant flycatchers' varied diet determines their wide range of forms – few characteristics apply to all the species. Mostly with relatively large heads, and tails which range from moderately long to spectacularly long, they also generally have well-developed rictal (gape) bristles which are thought to protect the eyes in dense vegetation. Some of the pygmy-tyrants have wide, spoon-shaped bills with which they scoop insects from the undersides of leaves while darting rapidly through generally thick vegetation. The short-tailed pygmy-tyrant (*Myiornis escaudatus*) is the smallest of all tyrants at just 6 cm (2.5 in) long and weighing 4.5 gm (0.16 oz). The largest tyrants reach 50 cm (19.7 in) and weigh up to 80 g (2.8 oz).

Because many of the species are so small and very restricted in range, they have gone unnoticed by science until quite recently. In some of the humid forests of the Amazon basin and eastern Andes some 70 tyrant species may occur together. One species (still unnamed) remained undetected in the rainforests of southern Peru until 1981 because, although locally common, it weighs just 7 g (0.24 oz) and lives high in the treetops. And the tiny cinnamon-breasted tody-tyrant (*Hemitriccus cinnamomeipectus*) of extreme northern Peru was only discovered in 1976 when ornithologists first began to explore the cloud-covered summit of a mountain ridge where the species is restricted to the mossy, stunted forests on a handful of isolated peaks.

THE RAREST BIRDS IN THE WORLD

So little is known about several hundreds of species that it is not possible to say whether or not they are truly endangered. Each year new species are discovered – for example, three in Ethiopia alone in the last 20 years. Even relatively large birds continue unnoticed, such as the **pheasant** (*Lothura haitinensis*) which was discovered in Vietnam in 1986. Also some species have been rediscovered many years after they were said to be extinct.

A tiny population does not necessarily mean that a species is endangered. For example, the **St Kilda wren** (*Troglodytes t. hirtensis*) has happily existed on the small Hebridean island for probably several thousand years with a meagre population of only around 230 pairs. Such a population is viable, but vulnerable owing to the very restricted range. Another example is the **giant grebe** (*Podilymbus gigas*) of Guatemala. Confined to the 130 sq km (50 sq miles) Lake Atitlan, it has enjoyed habitat protection since 1964 and the population has risen from only

80 birds to approximately 100 pairs.

In recent years a number of species have been saved from extinction by captive breeding programmes, but the main difficulty remains determining and correcting the factors which led to the decline before realistic reintroduction programmes become worthwhile. It is impossible to state without question which is the world's rarest bird, but there are several likely contenders.

We can never be sure how accurate our rare bird reports are. Some species are particularly noisy when pairing but quiet and elusive later on. Others are big, bright and bold while their cousins are tiny, dull and secretive. It is inevitable therefore that reports will be biased towards more evident species.

THE LONGEST INTERVALS TO REDISCOVERY
THE RECORD HOLDER – THE CAHOW

Found in 1916 after having gone unnoticed since the 1660s, there were then further periods during which the **Cahow** or **Bermuda petrel** (*Pterodroma cahow*) was not seen, the last rediscovery being in 1951 – just 18 pairs on a small islet.

Sometimes considered to be a race of the **black-capped petrel** (*Pterodroma hasitata*), the cahow, which gets its name from one of its calls, has always been restricted to the islands of Bermuda. With human settlement it became a valued food source, as it had already been for travellers, but it suffered major exploitation during periods of famine in the 17th century and was soon reduced to nesting on a few small offshore islands near Castle Harbour. Pigs and other domesticated animals also contributed to its decline.

In the late 1960s it was thought that the effects of DDT would doom the bird to extinction. Fortunately Bermuda conservation officer David Wingate instituted a plan of action, one of the most important aspects of which was control of the **white-tailed tropicbirds** (*Phaethon lepturus*) which share the breeding habitat with the petrel. These tropicbirds arrive about two weeks later than the petrels and when they find an occupied nesting burrow they kill the cahow chicks inside and take over the site. Fortunately the cahow can use slightly smaller holes than the tropicbird so obstructions were inserted into the entrances to keep the larger birds out. This was immediately successful and by the 1980s cahow chick production was averaging 12 per year. But the population has not risen above 26 pairs.

THE RUNNERS-UP
CHATHAM ISLAND TAIKO

The **Chatham Island taiko** (*Pterodroma magentae*, see page 42) was known only from a specimen collected in 1867 until it was rediscovered in 1978.

EYREAN GRASSWREN

This 15 cm (5.9 in) bird (*Amytornis goyderi*) of the cane grass-covered high sand dunes of the Australian interior was unseen between 1875 and 1961 – a total of 86 years. The eight species of **grasswren** are all birds of the arid shrublands, desert and rocky plateaus and not surprisingly they are rarely seen in these remote regions. In fact, the **gray grasswren** was not discovered until after World War II. The **carpentarian**, the **white-throated** and the **black grasswrens** were unseen for over 50 years.

THE TAKAHE

This heaviest – 3.3 kg (7.3 lb) – member (*Notornis mantelli*) of the large rail family, most of which are very secretive by nature, was rediscovered in some inaccessible valleys in the mountains of New Zealand's South Island in 1948, after not having been seen since 1898.

THE RAREST RACE OF ALL
DUSKY SEASIDE SPARROW

As far as we know, there are no **dusky seaside sparrows** (*Ammospiza maritima nigrescens*) left in the wild, and as there is only one male left in captivity the race must be the rarest in the world and doomed to extinction. The dusky is one of nine races or sub-species of seaside sparrow, all found in the USA, inhabiting Atlantic coastal marshes from Massachusetts to Texas.

Up to the 1940s the number of duskies on Merritt Island, Florida was estimated at about 4,000, and a few miles to the west thousands more thrived in the marshland of the present-day St John's National Wildlife Refuge. Then, in the mid-50s, disaster struck: Cape Canaveral and the NASA Space Center across from Merritt Island were being developed and Merritt Island was dyked for complete mosquito control, stopping the tidal flooding of the marshes, something the duskies needed for survival. Thus many sparrows were sacrificed to

The dusky seaside sparrow was sacrificed to man's conquest of the moon. (National Audubon Society, USA)

man's conquest of the moon. At the time one local newspaper suggested that a sign be posted at the John F. Kennedy Space Center, proclaiming 'Welcome to Cape Canaveral, home of the successful moon shot. We also sent a bird farther than that.'

In 1975 five females with young and 47 males were counted on the St John's Wildlife Refuge, the females being much more secretive and rarely heard. But in December of that year fire destroyed the habitat and not another female has been seen since.

When the population dropped to just six males in 1980 five birds were captured and confined to two federal cages while various experts argued about the best course of action. The International Council for Bird Preservation called upon the US Fish and Wildlife Service and Florida Freshwater Fish and Game Commission to perpetuate the race by breeding the five captives in repeated back-crosses with females of the closely related **Scott's seaside sparrow** (*A.m. penin-sulae*). In this the 'pure' males would mate with their own hybrid young and after only three generations of back-crosses the resultant offspring would harbour 94% of the genetic make-up of the dusky males. When released back to the St John's River Refuge these would stand virtually as good a chance of survival and increase as the original stock. The Government spent $2,625,000 from 1971 to 1979 buying up 6,250 acres on Florida's east coast to create the St John's River Refuge for dusky sparrows (Florida then being third among US states, after Hawaii and California, in having the most endangered species).

The cross-breeding scheme had many opponents who said that a 94% cross was not the 'real thing'. Supporters pointed out that it made no sense to speak disparagingly of hybrids between sub-species, for intermediates could occur naturally anywhere in a species' range. The duskies shared a common gene pool with other sub-species and mating between them had undoubtedly taken place. Unfortunately a US Department of Interior solicitor ruled that anything less than a 100% dusky was not a dusky and did not qualify for expenditure of federal funds under the Endangered Species Act of 1973, the source of most funds previously expended on the bird. Eventually, the release of the birds back into the wild was abandoned and the 28 g (1 oz) birds with a life expectancy of nine years entered a committee-organized breeding project. They were kept at Disneyworld's Discovery Island in a habitat that closely resembled their natural home.

In October 1986 just one 100% dusky called 'Orange' remained alive and it was already over 10 years old. Pure dusky 'White' died earlier that year. But also at Disneyworld there were five birds with dusky genes as a result of hybridization with females of another sub-species from Florida's west coast, including a 75% dusky male and females with varying dusky genes of 25–88%.

THE RAREST SPECIES OF ALL
IVORY-BILLED WOODPECKER

Of those birds reliably recorded within the last few years, the **ivory-billed woodpecker** (*Campephilus principalus*) appears to be the most endangered *entire* species (i.e. not just a sub-species or race). There are/were two sub-species – *Campephilus principalus principalus* of south-eastern USA, of which most experts have not accepted records since 1951, and *C.p.bairdii* of Cuba, which was rediscovered by Cuban biologists on 16 March 1986. Just two birds were clearly identified by the white stripe down the back, and in the autumn another pair were seen. The US ivory-bill race was very, very similar to the Cuban race, the latter having 5 mm (0.2 in) more white on the face but no other distinguishing feature.

The former range of the US main-land race was from east Texas to south-east North Carolina, south and up the Mississippi drainage to southern Illinois and Ohio. Its last stronghold seems to have been in the wilderness areas of South Carolina, Florida and Louisiana, where the preferred habitat was mature southern-hardwood forest, each pair requiring a very large territory of about four square miles.

In these extensive forests, where the birds nested high up in tree holes, the ideal habitat was in diseased trees where ivory-bills fed principally on the larvae of wood-boring beetles.

Many of the mature forests were cleared very early in the USA (pre-naturalists) so all the ivory-billed woodpecker records which came in were from the big timber and swamp forests. Hunting contributed to decline but habitat destruction was the main factor as extensive felling removed old and diseased trees and increased disturbance. 'Clean' forests were useless for specialist-feeding ivory-bills which needed big hardwood trees or large dying pines to maintain a family of two adults and two young weighing 1 lb (0.45 kg) each. However, these new forests favoured the **pileated woodpecker** (*Dryocopus pileatus*), which overlaps in feeding with the ivory-bill, is less demanding and certainly competed with the ivory-bill once the latter's prime habitat and population were reduced.

In Cuba, too, habitat destruction was the major factor in decline, though hunting pressure was more significant than in the USA. In eastern Cuba (Oriente Province) the ivory-bill became restricted to mixed montane/pine/hardwood forest where just 12–13 pairs were known in 1956, falling to six pairs in 1974 and none located in some subsequent years.

The 1986 sightings in the mountains 500 miles east of Havana were later confirmed by Dr Lester Short, chairman of ornithology at the American Museum of Natural History. A male crossed his path but there was insufficient time to take a photograph. The Cuban Ministry of Agriculture ordered an immediate end to forest logging within 6.4 km (4 miles) of where the birds were seen.

Aerial surveys indicate that apparently suitable habitat in the zoologically little-known Jaguani forest reserve, east of the rediscovery area, may hold another small group of ivory-bills. If so they would be from another distinct genetic group and that would bode well, greatly increasing the species' chances of survival, which must otherwise be viewed as very low. There is certainly some hope as the birds have held out in Cuba, where there is no competition with pileateds or other species in cut-over pinelands, but with considerable help from the Cubans.

A few people insist that one or two birds survive in the USA, but none have been photographed. Hundreds of pictures have been submitted to Dr Short and his colleagues for scrutiny, but they have all been of pileated woodpeckers or unclear.

The ivory-bill's allospecies (very close relative), the **imperial woodpecker** (*Campephilus imperialis*) of the Mexican high pinelands, has not been certainly seen since 1950 and may well be extinct. The odds against the imperial woodpecker are even greater than those restraining the ivory-bill, for a pair of imperials needs 15.5–18 sq km (6–7 square miles) of territory and they have traditionally been shot and eaten in western Mexico by numerous gunners. At 58 cm (22.8 in), the imperial is the world's largest woodpecker.

OTHER GREAT RARITIES
KAUAI O-O-AA
There is no very recent estimate of the population of the **O-o-aa** (*Moho braccatus*), a 19–21.5 cm (7.5–8.5 in) Hawaiian honeyeater, though one or two were seen at the end of the 1970s and a handful may remain on Kauai Island. A population of 'less than 10' was suggested in 1985.

Honeyeaters generally have been a very successful family, with 167 species (450 sub-species) in 38 genera, concentrated in Australia, New Guinea, New Zealand, the south-west Pacific, Indonesia and South Africa. There were once at least five species in Hawaii, but the kioea and one Moho became extinct in about 1840. Another species of Moho has not been seen since the beginning of this century and is presumed extinct. *Moho braccatus* is thought to survive in the more remote and inaccessible forests where its diet is predominantly insectivorous. It climbs the moss-covered tree trunks in the manner of a woodpecker, aided by its stiff tail, looking for insects and spiders, beetles and small snails. They have also been seen to take laplapa berries.

All honeyeaters have a long, protrusible tongue with a brush-like tip which can be used to extract nectar, and in some countries they are important pollinators of flowers – in fact some species have co-evolved with certain species of plant. The tip of the tongue is deeply cleft into four parts which are delicately frayed on the edges, forming the so-called brush. The tongue is extended into the nectar or other liquid about 10 times a second and the liquid drawn up by capillary action. When the tongue is withdrawn the mouth is closed and projections on the roof of the beak appear to compress the liquid from the brush along the two grooves at the base of the tongue leading to the throat. Despite this common characteristic honeyeaters are very variable in size and habits.

It is not clear what has caused the decline of the Kauai O-o-aa. Between 1968 and 1973 the population was estimated at 22–36. For many years it was thought to be extinct, but was rediscovered in 1960 in the depths of the Alakai Swamp region, in the undisturbed native ohia forest between elevations of 1,143 m (3,750 ft) and 1,295 m (4,250 ft). There the birds preferred the thick forest habitat and more were seen or heard in high canyons than on the forested ridges. A few nests with two young

were subsequently found high up in tree cavities.

Hunting for honeyeater plumes was once extensive among Polynesians, who used such feathers to adorn ceremonial garments, but the tribesmen are not likely to have been significantly responsible for the decline of the largely inaccessible *Moho braccatus* population as the species has relatively inconspicuous plumage. Also birds were generally caught in the moulting season, plucked and then set free. Shrinking forests and associated disturbance are likely to have been more influential factors. And even in the most remote areas the forests are increasingly infiltrated by exotic plants which displace the indigenous nectar sources. Introduced birds compete for food and territory and the increasingly common black rat can climb trees to take eggs and chicks.

There is a possibility that a second *Moho* – *bishopi* (**Bishop's Oo**) – survives in the dense Hawaiian rainforest. It was rediscovered in 1981 after going unrecorded since 1904. An American ornithologist called Mountainspring spotted it on Maui, on the windward slope of the eight-mile-wide crater Haleakala, on the powdery floor of which the Apollo astronauts had trained for their missions.

THE RAREST WADER
ESKIMO CURLEW

Like the passenger pigeon, the **eskimo curlew** (*Numenius borealis*) was once extremely numerous, but was brought to the verge of extinction largely through excessive hunting. It was renowned for its great abundance and delicious flavour and was shot in vast numbers in the USA while on migration from tundra breeding grounds to South American winter quarters. In the mid-19th century immense flocks were encountered on the Texas coast and as late as 1863 over 7,000 were shot in one day on Nantucket Island (Massachusetts) alone.

There were no large flocks at all

after the 1880s and the possibility of extinction was raised as early as 1900. It seems likely that habitat destruction also contributed significantly to the decline as much grassland with its associated food supply was lost to agriculture along the bird's migration route.

The main breeding area was on the tundra of northern Mackenzie (North West Territory), west to western Alaska and possibly eastwards to Norton Sound. In the autumn the bird flew south-east to Newfoundland and Nova Scotia where, among other things, it fed voraciously on ripe crowberries before working its way down the New England coast. By the start of the migration it had put on so much weight it was nicknamed 'doughbird' because the skinned breast revealed a thick layer of fat resembling dough. It needed good reserves of energy before making its arduous journey across the western Atlantic to winter in southern Brazil, Paraguay, Chile, Uruguay and on the pampas of Argentina.

Much smaller than the common Eurasian curlew, the 30.5–37.5 cm (12–14.8 in) eskimo curlew is not especially conspicuous and it was easy for the tiny remnant population to go unnoticed for many years: some recent authorities even considering the species extinct. However, some have been seen on migration in the last few years and there is growing evidence of breeding success although no breeding sites are known at present, all previous records having come from northern Canada. The species has been recorded in 22 years since 1945. All sightings were for North America except a 1963 Barbados specimen and a 1977 Guatemala sighting. Usually just one or two birds were seen, and never more than six together except for a group of 23 in Texas in 1981.

JERDON'S OR DOUBLE-BANDED COURSER

Generally thought to be extinct, the lapwing-sized **Jerdon's** or **double-banded courser** (*Cursorius bitor-quatus*) was rediscovered in India in January 1986 after having gone unnoticed by naturalists since reliably reported by Howard Campbell in 1900.

There are just nine species of courser in three genera, and they are all plover-like in size and shape, but rather long-legged and with a noticeably upright stance. Most are fairly active at night, but until the rediscovery of Jerdon's it was thought that only one other species was truly nocturnal. They are all running birds which fly only if forced to.

First procured and recorded for science by Dr Jerdon in about 1848, Jerdon's courser was considered to be a permanent resident with an extremely limited geographical distribution in eastern India. Yet there appeared to be plenty of suitable thornscrub jungle habitat and several serious surveys have been carried out to try to establish the bird's continuing presence. They all failed, bar one, including those organized in 1975/76 by the Bombay Natural History Society with the collaboration of the Smithsonian Institution and World Wildlife Fund-India. The successful survey was launched by the Bombay Natural History Society in 1985 and funded by the Fish & Wildlife Service of the USA. Target area was the Pennar river valley in southern Andhra Pradesh.

The BNHS circulated a poster showing a colour painting of both the Jerdon's and Indian coursers, with accompanying notes written in English for Andhra Pradesh and adjoining states. It was later found necessary to write a Telugu note for the Pennar river-valley areas, and the Godavari river-valley areas would require notes in the Telugu, Marathi, Oriya and Urdu languages. These were circulated to concerned individuals such as forest officials, local shikaris and tribals proficient in bird-trapping. Also Ali and Ripley's book *Pictorial Guide to Birds of the Indian Sub-Continent* was used to test each informant's depth of knowledge.

As a result of 'all this three shikaris gave versions of possible sightings. One man had recognized the courser from the poster and said that it was known as the 'Kalivi-kodi'. Kalivi is the Telugu word for *carissa*, the common scrub vegetation along with *zizyphus* and *acacia* in the area. Kodi means fowl. Kalivi-kodi was an apt description for the bird on account of its habit of hiding among the thorny *carissa* bushes.

The same tribesman reported how the bird walked for a short distance, stopped to look at the intruder and then flew away. He had always seen the coursers in groups of seven to eight birds, but never near cultivation, artesian wells or other water. He described the call as a single, soft, very 'sad' note. He also claimed that he saw the birds feeding at night, an important discovery as they were not thought to be truly nocturnal. During the day they would rest in the shade of a thorn tree.

Another shikari claimed to have seen the courser at night when after his main quarry – grey partridges and hares. Then, on 12 January

The Jerdon's or double-banded courser of India went unrecorded for 86 years. (Bombay Natural History Society)

1986, in the beam of his torch, he saw a Kalivi-kodi standing confused and motionless. Before the bird could react he ran up to it and scooped it up in his hand. He kept the bird alive in his house, feeding it on powdered rice, termites and black ants, and it was still alive on the 15th when he showed it to Bharat Cushman of the BNHS. Sadly the bird died on the 19th, just hours before well-known ornithologist Dr Salim Ali was able to see it. But on subsequent forays several more birds were seen in the area by Cushman and it is hoped they will not be harassed unnecessarily and no further deaths will occur.

As a result of the survey's findings the Andhra Pradesh forest department agreed to preserve the area to protect the species, and spurred on by this success, ornithologists may well mount searches for other supposedly extinct Indian species such as the forest little owl and mountain quail.

THE WORLD'S RAREST WARBLER
BACHMAN'S WARBLER

The only **Bachman's warbler** (*Vermivora bachmanii*) seen in 1986 was in Cuba and no more than six birds have been recorded anywhere since the 1950s. The former range was from southern Indiana and southern Missouri east to Virginia, south to northern Arkansas and Alabama. Nests have been found in just five states and the winter quarters are in Cuba and perhaps the Isla de Pinos, Bahamas. The favoured habitat is mature swamp woodland, and breeding is in marginal thickets, mainly cane. Enough breeding habitat still exists to support a healthy population so the most likely cause of significant decline must be destruction of the species' winter habitat.

Most of the world's warblers are very numerous. For example, the autumn population of the **willow warbler** has been estimated at 1,000 million birds, making it the most abundant of the Palearctic passerines which winter in Africa.

However a few island endemics are particularly vulnerable, including the **Aldabran brush warbler** (*Nesillas aldabranus*), which was down to 11 individuals in 1983.

Another American species which has entered a severe decline is **Kirtland's warbler** (*Dendroica kirtlandii*). This larger bird has one of the most restricted breeding ranges of non-insular birds and nests only in an area of about 100 × 130 km (62 × 80 miles) in lower northern Michigan. Even within this small area it is confined to woods of jack pine 8–22 years old and 1–6 m (3–19.5 ft) high. In winter it is confined to the Bahamas and adjacent Turks and Caicos Islands.

The main threat to the Kirtland's warbler was, for once, a natural one – the sudden spread of the parasitic brown-headed cowbird (*Molothus ater*) against which it has no defences. The cowbirds were trapped and removed and the threat receded, but the habitat requirements are still not secure and the Kirtland's population is only 400–450 birds.

THE WORLD'S RAREST PARROT
ECHO PARAKEET

In 1986 only 8–12 **echo parakeets** (*Psittacula echo*) survived, on Mauritius, and most of them were males. It was recommended that the last few birds be secured for a captive-breeding project and in July and August 1984 Don Merton of the New Zealand Wildlife Service visited the island to organize the work. Unfortunately, after two weeks' hard work camping in the forest he was unable to capture any. Then, in August 1985, an apparently young bird was seen and raised hopes for breeding success in 1986. It was then felt that the best hope for the species was to provide it with every opportunity for successful reproduction in the wild and to harvest eggs or young for the captive-breeding project.

In April 1986 a pair was seen on the Macchebée Ridge and the Forestry Service began to provide the birds with additional food and suitable nestboxes and to control nest predators and competitors such as black rats (*Rattus rattus*) and common mynahs (*Acridotheres tristis*). If these measures are successful the parakeet has a good chance of surviving in a country which has seen the decline of many species and the extinction of others such as the now-famous **dodo** (*Raphus cucullatus*).

Another critically endangered member of the large and diverse parrot family is the **Puerto Rican parrot** (*Amazona vittata*) of the Greater Antilles. Island species of parrot are particularly vulnerable to human activities, especially as they have mostly small populations and relatively slow breeding rates. And because they have evolved in isolation they tend to be less able to cope with habitat destruction, introduced competitors, disease and predators.

Through a combination of such factors there were only 13 Puerto Rican parrots left in the wild in 1975 and it looked as though the species was doomed to extinction, but an emergency conservation programme involving strict control of hunting and trapping saved the day. In addition, the number of nest-sites was artificially increased and there was cross-fostering of eggs and nestlings between the Puerto Rican parrot and the closely related but non-endangered **Hispaniolan parrot** (*Amazona ventralis*). It was also necessary to reduce attacks by the **pearly-eyed thrasher** (*Margarops fuscatus*), a recent immigrant, on nest-sites, eggs and young.

Success was immediate and by October 1982 the wild population had more than doubled, with a further 15 birds carefully maintained in captivity. By June 1986 the wild population had risen to 20 plus a further 20 in captivity. This clearly shows what can be achieved when man applies all his knowledge and resources. It is a tragedy that such techniques were not available earlier this century to save other species, such as the **Carolina parakeet** (*Conuropsis carolinensis*), then the most northerly representative of the family, from extinction. This bird was once very common throughout most of eastern USA but was shot unmercifully as an agricultural pest and its habitat decimated by forest swamp clearance.

THE WORLD'S RAREST BIRD OF PREY
MAURITIUS KESTREL

Despite intensive efforts to help this little falcon, the tiny remnant population in the native evergreen forests of south-west Mauritius remains at only about 15–25 birds in the best years.

In 1966 there were just 20–25 individual **Mauritius kestrels** (*Falco punctatus*) and they had declined to only six in 1973 when for the first time a pair was trapped and mated for propagation. The wild birds hung on in the Black River gorges and similar environs – rugged country which miraculously escaped the wholesale forest destruction brought about by pressure from one of the densest human populations in the world.

The species, slightly shorter and heavier than the **common kestrel** (*Falco tinnunculus*), appears never to have been common. Consideration of present territory requirements suggests that even when most of the island was covered with forest in the mid-18th century (estimated suitable habitat then 1,644 sq km/ 630 sq miles) there were only 164–328 pairs.

Unusually among kestrels, the male and female *punctatus* have identical plumage, but they exhibit marked sexual dimorphism, the males weighing just 178 g (6 oz) and the females 231 g (8 oz).

The short, rounded wings are not very good for hovering so hunting concentrates on searching for prey from a perch or slowly quartering the forest canopy. Arboreal prey, such as the main food item geckos (*Phelsuma*), is stalked by rapid hops along branches. Small insects, dragonflies, locusts, small birds and rodents are also taken.

Rather confiding birds, sitting Mauritius kestrels sometimes allow approach to within a few metres of the nest, usually in a tree cavity. Unlike all other kestrels, the young remain with their parents near the nest-site until the next breeding season.

Nests in tree cavities tend to be depredated by introduced macaque monkeys, which have become a great menace to all arboreal-nesting birds on the island. Fortunately, when the kestrel's population was at its very lowest in 1974, one pair chose to nest out of the monkeys' reach on the sheer face of a tall cliff. They fledged three young and thereby increased the population by a third! The progeny of this pair

The Mauritius kestrel has been threatened by introduced macaque monkeys. (©Philippa Scott)

continued to nest in such inaccessible places, and by 1976 there were 12 birds. Sadly, the tree-nesters continued to be unsuccessful.

Intensive research really began during the 1981/82 breeding season, but by 1983/84 only six or seven pairs were known, eight or nine in 1984/85 and seven or eight in 1985/86. Despite all the efforts the number of birds has not increased much since the 1960s. But although breeding success is on the whole poor, there is considerable variation from year to year: in the 1984/85 season 11 young fledged but in 1985/86 just five. Also, the number of breeding pairs is limited by the number of breeding territories holding adequate food.

In addition to habitat destruction, human persecution aided the decline and when the population was critically low the monkeys kept it down. This inevitably led to considerable inbreeding and it has been suggested that as a result there has been genetic deterioration, resulting in reduced reproductive capacity and increased susceptibility to disease and other stresses.

The remaining habitat of just 3,035 ha (7,500 acres) will never support many more pairs, even without the monkeys. Unlike other species in the sub-genus, such as the **Seychelles kestrel** (*Falco araea*), *punctatus* has shown no adaptability to its changed environment, including utilization of man-made structures or exotic stands of trees as nest-sites. It seems tied to the native evergreen forest and the greatest hope for species survival might be in transferring some birds to islands such as Reunion where sizeable native forests remain.

In the meantime active management has been stepped up and the productivity of a pair that had supplementary feeding has improved. During the 1985/86 breeding season 14 birds were bred in captivity and four of them were released in January 1986 in an area of rather suitable lowland forest that did not already have kestrels. Release techniques had been perfected on other falcons and the young birds were being fed daily on white mice, gradually gaining their independence.

Among the world's other rarest birds of prey are the **Madagascar serpent eagle** (*Eutriorchis astur*) and the **Madagascar fish eagle** (*Haliaeetus vociferoides*), both of which struggle on in very small but unknown numbers in isolated reserves and remote areas. Before the coming of man 3,000 years ago, Madagascar was mostly forested but since then settlement by many peoples with varieties of agriculture has robbed this great island (larger than France) of much of its richness and diversity of wildlife.

CALIFORNIA CONDOR

Now rarer in the wild than even the Mauritius kestrel, and in some ways more endangered, this magnificent New World vulture really grabbed world headlines in 1986 when its struggle for survival seemed to epitomize the growing conflict between human proliferation and Nature. After a long and steady decline through many suggested (but largely unproven) factors, it was decided in recent years that the best way to avoid almost certain extinction was through a captive-breeding programme. Hopefully this will lead to a release of 'surplus' birds into suitable areas once the causes of decline are better understood and significantly halted.

By October 1986 24 of the known 27 remaining birds (12 males, 14 females and one unknown) were in captivity, the main method of capture being rocket-propelled nets at meat baits. Capture efforts for the three remaining birds (all radio-marked males) were then in progress. Two of these would join 12 other birds at the San Diego Wild Animal Park and the third would join 12 at Los Angeles Zoo. An adult captive female was to be transferred from San Diego to Los Angeles for pairing with one of the wild males, as the same pair had bred in the wild in the spring of 1986.

The **California condor** (*Gymnogyps californianus*) is North America's largest flying landbird with a weight of 8–10.4 kg (18–23 lb) and a wingspan of 2.92 m (9.5 ft). Its historical range extended from southern British Columbia south through Washington, Oregon and California, generally being found west of the summits of the Cascades and Sierra Nevada, but it has been known as a breeding bird only in California. And even in its recent range it has been found in less than 20% of the vast area it occupied in the 19th century.

Concern for the condor began early: the 485.64 ha (1,200 acres) Sisquoc Sanctuary was established in 1937 and the 14,164 ha (35,000 acres) Sespe Wildlife Area (later renamed the Sespe Condor Sanctuary) in 1947. But care of birds which forage only for carrion over millions of acres is extremely difficult, especially when all the success achieved on public-owned land is negated by irresponsible actions on private ranches. And while legislation has improved in many directions, law enforcement has been very difficult over such large areas needing regular patrol.

Perhaps the chief failure of condor habitat management has been the research and control of toxic chemicals used to kill agricultural pests on private rangelands. Strychnine, DDT, compound 1080, cyanide and zinc phosphide have all been or still are common in condor territory.

Condors feed only on the carcasses of dead animals, and before the great herds of mammals were exterminated these probably included deer, elk, pronghorn and smaller species as well as whales and sea lions. But for many years domestic cattle have constituted by far the most important food source for condors, particularly since sheep farming declined in California. Recently, however, extensive conversion of rangeland to other more profitable uses has reduced the cattle carcass supply and in the long term grazing lands could be so diminished and fragmented that revived condor populations may be unable to find sufficient food.

While all known condor nest-sites since 1930 have been on public-

Wild condors feed only on the carcasses of dead animals. (Condor Research Centre)

In a bid to save the species from extinction it was decided to round-up remaining California condors for a captive-breeding programme. (Condor Research Centre)

owned land, major foraging and roosting areas have been on private range, and this has led to direct persecution of the birds through continued shooting and poisoning until very recently. In an effort to prevent ingestion of meat from poisoned carcasses, the Condor Research Center helpers have been swamping forage areas with 'clean' food.

Lead toxicosis has been suspected of being a major mortality factor in recent years, though the evidence is inconclusive. The last three known mortalities of wild condors have been through lead poisoning, ingestion of lead bullets from rifle-killed carcasses being a possible route of entry into the body. As well as cattle, condors show a distinct preference for deer carcasses and there is little doubt that many wounded deer carrying bullets or even shotgun pellets have eventually been eaten by condors.

Today fresh carcasses (mainly stillborn dairy cattle) are supplied daily at specific feeding points within the main foraging range to provide the birds with high-quality contaminant-free food. In captivity adult birds are fed chunks of horse-meat supplemented by commercially prepared bird-of-prey and feline mixtures. Young birds are fed chopped-up rats and mice.

Life expectancy of California condors may be as high as 50 years or more in captivity, though very little data exists on the age of wild birds. Age to maturity is approximately six years. In the spring of 1986 a six-year-old male – one of the last three in the wild – successfully mated with a female which has since been captured. This event was considered to be of great biological significance as previously it was believed that the breeding age commenced at 7–11 years.

Birds mate for life and produce a single egg approximately every other year. If the egg is destroyed a second or even a third egg may be laid, and making use of this double- and triple-clutching phenomenon field biologists were able significantly to increase the condor population during the period that wild birds were producing eggs. Thirteen of the birds currently in captivity were collected as eggs in the wild and later hatched in zoo incubators.

To date there have been no successful matings of these condors in captivity, due mainly to the fact that male and female birds have only recently been paired by the zoos. Whether or not these pairings will ultimately prove successful is not known, but aviculturalists experienced in the captive-breeding of the closely related **Andean condor** (*Vultur gryphus*) are optimistic that California condors will behave similarly in a captive-breeding programme.

There have been no successful reintroductions to the wild so far and there are not likely to be any for some time until targets have been achieved and there are enough 'surplus' birds. The Condor Recovery Team, a scientific advisory body to the Fish and Wildlife Service, is currently pondering the issue. There is certainly great public support for this programme and in 1984 and 1985 Congress appropriated $9 million for acquisition of a 5,670 ha (14,000 acres) critical condor foraging and staging area, which at the moment is also first choice for a release site. Such an ambitious scheme is essential as once the last birds are removed from the wild there will be less general incentive to protect habitat and consequently reintroduction would be more difficult.

Downtown Los Angeles is less than 75 km (45 miles) from the principal condor nesting areas in Ventura County, but the condor range itself is sparsely populated and is disturbed relatively little now, 36% of the land being in public ownership. Aircraft disturbance and mineral/oil extraction are unlikely to have been significant, but there have been deaths through collision with overhead wires. Indians once killed many birds for sacrifice and feathers but those days are long gone, as is lawful collection of skins and eggs, and habitat protection and poison/pollution control remain top priorities.

Despite everything, flying condors show little fear of man and apparently the more conspicuous and noisy a person is the more likely a condor is to approach. Let us hope that the 'blind faith' of this magnificent bird is repaid with a permanent place in American skies.

THE WORLD'S RAREST PIGEON
PINK PIGEON
The Mauritius **pink pigeon** (*Columba mayeri*), the rarest of the world's 255 pigeon species, has a population that has declined from 50–60 in the 1950s to less than 20 today. This shrinkage is the direct result of habitat loss, resulting in a range contraction of about 80% in just two decades.

Productivity in the wild population is low and it is suspected that only 10–20% of nests produce young, due to high predation upon the eggs. Wild breeding is seasonal, with a peak in egg-laying during the wet summer months and only a few or no birds breeding in the cool, dry winter. In captivity, however, the pigeons breed throughout the year and it is suspected that food shortages at the end of winter (September to November) prevent breeding at this time of year. If food shortages *are* limiting the population then artificial winter feeding should do much to increase the number of birds.

The captive-breeding programme at Black River, in Mauritius, has been very successful and between 1977 and the end of 1985 152 pink pigeons were bred (19 in 1984 and 20 in 1985). Many of the surplus birds have been circulated to zoos in Europe and America, and by 1984 enough birds had been bred in captivity to allow some to be released.

The first release site chosen was the Royal Botanic Gardens at Pamplemousses, Mauritius, because there the birds could be closely watched and monitored. Twenty-two birds were released, but although eggs were laid and young hatched, the population was not self-sustaining, due primarily to poaching. The main purpose of this study was to develop techniques for releasing pink pigeons into the wild, a project about to get underway.

In recent years hurricanes also reduced the tiny wild population and it is as well that there was a second captive-breeding project at Gerald Durrell's Jersey Wildlife Preservation Trust. Now, thanks to the same trust, telemetry studies are being undertaken on wild pink pigeons and wild birds released in the Macchebée Forest, Mauritius. In the fairly recent past this area held a small population of pink pigeons. It is hoped that this work will include supplementary feeding and other forms of direct management.

Another endangered race is *Columba inornata wetmorei*, the Puerto Rican sub-species of the **plain pigeon**, whose population in June 1986 was just 50–100 in the wild and 10 in captivity.

CHATHAM ISLAND ROBIN

Also confusingly called the Chatham Island robin-flycatcher or the Chatham Island black robin, the **Chatham Island robin** (*Petroica traversi*) has enjoyed a remarkable comeback after the population sank to just five in 1980. The New Zealand Wildlife Service developed a programme which entailed removing the eggs from the robins' nests and transferring them to the nests of the closely related Chatham Island tit. The robins continued to lay to replace the removed eggs and in this way it was possible to increase each season's production. The technique had already been used with other species and in this case the tits proved to be perfect foster-parents.

A critical turning point came in 1983/84 when some birds laid three clutches and the three pairs produced a total of 22 eggs. Eleven young survived, more than doubling the population. After that a 13-year-old female named 'Old Blue' was retired from the programme as a mother of six and grandmother of 11.

The few remaining robins were confined to the tiny 1 acre (0.4 ha) Little Mangare Island and were thus very vulnerable to natural disaster. But 19 fledglings were reared in 1985, bringing the total population to 38, the highest number at any time this century, and by the spring of 1986 the programme had been so successful it was thought that only one more season of assistance with breeding would be needed. But there followed a severe setback when storm and bird pox reduced the population to 23. However, 11 chicks were raised in the following season and the latest total was 30 birds.

Chatham and neighbouring islands are inhabited New Zealand protectorates to the east of the mainland and human settlement has made many inroads into the wildlife. Other endangered birds

'Old Blue', a 13-year-old female Chatham Island robin at the centre of a New Zealand Wildlife Service species-survival programme. (New Zealand Wildlife Service)

living there are the **Chatham Island oystercatcher** (*Haematopus unicolor chathamensis*), a race of the New Zealand sooty oystercatcher, the **Chatham Island pigeon** (*Hemiphaga novaeseelandiae chathamensis*), a race of the New Zealand pigeon, and the **Chatham Island taiko** (*Pterodroma magentae*), one of the world's rarest seabirds.

Also called the magenta petrel, the taiko was, until recently, known only from the type specimen collected in 1867. It was rediscovered in 1978, but it still remains a mystery as its breeding locality has not yet been discovered. However, some 26 individuals have been caught, ringed and examined, including a few recaptures, and a population of 70–100 birds has been suggested.

GUAM RAIL
Eight of the world's 124 species of rail are threatened by disappearing marshland habitat and introduced competitive domestic or predatory mammals. A few struggle on in the wild in tiny numbers but the **guam rail** (*Rallus owstoni*) is the only species whose entire population (just 33 birds in 1986) is confined to captivity.

Guam is a USA territory in the Pacific, about midway between

The Japanese crested ibis is now extinct in the wild in Japan. (Wild Bird Society of Japan)

Japan and New Guinea. The Australian brown tree snake and the Philippine rat snake, both bird and egg eaters, have been introduced to Guam since World War II and are now thought to be the main cause of a dramatic decline in native forest birds. Human disturbance of the island has also been great.

SAN CLEMENTE LOGGERHEAD SHRIKE

The future of this race (one of 11) of **loggerhead shrike** (*Lanius ludovicianus meransi*) is very uncertain. Restricted to one small island off the coast of southern California, it has suffered severe habitat alteration since the introduction of goats this century. Only 16 birds remained in 1974 and their reproductive success is very poor.

The population has increased under careful management but remains very unstable, for example falling from 50 to 28–36 between June and August 1986.

JAPANESE CRESTED IBIS

Six of the world's 31 ibis species are threatened, but the **Japanese crested ibis** ('**Toki**') (*Nipponia nippon*) is the most endangered of all. No wild bird exists in Japan any more and up to 1985 only 21 had been confirmed officially in China, though the total population might be 40–50. Hunting of the beautiful white and pink Toki for its feathers was widespread in former times and the species was thought to be extinct between 1890 and 1930, but then small numbers were found breeding in central Honshu on the Noto Peninsula and a few others on Sado Island in Niigata Prefectuna.

During the 1940s clearance of vast areas of forest destroyed much of the bird's natural habitat and by 1960 only some 12 birds remained in Japan. They were also recorded in Korea before World War II.

Today two males and two females are caged on Sado Island for the purpose of captive-breeding. Three of these were captured on Sado in 1981 and one male has been loaned by the Chinese government for three years from October 1985. All Japan's five remaining wild ibises were captured in 1981 (another was already in captivity) but three females have since died and failure of the breeding project so far is put down to the limited number and advanced age of the birds. Therefore the Japanese and Chinese governments decided that their closer co-operation was essential.

Decline was equally severe in China and not a single bird was seen between 1964 and May 1981, when seven were found in Yangxian Country, Shannxi Province in central China.

In the spring of 1986 the Japan International Co-operation Agency sent a survey team to Yangxian and as a result of their report the Japanese Ministry of Foreign Affairs will consider technical assistance for the Chinese Ministry of Forestry in managing these birds.

KAKAPO

The owl parrot or **kakapo** (*Strigops habroptilus*) is not only New Zealand's most endangered bird but also one of the world's most fascinating species. In 1980 only 15 individuals were known – all males – and although the position has improved since then the species remains top priority for the NZ Wildlife Service.

The kakapo is an extremely specialized bird and it seems likely that numbers were declining before the arrival of European settlers accelerated the process. Habitat destruction was disastrous, as was the introduction of domestic animals, especially the cat, as the kakapo has very short wings and is the only entirely flightless parrot. Sometimes it opens its wings when threatened or while climbing in trees when it may glide to the ground. It is also the heaviest member of this very large family of some 332 species in 82 genera, 30 species of which are threatened, many through wholesale exploitation as cagebird pets.

Like its New Zealand relative the kea, the kakapo is polygamous and the mating of this nocturnal bird is highly unusual. Males gather at night in traditional areas known as leks and advertise their presence with loud booming calls to attract the females who cannot see them easily in the dense cover. As with many other lekking animals, the male is not known to take any part in parental care.

The kakapo is unique in the way it feeds: it takes a blade of grass in its bill and chews it without severing it from the plant, extracting the juices but leaving the blade as a bundle of tangled fibres which dry white. After roosting by day under a rock or tree, the parrot wanders by night through the forest and next morning it is relatively easy to spot where it has been for it follows regular trails and these are marked by the pale, chewed grass-blades left behind.

The species soon became extinct on North Island and later confined to Fiordland. But in recent years some were rediscovered on Stewart Island off the south coast of South Island and some of these were later transferred to Little Barrier Island. And even more recently kakapos have been rediscovered in north-west Nelson.

THE RAREST BIRDS IN BRITAIN

Britain is no different from most countries in having a bird population changing in diversity and numbers all the time. In any year various species are contracting in range and numbers as factors such as habitat destruction, pollution and even long-term climatic change take their toll. Some may be declining as a direct result of the ascendency of others which are gaining control of particular niches.

On the other hand, incidental habitat alteration by man can assist some species – witness the proliferation of various gulls in response to an increased number of refuse tips, or water birds such as the tufted duck as flooded gravel pits have appeared in many places. And long-term climatic change can assist colonization by species from neighbouring countries. A trend towards a more continental-type climate, with more extreme summer and winter temperatures, is likely to bring breeding species from both north and south, as well as east, as indeed has been happening in recent years. As winters become more severe regular winter visitors to Britain from more northerly countries may stay to breed in increasing numbers, and as summers get hotter birds from more southerly countries might be more inclined to raise families in Britain.

In addition, there are more complicated factors such as eruptions – irregular migrations in response to fluctuating food supplies – which bring birds to Britain in varying quantities from neighbouring countries. Sometimes such species will stay to breed even when the food supply at home is adequate once more. But why some species such as the collared dove make sudden dramatic range expansions is largely a matter for conjecture.

To compare rarity requires some sort of determination of regularity, but this is not possible as some of Britain's very rarest breeding species have bred only occasionally over the last few decades whereas more recent colonizers have bred in Britain every year since their first arrival. Some may seem settled, but then suddenly stop breeding, so whatever list is put forward this year will be out of date next year.

It is also not possible to deal in absolutes when it comes to discussing non-breeding species for many birds do not occur in every year. We can offer suggestions as to the rarest winter visitors and passage migrants which have turned up in Britain in *most* years of recent decades, but there is also a list of well over 40 vagrants which have been recorded in this country only once. These have generally been blown off course or become disoriented en route to other countries and did not, as it were, set out to visit Britain.

On top of all this we have further complications in that birdwatching, despite its rapidly growing popularity, is still very much a developing interest. We will always have a widely varying range of skills, even though many fine visual aids, guidebooks, binoculars and telescopes are now available. Thus the ease with which a bird spotter can get his new record accepted by the rarities committee of the day will depend very much on his reputation and credibility. For example, when the report on rare birds in Great Britain in 1985 was published in autumn 1986 (there is always such a delay for reasons of both logistics and safeguarding sites), the British Ornithologists' Union Records Committee was still considering 337 records for 1985 and earlier years.

This was the 28th annual report of the committee and in 1985 they dealt with 894 records, 85% of which were accepted. These included 38 vagrants of 15 species from the USA – by far the best year ever, but no doubt this was linked to increased observation and not necessarily related to natural trends in bird movements.

Finally there is the problem of exotic species which have escaped from collections. Others have been deliberately released and have enjoyed surprising success. Some, such as the rose-ringed parakeet, have bred as feral birds for many years.

A few species, such as the great bustard and white-tailed sea eagle, have been the subjects of captive-breeding programmes and concerted efforts towards re-establishment in the wild, but others have recolonized Britain naturally, though often only through a great deal of assistance from man in the way of direct protection and habitat management.

Additions to the British Isles list, which certainly reflect the sociological aspect of birding, were as follows:

1901–1910 – 20
1911–1920 – 5
1921–1930 – 5
1931–1940 – 4
1941–1950 – 5
1951–1960 – 29
1961–1970 – 27
1971–1980 – 20

And a similar very high rate of 'discovery' is continuing in the 1980s.

BRITAIN'S RAREST OF ALL
BLACK-BROWED ALBATROSS

If we take numbers of *resident* individuals as our sole criterion then Britain's rarest species must be the **black-browed albatross** (*Diomedea melanophris*), a single specimen of which many birdwatchers have travelled to see every year since it joined gannetries at the Bass Rock in the Firth of Forth in 1967, later transferring to Hermaness, Shetland. There are over 20 records of the species in Britain, but so far this lonely individual has failed to attract a mate, and it is hardly likely to do so.

This species behaves like the wandering albatross and after breeding in the Sub-Antarctic migrates north in winter. Sometimes it reaches the northern hemisphere and can become marooned.

With its 229 cm (90 in) wingspan and 81–86 cm (32–34 in) length, this great bird, resembling an exceptionally large and stiff-winged great black-backed gull, is hardly likely to go unnoticed, though immatures are difficult to distinguish from immature grey-headed albatrosses. But it is the only albatross which occurs with any frequency in north-western Europe, mainly off Britain and Ireland.

Albatrosses are the world's

greatest gliders, depending on air currents for sustained flight. The region of very light winds and calms near the Equator, sometimes called the doldrums, more or less confines albatrosses to the southern hemisphere, but occasionally birds are carried over this invisible barrier on freak winds, when they end up stranded and have little hope of getting back to familiar haunts.

LONGEST PERIOD WITHOUT A BRITISH SIGHTING
BLACK-CAPPED PETREL – unseen since 1850

The vagrant which has not recurred in Britain for the longest period, but which still exists elsewhere, is the **black-capped petrel** (*Pterodroma hasitata*) of Dominica and the Caribbean. The last record is of a

The black-browed albatross occasionally gets marooned in Britain, one attracting birdwatchers to the Scottish islands for over 20 years. (Doug Allen, Oxford Scientific Films)

specimen caught alive on a heath at Southacre, near Swaffham, Norfolk, in March or April 1850.

Members of the genus *Pterodroma* have a forceful flight and it is generally young birds which travel great distances. This 41 cm (16 in) very rare bird, known to breed only in Hispaniola, occasionally wanders northwards and is found off Florida and South Carolina.

Whether the bird which visited Britain was the sub-species *P.h.hasitata* or the Jamaica petrel *P.h.caribbaea*, now possibly extinct, is not known.

Similarly, it is not known which sub-species of **rednecked nightjar** was shot at Killingworth, Northumberland on 5 October 1856, but none have been seen since. *Caprimulgus ruficollis ruficollis* breeds in Portugal, Spain and Morocco but *C.r.desertorum* in Algeria, Tunisia and south Sahara.

Ruficollis is fairly distinctive among some 70 species of nightjar as it has a yellow-rufous collar. The **British nightjar** (*Caprimulgus europaeus*) winters mainly in Africa, from the Sudan south to Cape Province.

BRITAIN'S RAREST NON-BREEDING ANNUAL VISITOR
GYRFALCON
This beautiful bird has been the most prized species in falconry for hundreds of years and Arab enthusiasts have paid enormous sums for this largest of all falcons. Because of the falconry interest it appears to have declined earlier than other falcons, though it is still just about an annual visitor to

Britain from its more northerly breeding range.

Most birds which visit Britain originate from Canada and Greenland and are of the *candicans*, an almost pure white variety of *Falco rusticolus*. The bulk of the western Palearctic population, recently estimated at 600–1,000 pairs excluding the Soviet Union, is basically sedentary, though some wandering does occur. Further east, Russian birds move south more frequently and there is no evidence that Icelandic birds leave the country. It is generally birds from Greenland which come to Britain via Iceland, white birds having been recorded as far south as Portugal, Spain and northern Italy. Some southern European records are undoutedly escapes from falconers. Gyrfalcons come mostly to western Britain and Ireland. They are most likely to be seen in Shetland, northern Scotland, Cornwall, Devon and the Isles of Scilly in March, but there is a further peak in November-December.

Recent studies have shown that the species is not as scarce as once thought, for it is very secretive throughout its circumpolar range. Nest-robbing for falconry has been prevalent in some areas but overall the population seems to have stabilized. Environmental poisoning has not been significant as the species mostly lives in very remote areas.

Inland the gyrfalcon's main prey consists of about 92% ptarmigan and grouse by weight, but there is considerable local variation, and cyclical abundance of rodents such as lemmings can contribute to greater breeding success, with more young fledging. Some birds concentrate on prey from large seabird colonies, and coasts are a favourite haunt of wandering birds in winter.

The gyrfalcon has deceptively slow wingbeats but in level flight it can overtake a peregrine, and prey is often caught on the wing. Some species such as owls, skuas and gulls try to rise up above the falcon, but when the prey is sufficiently tired the gyr then takes them

spectacularly through rapid ascent.

BRITAIN'S RAREST BREEDING BIRDS

Britain's very rarest breeding birds include a number of species which have established toeholds in these islands as a result of recent range extensions from nearby countries. Most of these have colonized Scotland from the north, though a few have come from the south, and climatic change is often put forward as the most likely cause. Temporary weather patterns are important too in that unusual prevailing winds can bring 'falls' of birds, some of which stay on to explore the potential. Exceptional eruptions related to failure of food supplies overseas may be important too.

Some species have colonized whereas others (some closely related) from similar latitudes have not, so genetic rather than climatic change may be more relevant. But whatever the reasons, we have no way of assessing the permanency of these changes. Many colonizations have gone unnoticed and unrecorded in past centuries and apparent recent increasing incidence of colonization may be at least partly related to the growing number of experienced birdwatchers at large. Generally, strict secrecy is observed with recent colonizations and locations are not given, at least until the species are well-established and secure. There are birdwatchers and landowners who do not even report rare finds to bird-interest organizations.

Some species have bred in Britain on a very small number of occasions, perhaps even just once, but the following are likely to include the rarest *regulars*. Some may not breed in *every* year.

PARROT CROSSBILL

Previously only an irregular visitor to Britain with common crossbill invasions from Scandinavia and northern Siberia, the **parrot crossbill** (*Loxia pytyopsittacus*) first bred in north Norfolk in 1984, when a

The gyrfalcon is the largest of all falcons and a rare visitor to Britain. (P. Morris, Ardea London)

The brambling is one of a small number of Scandinavian species which have colonized Britain, in Scotland, in recent decades. (Eric Hosking)

pair reared four young and fledged a second brood. The established breeding range of the parrot crossbill is in Scandinavia, Estonia and north-west Russia, and this species is much less common than the other crossbills.

This is a bird of mature, open pine forest and mixed conifer forest with pines. The male is brick-red and the female olive-green and the huge head has a very heavy bill. Unlike the smaller-billed common crossbill, which concentrates on spruce-cone seed, the parrot crossbill favours pine seed, though neither is rigid in diet.

Breeding is well-timed so that hatching coincides with the opening of the hard pine cones in the early spring warmth, thus ensuring that seeds are easier to obtain. This programme means that the nest is completed in February and the female is sitting in March, often in sub-zero temperatures with lying snow.

The young are fed on a paste formed from pine seeds and water, which explains the adults' constant need to visit puddles. The young's bills do not become crossed before leaving the nest, thus facilitating easy feeding by the parents.

A further two broods were reared in Norfolk in 1985 and the pair returned to the site again in 1986. All crossbill species are quick to take advantage of new breeding sites but the parrot crossbill is much less prone to wandering than the others and the colonization might be short-lived, without further birds to produce a viable population.

SCARLET ROSEFINCH

Also known as the common rosefinch, the **scarlet rosefinch** (*Carpodacus erythrinus*) has been gradually extending its range westwards in Europe. It occurs through most of northern Eurasia from the Baltic east. Favourable winds have carried birds surprisingly long distances from Eurasia into Scandinavia on the autumn migration, and from there it is but a short hop to Britain. Birds are also brought to Britain through overshooting when they head northwards on the spring migration.

It is still generally only a summer visitor to Britain, retreating in winter to its ancestral Asian home. However, an increasing number of Norwegian birds turns up on passage each year, mostly in August/ September, the majority settling on Fair Isle between the Orkneys and Shetlands. Such range extension might well reverse in the future as the species performed a similar but temporary movement west earlier this century.

BRAMBLING

This species has long been a common winter visitor to Britain, where it is often seen in large flocks of the closely related chaffinch, but there was no recorded breeding between 1920 (Sutherland) and 1979 (Scotland). Since then there have been up to four pairs in most years.

The population of the **brambling** (*Fringilla montifringilla*) expands and contracts with the varying seed crop and only when this is exhausted does it usually appear in Britain. Its range overlaps with that of the chaffinch and when one spreads the other always seems to contract proportionately.

Most visitors to Britain come from Scandinavia and are seen from October to March throughout England, Wales and Scotland. This is just one in a steady flow of Scandinavian colonists in Scotland, following redwing (1925), wood sandpiper (1959) and fieldfare (1967). But in the case of the brambling there have been accepted breeding records from as far south

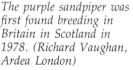

The purple sandpiper was first found breeding in Britain in Scotland in 1978. (Richard Vaughan, Ardea London)

as Buckinghamshire.

PURPLE SANDPIPER

This rocky-shore specialist feeder, *Calidris maritima*, with a wintering population of some 20,000, was first found breeding in Britain in Scotland in 1978. Since then at least one pair has bred at the same site in three consecutive years. An arctic/alpine breeder, it is seen mostly in the north-east, from Yorkshire to Scotland, and has little fear of man.

LAPLAND BUNTING

The **Lapland bunting** (*Calcarius lapponicus*) was only a scarce passage migrant and winter visitor to Britain until 1977, when 14 pairs were found at six distinct Scottish sites. Some nested successfully, but others failed to raise young. It was suggested that this could have been a freak occurrence as the winter of 1976/77 had been severe and protracted in Scotland, with snow remaining on the ground even in June, but pairs have been found in subsequent years, with a maximum of 16.

This colourful bunting breeds in arctic and sub-arctic Eurasia and North America, but only in Scandinavia and Finland elsewhere in Europe. As a winter visitor to Britain it is very scarce, for it generally moves further down into even

The Lapland bunting appears to have colonized Britain in the wake of climatic changes. (Kevin Carlson, Nature Photographers Ltd)

more temperate areas. Small numbers of Lapland buntings are seen on passage from September to early November in Shetland and on the east and south coasts.

It does seem as if a climatic change has brought this bird – which generally breeds on shrub and moss tundra – to nest in Britain. In Scotland it is found on the barren mountain tops and screes, but wintering birds frequent shore and marsh.

SHORELARK

Scandinavian **shorelarks** (*Eremophila alpestris*) have wintered on the east coast of England for a long time, but the first summering was not noticed till 1972, and then in Scotland. Pairs were recorded from 1973 in the Highlands, but some subsequent years were missed in the colonization.

The shorelark is widespread in the higher northern latitudes of Europe and Asia. In North America, where it is known as the horned lark because of the black tufts on the crown, it is the only lark present and consequently has exploited a much wider range of habitats. Another extraordinary feature of its range is that in Europe there is a thousand-mile break in its continuity, with birds well-established in southern mountains.

Shorelark is an appropriate name for this bird during the winter, especially January, but otherwise it favours inland haunts, in Britain at least.

TEMMINCK'S STINT

The first British breeding of the **Temminck's stint** (*Calidris temminckii*) was recorded in 1934, but there were only another three nests up to 1968, and none of these hatched off successfully. Then a couple of nests were found in Scotland and since then it seems to be getting established north of the Border, with a few more in Yorkshire. Whereas many of the early nests were deserted, fledging is now more frequent.

Britain is at the extreme western edge of the species' range, most breeding being in the tundra from Norway east to Siberia, but it is also a scarce passage migrant to Britain.

Temminck's stint has a very interesting breeding cycle. The eggs are laid very late, from the second half of June, but each female pairs in rapid succession with two males on different territories and lays one clutch on each. Every male also pairs successively on the same territory with two females and fertilizes one clutch of each. The first clutch is incubated by the male, the second by the female, and both take sole responsibility for their broods. Such behaviour no doubt makes best use of the short northern breeding season.

The eggs are remarkable too. Wader eggs generally are large for the size of the birds and in most

A relative of the canary, the serin was not found breeding in Britain between 1852 and 1967. (Heinz Schrempp, Frank Lane Picture Agency)

the complete clutch is 50–70% of the female's bodyweight. But in stints it reaches 90%, so that in Temminck's, which produces two clutches in a very short period of time, the total weight is an amazing 180% or so of the female's bodyweight, the latter shrinking dramatically during the egg-formation period.

SERIN

This relative of the canary, which is commonly kept as a cagebird in southern Europe, is said to have been on the move for over 200 years. At the beginning of the 19th century it started to spread north and east from its native home in the Mediterranean, Greece and Iberia to colonize most of Europe, including France to the Channel coast. There was a record of breeding in Hampshire in 1852, but the first British record this century was from Dorset in 1967. Since then it has been found breeding throughout the south, including Sussex, Devon and Worcestershire.

Climatic change was suggested for the spread, but, in view of the fact that it occurs over a very wide climatic range and other species have not followed suit, genetic change in migratory habit seems more likely.

In view of the species' history, British records have been less numerous than expected, despite the fact that the **serin** (*Serinus serinus*) is relatively easy to monitor, being a bright, green-and-yellow bird with a distinctive tinkling song, frequently found around gardens and villages. However, the incidence of passage migrants is increasing, November and May being the best months for the autumn and spring migrations respectively.

SPOTTED CRAKE

This well-camouflaged bird has been particularly difficult to observe because it is extremely elusive and lives in the densest mixed fen swamps. It was probably fairly common before the extensive drainage of the 19th century, which has continued into recent times. Now it is restricted to odd patches of suitable habitat. Very few nests have ever been found, and these by chance. The best way to locate the bird is through its 'whiplash' call at night.

A summer visitor to Britain, the **spotted crake** (*Porzana porzana*) breeds across Scandinavia and Finland south to France, Italy, Yugoslavia and western Asia and winters in the Mediterranean and North Africa. It is found throughout the UK mainland, but not in Ireland.

Two British species have been in protracted, apparently irreversible, decline in Britain and their extinction in these islands looked imminent. But an odd thing happened – as their southern populations tumbled other birds, apparently from Scandinavia, colonized Scotland. But these two species, detailed below, still remain among the very rarest British breeders.

RED-BACKED SHRIKE

The **red-backed shrike**'s (*Lanius collurio*) population has been declining in much of western Europe, including Britain, since the 19th century. This has been linked to climatic deterioration, with cooler and wetter summers this century reducing the shrike's main insect prey. Yet the decline has been steadily accelerating through both relatively warm and cool periods. Habitat loss may be a more significant reason, especially sacrifice of heathland to farming.

In 1952 there were over 300 pairs, in 1960 250, in 1971 80–90, 52 in 1974 and just 10 in 1984. But whereas the species seems to have deserted its traditional strongholds in southern and eastern England, there have been recent records of birds in Scotland, apparently from a healthy Scandinavian stock unaffected by the factors causing general decline. A periodic world-wide range shift is also suggested.

The shrike is more familiarly

known as the 'butcher bird' through its habit of impaling larger prey (such as bees, young birds and small mammals) on thorns and barbed wire, for later consumption, though it does not use such a 'larder' in its African winter quarters. Shrikes are usually present in Britain from May to September.

WRYNECK

Just nine breeding sites were reported for the **wryneck** (*Jynx torquilla*) in 1984, and all but one

The wryneck now seems to be lost as a British breeder south of the Scottish border. (J. Bottomley, Ardea London)

were from Inverness-shire, whereas the species' traditional stronghold was southern England. Now it seems to be lost as a breeding bird south of the Border, though the reasons why are not understood. Decline has been steady throughout much of western Europe for over 150 years: it could be due to climatic change, but habitat loss resulting in a major reduction in the staple ant diet could also be implicated.

Now the wryneck visits England only on the east coast as a displaced migrant, mainly in late August and early September if strong easterly winds blow during the southerly migration to winter in Africa.

Oddly, when the wryneck was common in England it never bred in Scotland, where the first two pairs were located in Inverness-shire in 1965, individuals having been seen there throughout the early sixties.

There is hope that the population is larger than apparent as this species is particularly hard to monitor. The colouring is cryptic and the birds, though noisy when attracting a mate, are very quiet and secretive after eggs are laid. Unless young are seen, breeding is most difficult to prove.

The wryneck is related to the woodpeckers, having two toes on each foot directed forward and two backward, but it does not have the woodpeckers' stiff tail to help in climbing trees, and its bill is weak, insects being taken from the bark or on the ground. Its name comes from one of the displays in which the head and neck are contorted in unlikely fashion.

BRITAIN'S RAREST BREEDING SEABIRD
MEDITERRANEAN GULL
Also known as the Mediterranean black-headed gull (the species is

distinguished from the black-headed gull by its black rather than dark-brown head), this bird first bred in Britain in 1968 at Needs Oar Point Nature Reserve on the Hampshire coast.

It has been spreading slowly north-westwards across Europe from its somewhat restricted range in south-east Europe, central and western Asia, though evidence of a long-term colonization in the north-west is not clear. However, it has also been increasing in numbers as a non-breeding visitor since the early 1960s, some birds staying on through the winter.

The **Mediterranean gull** (*Larus melanocephalus*) is easily overlooked among the large colonies of black-headed gulls, where most of the nests have been found, and it is probably the increasing interest in bird spotting which has led to these records. Mediterranean/black-headed hybrids have also been found inter-breeding with pure black-heads in the colonies. Mediterraneans, like most other gulls, have enjoyed a population boom in recent years and a range extension is a likely consequence of 'surplus' birds seeking out new nesting territories.

Outside the breeding season Mediterranean gulls are most easily found along the coast, but some occur inland at rubbish tips and reservoirs.

BRITAIN'S RAREST BREEDING BIRD OF PREY
MONTAGU'S HARRIER
All British birds of prey, including the owls, have suffered prolonged persecution by man through shooting, trapping and poisoning in the mistaken belief that these species made significant inroads into stocks of game and farm animals. But now, as in most developed countries, these days are past and the new battle is to preserve sufficient suitable habitats for these spectacular predators. Another major problem has been the continuing battle against egg collectors, for whom our birds of

prey seem to have had a special attraction. And, of course, the rarer a bird becomes the more its eggs are sought after.

In recent years Britain's most endangered bird of prey has been the **Montagu's harrier** (*Circus pygargus*). In England it has never been numerous, being at the north-western limit of its range which fluctuates with minor climatic variations. It is a summer visitor to Europe, where much of its favoured marsh, heath and moorland habitat has been eradicated. Recently, drier situations, especially among young

The Mediterranean gull was not known to breed in Britain before 1968. (J. B. & S. Bottomley, Ardea London)

The Montagu's harrier reached a low point in 1974 when no breeding pairs at all were found in Britain. (M. England, Ardea London)

forestry, have been favoured. Being a migrant, recolonization should be relatively easy but habitat decimation remains a problem. The species also breeds in southernmost Sweden, Estonia, North Africa and west-central Asia, wintering from the Mediterranean to southern Africa.

Oddly enough, at the beginning of this century when it was almost shot and collected out of existence in Britain, this harrier was expanding northwards. For example, it first bred in Denmark in 1900 and three years later there were about 200 pairs there.

There was a sudden upsurge in numbers in Britain after the last war, but the reasons for this are not clear, and the centre of population shifted from East Anglia to south-west England. By the mid-50s there were thought to be 40–80 pairs, but from then on the trend was downhill, reaching a low point in 1974 when no breeding pairs at all were found, although a small trickle of passage migrants continued from late April to late September in most years.

From 1974 onwards small numbers were reported in most seasons and there has been an increasing tendency for birds to use agricultural land, as is more common in the rest of the range. Some nests have even been found in standing corn and this presents a new problem in that harrier conservation now depends very much on the goodwill and vigilance of farmers.

In 1986 there were seven pairs in Britain, six of which were successful in rearing 13 young. One nest fell victim to a combine harvester because the farmer did not know of its existence, but one chick survived and successfully fledged. Abroad there has been a special problem when the birds breed late, for the fields may be harvested before the young are fledged. In an instinctive attempt to protect themselves when the combines approach, they lie on their backs and often get their feet chopped off.

Internationally the population seems to be declining, though there are exceptions. Poisoning is still common in winter quarters, where the birds commonly spend the night on paddy fields sprayed with dieldrin, and the fight to stop British migrants being shot in France has been difficult.

ENGLAND'S RAREST BREEDING BIRD OF PREY
GOLDEN EAGLE

The **golden eagle** (*Aquila chrysaetos*) was exterminated in England and Wales by about 1850, and in Ireland by about 1912, but in 1969 a pair returned to breed in the Lake District, the first English record for over 100 years. In July 1986 one bird was fledged from this site, the 14th since it was first occupied. And in recent years there has been a second pair breeding in England.

The British decline began in the 18th century when sheep farming became popular and many eagles were shot by ignorant farmers who thought the birds took many healthy animals. The situation was aggravated by even more shooting from the 19th century as gamekeepers sought to protect grouse and other gamebird stocks. There was some revival when the intensity of keepering lapsed during the two world wars, but a further major decline came in the 1950s and 1960s when chlorinated hydrocarbons used in sheep dips and on seed dressings worked their way through the food chain to become concentrated in the fat of eagles and other birds of prey, resulting in loss of fertility and egg-shell thinning. And while skin collecting had more or less disappeared, egg collecting continued into recent times.

After these persistent chemicals were banned a steady population increase began and there are now some 425 pairs plus about 90 individuals in Scotland. The species ranges widely over Europe, Asia, the Middle East, Mediterranean, North Africa and North America, but nowhere is it very common.

Ringing records show that British birds do not move south of their

Only two pairs of golden eagle are known to nest in England but the species is recovering well in Scotland. (Niall Rankin, Eric Hosking)

breeding range, even in severe winters. Birds pair for life and generally have two or three nest-sites, but up to 14 have been recorded for one pair. Large, old trees and inaccessible cliff ledges are favoured. Tales of very large animals or even children being carried away are to be viewed with scepticism as the maximum weight most golden eagles can lift is 4–5 kg (8.8–11 lb).

Sadly, there is a new threat to the golden eagle and other upland birds. Afforestation is becoming more profitable than sheep farming and many of the wild hills are becoming blankets of conifers, eradicating the eagles' preferred habitat.

WHITE-TAILED SEA EAGLE

In terms of successful pairs, the **white-tailed** or **sea eagle** (*Haliaeetus albicilla*) might be considered Britain's rarest breeding species as 1985 saw the first bird to be raised in the wild in Britain for some 70 years. But this was only as a result of 10 years' co-operation between the Nature Conservancy Council and the Norwegian Government to re-establish the bird in Scotland.

The sea eagle was last reported breeding in England on Culver Cliffs on the Isle of Wight in 1780, and in Ireland around 1898. It was once quite common and also nested in the Lake District and Devon.

Although primarily a scavenger throughout its range, the sea eagle occasionally takes healthy lambs and sheep farmers soon put a price on its head. In Britain its eventual extinction was a result of direct and sustained persecution by shepherds, gamekeepers, fishery owners, skin collectors and egg collectors. For once, its decline was not a question of significant habitat loss.

The last British breeding record is from 1916 when an English vicar took the eggs from a nest on the Isle of Skye. From then on there were reports of only rare vagrants. Perhaps the last British-bred bird was the almost white bird, said to be 30 years old, shot in Shetland in 1918.

Unfortunately, the choice of Fair Isle in the northern isles as the first reintroduction site in 1968 was a poor one and the few birds released there soon died or moved away. The Isle of Rhum in the Inner Hebrides was a much better prospect, sea eagles having last bred there in 1907, and since 1975 over 80 birds have been released on this National Trust reserve, in the hope that they would breed and the colony grow. Food has been provided at special dumps and includes fish, venison offal and gulls, the young Norwegian birds quickly learning to kill seabirds for themselves. Considerable patience was necessary as sea eagles take some five years to reach maturity, but finally, in 1985, four pairs made serious attempts to breed and one was successful. The same pair fledged two young in 1986, but up till then none of the others had bred. Three other pairs laid eggs in 1986 but they all failed through natural causes, one at the point of hatching. The position is less rosy over much of the bird's range where illegal poisoning and shooting continues, though the species is gaining ground in some countries.

The British breeding project has rather overshadowed the fact that England has enjoyed the sight of some truly wild sea eagles in recent years. One spent the whole winter in Buckinghamshire, and a German-ringed bird died in Norfolk in 1985. Most occur in eastern England from November to March and if trends continue, with successful breeding, more birds should wander to winter in southern England.

OTHER VERY RARE BRITISH BIRDS OF PREY – BREEDING OR OTHERWISE
SNOWY OWL

After all the excitement of the first-ever recorded British breeding of **snowy owls** (*Nyctea scandiaca*) in 1967, there has been disappointment as this handsome, white, high-arctic species has not bred here in recent years.

In the 19th century the snowy owl was a comparatively regular winter visitor to Shetland, but by the early 20th century it had become only a rare vagrant. Decreasing incidence in Britain in the 20th century could have been linked to a warming up of the Arctic 1900–40, which meant that the birds were more inclined to stay further north, but from 1963 birds were again seen regularly.

It was a memorable day indeed when, in 1967, a nest with three eggs was found on the open hillside on the tiny island of Fetlar in the Shetlands. Close protection was obviously essential as the crofters' sheep and ponies grazed there and a regular steady stream of bird-watchers might endanger the ground nest. So the RSPB mounted a round-the-clock guard and in the end seven eggs were laid, all of which hatched. Two of the young died, but five flew – a high success rate.

With continued close protection over nine years, what was presumably the same pair of snowy owls raised 21 young, but in 1975 the old male disappeared and no owls have fledged there since. The site has continued to be occupied by females, and unfertilized eggs have been laid in some years, but there has been no strong male nearby, though a few have been seen elsewhere in Scotland, including Fair Isle.

The males are considerably smaller than the females and it could be that as they are more susceptible to cold they find rabbit hunting in Britain difficult. Certainly when, in 1973, there were two nests on Fetlar, the lone male could not provide for both and the younger female deserted her nest and three eggs. It is hoped that another male will soon serve the waiting females (there have been up to five present at one time).

Some of the Shetland Islands are close in appearance to the high-arctic tundra, where the snowy owl needs its exceptionally dense and downy plumage to keep warm. Also its feather cells are filled with air for extra insulation, and the short bill and legs are largely concealed by feathers, right down to the claws. Its range is across northern Asia, northern Canada and the Holarctic. Birds have been seen in

The return of the osprey as a British breeder has done much to promote the conservation movement. (Georg Nystrand, Frank Lane Picture Agency)

both summer and winter in Shetland.

Snowy owls fluctuate in abundance according to density of prey. In a good year clutches of 10–14 can be laid but in a poor one 2–4 or even none. Periodically the lemming and hare populations crash in the Arctic and then large numbers of snowy owls appear in the USA in search of food. Some of these birds have rested on ships and ended up in Britain!

OSPREY

The fish-eating **osprey** (*Pandion haliaetus*), has probably done more than any other species to stimulate interest in birdwatching and conservation in Britain. Yet it is one of the most widespread of all birds of prey, breeding in North and Central America, parts of the Mediterranean, northern and eastern Europe, much of Asia, sporadically in Africa and along the coast of much of Australia.

Like all the other large raptors, it was persecuted to extinction in many of these regions, and Britain lost it as a breeder in 1910, though it remained a passage migrant. When it returned to breed in 1954 it generated colossal public interest and in subsequent years many thousands of people have had the thrill of watching the pair at Loch Garten, Scotland, from a hide. But the RSPB had to mount a round-the-clock vigil against egg collectors, and in 1986 vandals actually tried to cut down the nest tree with a chainsaw! Nests are used for many years and are only deserted after repeated disturbance, and to everyone's relief the famous birds re-adopted the repaired Loch Garten tree.

In 1986 40 pairs were located in highland Scotland. Thirty-four pairs laid eggs and 24 succeeded in raising 47 young – only slightly down on 1985. Almost all European breeding ospreys winter in Africa south of the Sahara.

Now more and more passage birds are seen in southern England. They turn up regularly at certain reservoirs, even in suburbia, and can take fish up to about 57 cm (22 in), weighing 1,500 gm (3.3 lb).

RED KITE

Scotland might have the osprey but Wales alone can claim the **red kite** (*Milvus milvus*) in Britain. The fact that it never quite became extinct in these islands is partly a matter of luck, but also a tribute to the efforts of a small number of caring people. It is as well they succeeded for natural recolonization would have been most difficult.

In past centuries the kite was very common in Britain, especially in mediaeval towns where it scavenged freely. It was an everyday sight in London, which Shakespeare referred to as a 'city of crows and kites'. For a long time it was a capital crime to kill kites in London as they were said to help keep the streets clear of filth. But in the countryside the bird soon had a price on its head as it commonly took free-range fowls.

Still common in the early 18th century, the kite was soon to fall victim to man's ruthless persecution of raptors in so-called defence of game. Skin collectors took innumer-

Once common in London, the red kite now breeds only in Wales within the British Isles. (Eric Hosking/ RSPB)

able kites and the depredations of egg thieves have been particularly disastrous on the small stocks this century. The last English birds to be seen were in Lincolnshire in 1870 and Scotland's last went in 1900.

In 1905 there were just 9–12 kites left in Britain, in the upper Towy Valley. With tremendous help from a few people this tiny population has gradually grown. In 1986 48 Welsh pairs produced 29 young. Thirty-nine pairs laid that year but only 22 managed to fledge young. Some failed naturally but seven nests were robbed, despite the RSPB's use of a protection scheme employing sophisticated electronic equipment.

The red kite has a remarkably small range, breeding outside Europe only in very small numbers. It has declined almost everywhere as greater concern for hygiene has removed most carrion. On the other hand it is making a comeback in many parts where protection is now afforded and pesticides are being brought under control, and it has learnt to exploit the many wildlife fatalities along roads.

The isolated Welsh breeding population was thought to be totally sedentary but recent ringing recoveries have shown that some young move south-east into England in winter. And a ringed German bird has been recovered in the Welsh breeding range.

There are special problems for the kite in Wales. The country has the lowest-known rate of fledging success – an average of just 0.6 surviving chicks per breeding attempt, compared with a world-wide average of 1.44 and a maximum of 1.68 in West Germany. This could be linked to the difficulty of finding sufficient food in a rainy climate for the kite is one of those raptors which will remain at its roost all day in adverse weather. But it takes a wide variety of food – birds, mammals, amphibians, reptiles, fish and insects, a high proportion taken alive.

Outside the Welsh stronghold, there are occasional vagrants in Britain. An increasing number of kites have been seen in Devon and Scotland and these could well be the forerunners of potential colonization.

THE MOST ABUNDANT BIRD IN THE WORLD
RED-BILLED QUELEA

There seems to be little doubt that the **red-billed quelea** (*Quelea quelea*), a seed-eating African weaverbird, is the most abundant species on earth. In 1968 Crook and Ward estimated the population at 1–10,000 million birds, but their estimate was based on reported kills as a pest, which are always likely to be exaggerated. A more recent estimate by Clive Elliott was based on breeding reports and a continent-wide adult breeding population of 1,500 million is thought to be more accurate.

The bird's range covers the Sahel from Senegal to Sudan, and the savannah regions from Sudan south to the Transvaal in South Africa. The genus of queleas or diochs contains three species and there are three races of the red-billed.

A population within a region can breed up to five times in a year but there is no proof that the same individuals are involved. Wear and tear on the individual would make it most unlikely that it would breed more than twice a year, perhaps, exceptionally, three times. Ward gives a production figure of 2.3 fledged chicks per pair from an average clutch of three. The different populations throughout Africa have different breeding seasons so there is no seasonal peak population level overall.

Individual flocks seldom exceed more than 10,000 birds but night roosts and breeding colonies can be much larger. It is said that one roost in Sudan was counted and contained 32 million birds, but the largest seen by Clive Elliott was at Tsavo in Kenya and contained about four million. The word 'invasion' is inapplicable for *Quelea quelea* as the bird migrates according to regional fluctuation in food supplies and anyone claiming a feeding flock of more than a few thousands is likely to be exaggerating. Flocks leaving a roost at dawn might temporarily contain 100,000 birds but these would soon break up into much smaller units to feed.

In such vast numbers this 20 g (0.7 oz) bird is the world's worst avian agricultural pest (see page 180).

OTHER VERY ABUNDANT SPECIES

In 1951 Fisher proposed the **common starling** (*Sturnus vulgaris*) and **house sparrow** (*Passer domesticus*) as the world's most abundant landbirds, but it has been pointed out that while their distribution is exceedingly wide their occurrence is relatively localized. The house sparrow is undoubtedly the world's most successful introduced species and already occupies over two-thirds of the world's land surface. While not so widespread as the house sparrow, the starling is equally adaptable and assembles in impressively vast numbers.

Darwin suggested that the **fulmar** (*Fulmarus glacialis*) was the most numerous bird in the world. He was probably misled by his own encounters with fulmars at sea in the North Atlantic, where large assemblies do occur. Since his day the species has enjoyed a remarkable spread but in no way can fulmar numbers be compared with the abundance of other seabirds.

Fisher proposed the **little auk** (*Alle alle*) as the most abundant seabird, but auks are notoriously difficult to census. Several species, including puffin, guillemot, and least and crested auklets, are

The red-billed quelea of Africa is not only the most abundant bird in the world but also the worst avian agricultural pest. (Matthew Hillier)

thought to number several millions of pairs, but there is a tendency to overestimate the populations of colonial species. Few serious surveys have been made and there is much speculation.

The enormous colonies, large (Antarctic-Sub-Antarctic) breeding distribution and wide oceanic range, over much of which it is seasonally abundant, has led many people into suggesting that **Wilson's storm petrel** (*Oceanites oceanicus*) is the most abundant bird on earth. Again such a notion seems fanciful, though this species could be the most abundant seabird with an estimated population of some hundreds of millions. This very small, 18–19 cm (7–7.5 in) bird is rarely seen in large numbers but is fond of following ships.

Quite apart from the very wide distribution of many seabirds it is increasingly difficult to estimate their worldwide populations through fluctuating fortunes. Some have probably declined overall through pollution whereas others have exploited the vast increase in offal generated by an ever-expanding fishing fleet.

America's most numerous land-bird is probably the **redwinged blackbird** (*Agelaius phoeniceus*), which has been well-censused because of the great agricultural damage it inflicts. A US Fish and Wildlife Service roost survey during the winter of 1976/77 in Kentucky and Tennessee revealed 25 roosts containing over one million birds in each and a total of 47 million birds for these two states alone!

BRITAIN'S MOST ABUNDANT BREEDING BIRD
WREN

The abundance of resident species is related to the severity of recent winters, especially in a climate which is very unpredictable and to which some species do not appear to have become fully adapted. But after a run of mild winters our most numerous bird is the **wren** (*Troglodytes troglodytes*), with a population of 15–20 million.

The common wren is the only Old World representative of an extremely common New World family. It is a very widespread species with five races in Britain and seven in North America, where it is known as the winter wren, many of which migrate away from the more severe weather there. In northern Europe, too, the wren displays some movement south for winter, and exceptionally heavy birds (probably of Scandinavian origin) are sometimes caught in quite large numbers at ringing stations along the east coast of England. In southern England there is some local movement into better habitat in winter.

The wren is particularly suscept-ible to cold weather because it is largely insectivorous and its tiny body, with a proportionately greater surface area than that of

larger birds, is less able to stand heat loss and the subsequent drain on energy reserves. After the winter of 1962/63 (the most severe for 200 years) the wren's population was reduced by some 78%, though fortunately it had the ability to make a remarkable comeback, and between 1964 and 1974 its population multiplied tenfold to 10 million pairs. In recent years the number of severe winters has increased, those of 1981/82, 1984/85 and 1985/86 being costly in wren lives. That of 1978/79 reduced the wren population by 40% but the species almost fully recovered in just one season.

In order to mitigate the effects of a severe British winter the wren has evolved an unusual communal roosting habit, for when bodies are huddled together the exposed surface area is reduced and with it heat loss. Nine wrens have been found in an old song-thrush nest, 10 in a coconut shell and, incredibly, 41, 51 and 61 in different nest-boxes. A remarkable adaptation for a pugnacious bird which usually roosts singly. But the British wren-roost record is 96 in the loft of a house during a six-week period from January to March 1979, when numbers fluctuated according to the temperature and at times of peak numbers there was a queue to enter the hole!

It is thought that the British wren's sedentary behaviour has some survival value through intimate knowledge of winter territories in securing both food and warm roosts. After severe population cutbacks it was noticed that remaining birds concentrated in wooded areas and waterside vegetation, and recolonization took place in gardens and orchards before field hedgerows. Scrub and woodland may hold anything from 13 to 100 pairs per square kilometre.

The wren is dependent on the weather for breeding. It needs sufficient rainfall to ensure the compactness of its domed nest. The structure must be built with damp materials as tightness is achieved through shrinkage on drying. Wrens have been seen to commence building at the onset of a shower. The male builds up to four 'cock' nests and tries to attract a passing female into one. When a female chooses a nest she will then line it and lay her eggs.

OTHER ABUNDANT BRITISH BREEDING SPECIES
BLACKBIRD

After a hard winter, when the wren population is cut back, then the **blackbird** (*Turdus merula*) is probably Britain's most abundant breeding bird, with an end-of-breeding-season population of 10–15 million birds. As the largest of several very common species, the blackbird is better able to stand energy and weight loss in sustained frost. For example, during the winter of 1962/63 its population dropped by only 18%, yet even the **song thrush** (*Turdus philomelos*) suffered a 57% reduction.

At the beginning of this century the song thrush probably outnumbered the blackbird by 5 to 1. Favourable climatic conditions no doubt helped the blackbird during the first half of this century, as it did many other species, but the ability to adapt to changing habitats seems to have been more important. This favourite songster was once chiefly a bird of woodland edge and it found the proliferation of lawns and suburbia much to its liking, with an easy supply of invertebrate food such as earthworms.

Studies have shown that the blackbird's nesting success is higher on farmland and in suburbia (particularly gardens) than in woodland. And the higher productivity means that the population has been better able to maintain its level despite a high mortality rate through cats and road traffic.

The **chaffinch** (*Fringilla coelebs*) is probably the next most common, followed by **starling** (*Sturnus vulgaris*), **house sparrow** (*Passer domesticus*), **robin** (*Erithacus rubecula*) and **blue tit** (*Parus caeru-*

Berries help the blackbird survive severe winters, after which the species generally replaces the more vulnerable wren as Britain's most abundant breeding bird. (M.C. Wilkes, Aquila Photographics)

leus), all of which are thought to have peak populations of some five million pairs. These are all species which have adapted well to a wide range of man-made habitats over the last century and have taken advantage of garden food handouts and/or artificial nest-sites.

The **willow warbler** (*Phylloscopus trochilus*) could be Britain's most numerous summer visitor, with six million individuals, reflecting its great success throughout western Europe.

THE MOST WIDESPREAD SPECIES IN THE WORLD

Distribution is a very complex subject full of variables. It is forever changing as species success waxes and wanes in accordance with long-term factors such as climatic change and short-term influence such as habitat modification by man. Worldwide distribution is rare at the level of genera and species, but among the most widespread bird families are grebes, cormorants, herons, harriers, falcons, rails, pigeons, nightjars, pipits, thrushes and crows. This does not imply direct correlation with abundance as many widespread species are restricted to small pockets of suitable habitat across the world.

Several seabird and shorebird genera are virtually cosmopolitan, and a few non-passerines are nearly cosmopolitan, including the **osprey** (*Pandion haliaetus*), **peregrine** (*Falco peregrinus*), **Kentish plover** (*Charadrius alexandrinus*) and **barn owl** (*Tyto alba*).

THE MOST WIDESPREAD PASSERINE
SWALLOW

In terms of zoogeographical distribution the **swallow** (*Hirundo rustica*) is the most widespread 'perching bird', being found worldwide except in Antarctica and on some remote islands. There are 74 species of swallow in 17 genera.

The common swallow's migration is probably the most familiar of all bird movements as most swallows from the Western Palearctic move south of the Equator in winter in search of sufficient insect food. Sometimes unseasonal weather can cause widespread mortality among swallows which either leave rather late in the autumn or arrive early in spring.

Known as the barn swallow in many countries, *rustica* varies its diet according to location. In Britain it eats mainly large flies such as bluebottles and hoverflies but in its main wintering quarters in South Africa ants are favoured.

Swallows now rarely use natural nest-sites in Britain, but elsewhere in their wide range, where buildings are not available, cliffs, caves and even tree-sides are commonly used. It is thought that the swallow's range was much more restricted before mankind provided it with artificial structures on which to build its nests, unless tree-nests were more common.

Despite its wide choice of territory and habitat, the swallow will often return to the same farm in subsequent years, and ringing recoveries have proved that they will even return to the same nest.

The swallow is also the most widespread summer visitor to Britain.

BRITAIN'S MOST WIDESPREAD BREEDING BIRD
SKYLARK

Britain is indeed fortunate that its most widespread bird should be one whose magnificent song has inspired some of its most accomplished poets. And one of the reasons why the **skylark** (*Alauda arvensis arvensis*) has adapted so well to new open habitats is that it delivers the famous song from the air and is not dependent on a perch.

A breeding bird throughout Europe (except Iceland and northern Scandinavia), much of Asia and parts of North Africa, the skylark numbers 2–4 million pairs in the British Isles. And this population seems to have varied little in recent times, by under 30% since 1964. It is, however, affected by severe winters, the British population of 1963 being just 64% of the 1968 level after two exceptionally cold years. Nonetheless, many Continental skylarks join British birds in winter because the UK climate is far less extreme.

There are two species of skylark and 10 races of *arvensis*, *A.a.arvensis* being the most successful. It must have been far less widespread when Britain was largely wooded, a further spur to increase being the

spread of agriculture and extensive land drainage, for this is chiefly a species of dry country. Larger fields are preferred so the recent trend towards so-called 'prairie farming' will have helped too.

Skylarks nest in a very wide variety of habitats, from coast to mountain, from saltmarsh, sand-dunes and heaths to farmland and moorland even up to the arctic-alpine level in the Cairngorms, above 1,000 m (3,280 ft). Short veg-

The skylark has adapted well to agriculture's sweeping changes in the countryside and is now Britain's most widespread breeding bird. (Eric Hosking)

etation in which to feed is essential and one of the best skylark habitats is chalk downland. On arable farmland there are 10–50 pairs per square kilometre, but up to 70 on coastal dunes. Distribution is much more sparse over uplands.

A wide variety of foods is taken, including the seeds of wild plants and insects and other invertebrates, especially beetles, but in mid-winter it may feed almost entirely on the leaves of cereals. It also takes a little grain and some specialist growers have condemned it as a pest. But on the whole damage is insignificant and must be balanced against the good done by the species in consuming invertebrate pests.

The average annual mortality rate for adults is about 33% – low for a temperate small passerine, but in the 19th and early 20th centuries many further birds were killed for the table. The only naturally occurring lark in America is the shorelark, one of the world's most numerous birds.

In Canada the European skylark provides a remarkable example of range limitation. It remains confined all year to the campus of Victoria University and near Victoria Airport.

THE WORLD'S MOST WIDESPREAD LANDBIRD FAMILY
FALCONIDAE

There are 60 species in 10 genera in this family, but the most widespread genus is *Falco* with 37 species. Representatives are found in all continents except Antarctica, ranging from the tiny 15 cm (6 in) Philippine falcon to the spectacular 50–60 cm (20–24 in) gyrfalcon. *Falconidae* occur in a wide range of habitats from arctic tundra (gyr) to desert (North African sooty falcon). Some species, such as the common kestrel of Britain and Europe, have proliferated in recent years, making good use of man-made habitat such as roadway verges, but others have failed to adapt and now include one of the world's rarest birds – the Mauritius kestrel.

Many falcons have great dispersive abilities, 13 species breeding on two or more continents, and the peregrine is notable for having a worldwide breeding distribution virtually as wide as that of the entire genus.

The *Falconidae* also include caracaras, nine species of long-legged, buzzard-like New World birds.

THE WORLD'S MOST WIDESPREAD INTRODUCED SPECIES
HOUSE SPARROW

Though not the most numerous bird in the world, the **house sparrow** (*Passer domesticus*) is perhaps the most familiar for it has already colonized over two-thirds of the world's land surface, largely in the wake of man – it was the emigrant European's desire to retain the most familiar creatures around him that was responsible for much of the house sparrow's progress.

In the absence of suitable buildings house sparrows may make untidy, ball-like, domed nests in trees or bushes, but the provision of hay and straw stacks, farm buildings and cottages over the last few centuries were readily accepted as alternative nest-sites. Breeding close to man, sparrows were best able to take advantage of his food handouts. Towns were warm havens safe from many predators, and when horses provided the chief means of transport in towns and cities, sparrows were able to feed on corn spilt from nose-bags and among the litter on stable floors. Later, the spread of the motor car and increasingly mechanized and more efficient farming reduced the grain supply, but this was negated somewhat by the continuing spread of agriculture and increased cereal growing, and garden-bird feeding and rubbish tips provided further alternative food. But at the same time the species came to be a significant agricultural pest and as early as 1899 it was called the 'avian rat'.

A desire to control cankerworms

was said to be the reason for first introducing the house sparrow into the USA. Eight pairs were released in Brooklyn, New York in 1852, but they did not take. Later that year a further 100 birds were brought over from Europe. On arrival, 50 were released at the Narrows, but it was the 50 held in captivity and then released in 1853 at Brooklyn's Greenwood Cemetery which brought the first success. Many other introductions and transplants followed in America – partly through love of homeland birds and partly through desire to control insects.

From its natural breeding range in much of Eurasia, the house sparrow spread by taking advantage of favourable climatic changes, but it was chiefly deliberate introduction by man which took it all around the globe, particularly throughout the vast British Empire – Canada 1864 on (plus colonization from the USA), Australia 1863–72 (chiefly aesthetic reasons), New Zealand 1859–71 (chiefly insect control) and South Africa 1890–97. Other successful introductions include those to much of South America, the Falkland Islands,

Hawaii, Mauritius and Mozambique. In many of these countries its success was immediate and the house sparrow soon spread to neighbouring states.

It is now generally conceded that in sufficient numbers the house sparrow can cause serious damage to cereals at harvest time and to garden crops at other times, yet in many areas their control of insect pests is significant. They have also displaced some indigenous species and helped to spread disease by contaminating food stores with their droppings. Overall, the house sparrow is not considered to be a truly beneficial introduction anywhere.

The species' capacity for range extension has been greatly aided by its breeding cycle. In Britain, for example, eggs may be laid from March to August and 2–4 broods of 3–5 young reared.

The **common starling** (*Sturnus vulgaris*) has not spread either so widely or so rapidly. In some parts, such as the eastern USA, the starling is no longer seen in the vast flocks of 50 years ago and it appears that the world population has declined markedly after the initial

Having already colonized over two-thirds of the world's land surface, the house sparrow is the most widespread introduced species of bird. (M.C. Wilkes, Aquila Photographics)

'explosion' characteristic of introduced species freed for a time from the limiting factors, such as competition with other species in the natural range.

THE COUNTRY WITH THE MOST INTRODUCED SPECIES
HAWAII

Now the 50th state of the USA, Hawaii is an archipelago of eight large and over 100 smaller volcanic islands to which at least 68 species have been introduced by man. Sadly, the island's rich and diverse indigenous avifauna has had to compete with many of these aliens and has suffered greatly in the process.

Annexed by the USA in 1898, Hawaii became a port-of-call for trans-Pacific shipping and a wintering station for New England whalers. As a result many pest birds and mammals, such as rats, were introduced accidentally. In addition, other species were deliberately introduced from all around the globe, Hawaii's human population of some 965,000 being only about 2% full-blooded Polynesians; the rest are of Chinese, Korean, Japanese, Philippine and Caucasian origins.

New Zealand's introduced avifauna is remarkable in that 13 species were taken there by British colonists for aesthetic reasons alone. These are now the dominant songbirds there, much to the detriment of the more interesting native species.

THE MOST DYNAMIC RANGE EXTENSIONS OF MODERN TIMES

Natural range extension is not always easy to determine for the two most dynamic examples of modern times have been complicated by man's deliberate introductions. It is tempting to suggest that the collared dove's range extension has been the most phenomenal but this received great attention at the outset whereas the cattle egret's initial arrival and spread in the Neotropics was inadequately documented at the time.

COLLARED DOVE

Against all the odds imposed by man's proliferation, the **collared dove** (*Streptopelia decaocto*) has found a vacant niche in nature to exploit (possibly linked to the dovecote decline) and its world population has exploded since about 1930. Its range continues to increase.

The bird had spread to south-east Europe from northern India by the

The collared dove's ability to rear up to five broods in one season has greatly assisted its phenomenal range extension. (A. Butler, Aquila Photographics)

16th century, but expansion then ceased until 1930. Why this happened is unknown, though it has been suggested that a genetic mutation with less restrictive needs occurred. Increased arable farming in the wake of climatic improvements no doubt helped. During this century the species has spread north-westwards right through Europe from a range once restricted to Turkey, Albania, Bulgaria and Yugoslavia. Hungary was reached in 1932, Czechoslovakia in 1936, Austria in 1938, Germany in 1943, the Netherlands in 1947, Denmark in 1948, Sweden and Switzerland in 1949, France in 1950, Belgium, Norway and Britain in 1952 – nearly 1,000 miles in 20 years!

The first recorded British nesting was at Cromer, Norfolk in 1955 and during the first decade in the UK it spread at the incredible rate of 100% per annum. Towns, suburbs and villages were first to be colonized, particularly in the low-lying areas of coastal counties. As the best habitat was taken colonization slowed down, but still continued into rural areas and town centres. The Common Birds Census recorded a five-fold increase on farmland between 1969 and 1973 and early in the 1970s it was even breeding in the Faeroe Islands and Iceland. Strangely, pre-1950 attempts to introduce the species to Britain failed. But now it has bred in every county in the British Isles and is widespread, except in hilly districts, especially in the north and west.

There has also been a small spread into Turkmenistan, around the Caspian Sea, and Japan. Outside Europe the species is found in southern Asia and North Africa and there have been many introductions around the world.

Predominantly a vegetable feeder, the species' close association with human settlement has brought conflict with man and it is now shot as a pest in countries such as Britain where it has existed for only a few decades. Apart from wild foods, the main attraction is grain. They increasingly feed on stubble but damage to laid corn is probably negligible. Most complaints arise from assemblies of birds around stocks of harvested grain at mills, maltings, docks, farmyards, hen-runs and pheasant-rearing pens where there is often spillage. More seriously, they frequently get inside large stores where they foul grain and fodder crops.

The cattle egret has literally followed in the footsteps of cattle in its outstanding range extension this century. (Eric Hosking)

Fortunately for man, for reasons unknown, expansion through America has been slow and fairly restricted, for concern has been expressed that should this bird ever become established in the prairies around the world's greatest grain store the economic loss could be immense.

CATTLE EGRET

Unlike other members of the heron family, this bird concentrates on insects rather than fish, especially those disturbed by cattle hooves. As a result the **cattle egret** (*Areola ibis*) has enjoyed a phenomenal increase this century: from its original home in much of Africa, southern Asia, parts of Indonesia and southern Iberia, it has spread steadily, but the most dynamic gains have been in the New World.

Expansion into northern South America from about 1910 could have been by African colonists. In any event, from about 1930 cattle egrets extended their range explosively both north and south, through Central America, much of the USA and into Canada. In the other direction they have spread through Asia and all around the outer edge of Australia. The opening up of vast ranges for cattle ranching, the cutting down of forests and the draining of swamps has greatly increased the amount of habitat suitable for this bird.

Cattle egrets habitually follow a particular herd of cattle and feed on their own only when the cattle are at rest. In following cattle they have been found to expend a third less energy in walking (sometimes hitching rides on cattle backs) and catching 50% more insects than they would do on their own.

OTHER EXCEPTIONAL BRITISH RANGE EXPANSIONS
FULMAR
The **northern fulmar** (*Fulmar glacialis*) has been expanding its range for over 200 years but over the last century the Atlantic population has increased dramatically, particularly on the eastern side, where it has markedly extended its range southward. In the British Isles fulmars are known to have inhabited St Kilda, west of the Outer Hebrides, for over 800 years, and it was suggested that this was one of just two north-east Atlantic colonies in the Middle Ages.

Increase was first noticed in Iceland around 1750. Settlement of the Faeroes began in about 1820 and the Shetlands in 1878. Since then almost all the suitable cliffs of Britain and Ireland have been settled, north, south, east and west.

Many reasons have been put forward for the fulmar's increase, but all are conjecture. One suggestion is the increased amount of food (offal) available through more commercial fishing, but if this is so it is hard to explain the relatively slight increase and range extension in the western Atlantic.

BLACKHEADED GULL
Now the most common gull over much of Europe, the **blackheaded gull** (*Larus ridibundus*) has benefited enormously through close association with man, yet it was close to extinction in Britain in the 19th century. The British population of some 300,000 pairs is greatly augmented by winter visitors from the Continent.

The main reasons for increase are greater availability of food through more open rubbish tips and an increase in arable land, and widespread use of safe inland roosts on playing fields.

Other gulls too have increased for the same reasons, especially the lesser black-backed and herring, the latter's population having increased at a phenomenal 10% per annum in recent years. There are now colonies of herring gulls in remote moorland areas, yet they were rare inland at the start of this century. Others have learnt to nest on town rooftops, the habit apparently starting in Dover in 1920. Sadly, the increases have threatened some tern colonies and gulls have had to be destroyed by various conservation organisations.

Once ruthlessly persecuted in Britain for its underpelt or 'grebe fur', the great crested grebe has made a good recovery since 1900. (H. Arndt/RSPB)

GANNET

An extensive survey in 1939 revealed about 165,000 **gannets** (*Sula bassana*) breeding in the world. By 1969 this had almost doubled to 138,000 pairs, rising to about 213,000 site-holding pairs plus 70,000 non-breeding birds in 1976. Suggestions as to reasons for increase include less persecution by man and an increase in prey fish following climatic change and sea-current shift. Britain holds over three-quarters of the world population, mostly in inaccessible colonies. Some 33,000 pairs are found in Canada.

GREAT CRESTED GREBE

From less than 100 birds in the second half of the 19th century, the population of the great crested grebe (*Podiceps cristatus*) has grown dramatically to 2,800 in 1931, 4,500 in 1965 and 6–7,000 in 1975. And the trend seems to be continuing with birds taking full advantage of new waters created through the sand and gravel extraction industry. The population had been very depressed because the species was ruthlessly persecuted for its under-pelts, once fashionable as 'grebe furs'. In recent times pesticides have reduced breeding success, but now this is less significant than disturbance of waters through new leisure activities such as still-water yachting and sail-boarding.

THE GREATEST NORTH-SOUTH RANGE
McCORMICK'S SKUA

This is the only species of skua to breed on Antarctica; they arrive in October and adults and young leave at the beginning of April. It has been recorded from the South Pole to 69° 50'N in Greenland.

Also known as the **South Polar skua, McCormick's skua** (*Catharacta maccormicki*), has both dark and light phases (dimorphic plumage). Light-phase birds increase in frequency towards the Pole, but it is not known why skuas should benefit through having paler upperparts in regions with more snow and ice.

McCormick's skua feeds on offal and preys on the young of other species. Skuas have gull-like feet, but with prominent sharp claws, and the bill is well adapted for tearing flesh, being strongly hooked at the tip. As in birds of prey, the females are larger, but the male does most of the hunting, the female generally remaining in the territory to guard the nest and young.

MOST SOUTHERLY BREEDING

The most southerly breeding records are of **Antarctic petrels** (*Thalassoica antarctica*) in the Thiel Mountains at 80° 30'S, 25° 00'W, and **snow petrels** (*Pagadroma nivea*) on Mount Provender, in the Shackleton Mountains at 80° 23'S, 29° 55'W. These two birds are among about 40 species which breed regularly in Antarctica and on Southern Ocean islands. They favour ice-free cliffs, frequently some distance inland despite temperatures being generally lower on higher ground.

The pure-white snow petrel is remarkable for having two races – *nivea* and *major* – of very different size, and rarely ranges beyond the pack-ice whereas the Antarctic petrel commonly ranges up to 100 miles from the sea-ice.

These birds nest in some of the lowest temperatures on earth so the eggs and young are unusually resistant to chilling, chiefly to overcome the occasional forays for food undertaken by the parents – a disadvantage of breeding some 250 km (150 miles) inland away from the sea and food. But the species has other ways of beating the cold. Firstly, it is the only fulmarine petrel which nests under cover. Secondly, whereas most petrels appear to moult the juvenile plumage only when at sea and some of the larger species start a slow body moult during the breeding season, only the snow petrel completes the moult early, during the breeding season. Petrels range over all the world's oceans, but are most diverse and abundant in colder waters where marine life is especially prolific.

MOST NORTHERLY BREEDING
IVORY GULL

The beautiful **ivory gull** (*Pagophila eburnea*), distinguished by its all-white plumage, is usually seen on

The ivory gull is the world's most northerly breeding bird, which remains in the Arctic throughout the long polar winter when other species migrate southwards. (R.T. Mills, Aquila Photographics)

the fringe of pack-ice, but occasionally wanders south in winter. It breeds colonially on high-arctic islands in the presence of pack-ice and snow where only the hardiest vegetation survives. Most remain in the Arctic throughout the long polar winter when other species migrate southwards. An accomplished scavenger, it survives on the kills of polar bears during the most lean times.

The most northerly breeding landbird is the **snow bunting** (*Plectrophenax nivalis*), which nests as far up as the northern tip of Greenland. It breeds on bare, rocky lichen tundra, rocky coasts, rock outcrops in glaciers and snowfields and on high tundra-type mountain tops. A few birds nest regularly on the highest Scottish peaks.

The **ptarmigan** (*Lagopus mutus*) winters further north than any other landbird for, whereas snow buntings move south in winter, ptarmigans are resident in the Arctic. They survive by burrowing under snow in winter, but may descend to lower levels if forced to. This beautiful bird is white in winter, but its cryptic colouring changes with the seasons, providing excellent camouflage in countries such as Scotland, where it is hunted by man.

THE LARGEST BIRD ASSEMBLIES

The very largest of avian assemblies are winter roosts in which birds (mostly of single species) spend the night together. The main reason for communal roosting is to keep warm in the best possible spots. Body contact cuts down the surface area of each bird exposed to the cold air and this preserves energy reserves. Secondly, most large roosts are of species which feed together by day and the assemblies act as information centres, successful food-finders being followed at dawn. Thirdly, there is safety in numbers as there are always some birds awake to raise the alarm, though such bird concentrations do attract predators such as owls.

Generally, the more severe the weather, the larger the roost. In the winter of 1951/52 an estimated 70 million **bramblings** (*Fringilla montifringilla*) assembled every night for several weeks near the Swiss town of Hunibach.

One **red-billed quelea** (*Quelea quelea*) roost in the Sudan was said to contain 32 million birds but a maximum of several millions is more likely for the world's most numerous bird.

In America roosts of **red-winged blackbirds** (*Angelaius phoeniceus*) often contain over one million birds, those in reed-beds sometimes containing birds at a density exceeding 2.5 million birds per hectare.

Britain's largest roosts are of **starlings** (*Sturnus vulgaris*), some city 'hot spots' containing over one million birds, but reed-bed roosts of **martins** and **swallows** may also be spectacular prior to autumn migration.

Night roosts usually break up into much smaller feeding parties each day, though flocks may remain very large where food is unusually local or concentrated. Waders may be forced into exceptionally large feeding or roosting groups by the tides, but none compares with the feeding flocks of around one million **budgerigars** (*Melopsittacus undulatus*) seen in Australia. Such concentrations of these little parrots can cause serious agricultural damage, but are rare and usually brought under control by natural mortality through starvation and disease. Another spectacular feeding concentration is of the million or more **lesser flamingos** (*Phoeniconaias minor*) on Lake Nakuru in Kenya.

Breeding colonies, too, can be vast. Those of the **sooty tern** (*Sterna fuscata*) on oceanic islands have been estimated at 1–10 million pairs and the Antarctic rookeries of the **adélie penguin** (*Pygoscelis adeliae*) at over one million pairs.

Britain's largest breeding colonies include those of the **gannet** – St Kilda has 52,000 pairs, with the nests almost touching.

The Bird Machine

In looking at extremes of avian size, senses and anatomy it must be remembered that there is considerable variation among individuals in the bird world, just as there is among humans. But wherever possible records of extremes are given. Obviously, consistency in measuring is important in making comparisons and there are generally accepted methods of achieving this. For example, overall length – tip of bill to tip of tail while bird is lying on back; wingspan – distance from one wingtip to the other with bird lying on back and wings spread to fullest natural expanse. Opportunities to capture and measure live birds have increased enormously in recent years and it is quite likely that many of the statistics given now will be revised in the future.

Study of bird senses is more difficult and really only in its infancy. Recent research has already shown many previous assumptions and calculations to be either untrue or exaggerated.

Notwithstanding their great diversity on earth, *all* birds are feathered, warm-blooded, egg-laying vertebrates which have the forelimbs modified into wings (though some are flightless), the jaws covered with a horny sheath forming a beak, and a body temperature which is considerably higher than man's to facilitate a higher energy output in everyday life.

THE WORLD'S HEAVIEST AND TALLEST FLIGHTLESS BIRD
OSTRICH – maximum 156 kg (345 lb) and 2.7 m (9 ft)
Of the four remaining sub-species of **ostrich** (*Struthio camelus*) the race *S. c. camelus* of North Africa and the Sudan is the largest and tallest, cock birds often weighing up to 150 kg (330 lb) and standing 2.5 m (8.16 ft) high. The height at the back is about 1.37 m (4.5 ft). Extreme examples have weighed around 156 kg (345 lb) and stood 2.7 m (9 ft) tall. Hens weigh up to about 100 kg (220 lb) and stand 2.1 m (7 ft) tall. Domesticated and captive birds may get exceptionally fat, but these are more likely to be of the smaller sub-species.

There are several advantages in being such a large bird in African semi-desert and savannah. First there is the need for adequate defence in being a flightless species surrounded by predators. Related to this is the bird's ability to run very fast and when cornered give a very powerful kick. Ostrich victims have included men who have been disembowelled or killed through having their skulls fractured.

Secondly there is the necessity to cover great distances in gathering sufficient sparsely dispersed food. With its long legs the ostrich can walk tirelessly and its long, flexible neck has a good reach, thereby bringing more food within range. While it is almost entirely vegetarian and selects relatively nutritious foods among shoots, leaves, flowers and seeds, the ostrich must take in a lot of fuel to get enough energy and this in turn requires a relatively large digestive system. The ostrich pecks repeatedly with great precision and amasses the food in the gullet before passing it slowly down the neck in a ball which visibly stretches the skin.

Ostrich capacity to swallow weird and wonderful objects is generally exaggerated, but nonetheless remarkable. Stones and pebbles are regularly swallowed to aid digestion of vegetable matter, but if these are not available, usually in captivity, other objects may be substituted. One bird, which died in London Zoo, was found to have swallowed an alarm clock, 91 cm

(3 ft) of rope, a spool of film, a pencil, a cycle valve, three gloves, a comb, a handkerchief, glove fasteners, pieces of a gold necklace, a Belgian franc, a collar stud, four halfpennies and two farthings. And another bird on a South African ostrich farm had swallowed 484 coins weighing 3.74 kg (8 lb 4 oz)!

Great height is also usefully coupled with keen eyesight in the ostrich both to spot predators and food more easily and to locate other members of the species over a large area.

A disadvantage of bulk in a hot climate is increased risk of over-heating, but this is reduced through the ostrich having huge, bare thighs surrounded by loose, soft feathers without barbs. The thighs also serve as signals in breeding males when they develop a bright red or blue colour depending on race. The apparently bare, flesh-coloured neck is actually covered with minute downy feathers.

The ostrich is also the world's fastest-running bird and the species which lays the largest eggs.

THE WORLD'S HEAVIEST FLYING BIRD
GREAT BUSTARD—maximum 21 kg (46.3 lb)

It is not possible to state with great certainty which is the world's heaviest flying bird in the natural state as there is considerable variation within several species. Also, as some of these birds are thought to be near the theoretical weight limit for flapping flight, it is possible that some of the largest individuals measured had become so fat that they were incapable of flight. It also depends on *when* a bird is measured because many individuals feed fairly infrequently and may take on a considerable weight in one meal.

The theorists argue that flying weight is restricted to a formula based on the inter-relationships of physical limitations of muscle power, bone strength and wing-loading. And there is no doubt that some of our largest flying birds fly only when pressed, swans in particular finding great difficulty in taking off, which is obviously a great drain on precious energy. Yet

At weights of up to 21 kg (46.3 lb), the great bustard is the world's heaviest flying bird. (John Markham, Bruce Coleman Ltd)

Although approaching the theoretical weight limit for flight, the great bustard is powerful in the air. (Kevin Carlson, Nature Photograpers Ltd)

there have been and are very heavy birds which need to flap only rarely so that sustained soaring in the hunt for food is well worth the effort of take-off. Some have minimized the energy requirements of take-off through utilization of cliff thermals, and others have probably needed only to open their massive wings into the prevailing breeze to become airborne. Certainly the recent discovery of the massive bird fossil *Argentavis magnificens* (see page 12) necessitates a re-evaluation of the whole subject. It is largely a question of how worthwhile it is to devote a higher percentage of body mass to flight muscles when all other bodily functions still have to be maintained. However, there is a suggestion that the larger size of extinct birds is evidence that the atmosphere was more dense in former times, denser air making it easier for heavier birds to fly.

Of the species which do fly regularly in the wild the **great bustard** (*Otis tarda*) of Europe and Asia probably has the greatest average weight with cocks often reaching 16.8 kg (37 lb) and extreme examples recorded at 18–21 kg (39.7–46.3 lb). The bird's length is to 1.2 m (4 ft), with a wingspan to 2.5 m (8 ft). The female is usually under 75 cm (2.45 ft).

The **kori bustard** (*Choriotis kori*) of Africa is also sometimes credited with being the world's heaviest flying bird, but its average is less than that of the great bustard. Large cocks scale around 13.6 kg (30 lb) but one South African specimen weighed 18.2 kg (40 lb).

Other species of bustard are heavy too. They all have powerful flight with long, broad wings and in the air do not seem to be so laboured as the other heavyweights. Rather long legs are an asset in getting airborne from the ground, unlike the swans, which need a runway of water. Bustards are long-lived omnivorous birds with a slow reproductive rate which makes it hard for them to recolonize the many areas from which they have become exterminated in modern times.

Swans probably have the second-highest average weight among flying birds, and the North American **trumpeter** (*Cygnus cygnus buccinator*), generally regarded as a race of the whooper swan, is the largest with a wingspan of 3.1 m (10 ft 2 ins). The mute, trumpeter and other races of whooper all attain a length of 152 cm (60 in) and weights to 15 kg (33 lb) are common. Audubon reported a **trumpeter swan** weighing 17.2 kg (37 lb 13 oz).

The position of the **mute swan** (*Cygnus olor*) is much more difficult to evaluate as the species has been in semi-domestication in Europe for over 900 years, resulting in many birds which were fattened excessively for the table inter-breeding with wilder individuals. Tame birds are often lethargic, well-fed and have no need to fly off in search of food, and it is likely that the record weights recorded, such as the 22.5 kg (49 lb 9½ oz) of a cob from Poland, are from individuals which had, temporarily at least, lost the power of flight.

Similarly, it is difficult to give a maximum weight for truly wild North American **turkeys** (*Meleagris*

gallopavo) as the species has been bred to unnaturally large sizes in captivity and some of these birds have escaped or been deliberately released to provide sport. Interbreeding between wild and semi-wild birds has occurred and it is not known which of the resultant heavyweights could fly. Truly wild males generally reach 10 kg (22 lb) – only about 28% of the heaviest domesticated birds – though they can fly strongly for short distances and it is possible that much larger individuals retain the power of flight.

The male turkey is at its heaviest at the start of the breeding season for it then develops a store of fat and oil on which it draws during its extremely energetic courtship activities.

Some birds are at their fattest as juveniles. For example, a **wandering albatross** nestling weighed 16.1 kg (35 lb 7½ oz), but about a third of this fuel would be shed rapidly as the wings were exercised and the first flights undertaken.

BRITAIN'S HEAVIEST FLYING BIRD
MUTE SWAN – 14 kg (31 lb)
Though there are great bustards in Britain they remain in captivity as part of a reintroduction programme

Once underway the mute swan has a graceful flight. (F. Pölking, RSPB)

in Wiltshire, so the **mute swan** (*Cygnus olor*) is unquestionably the country's heaviest wild flying bird. Males or cobs commonly weigh in at 14 kg (31 lb). There have been larger domesticated individuals, but it is not clear whether these birds retained the power of flight.

The mute swan's total length is 145–160 cm (57–63 in), half of which is head and neck, and it is clear that the bird needs every centimetre of its 213 cm (7 ft) wingspan to take off. A good, clear stretch of water is needed to get airborne, and the run-up is very laboured; yet when the bird is underway the slow, powerful wingbeats are graceful and produce a musical, throbbing sound.

This great bird, a popular meal up to the 19th century, feeds chiefly on vegetable matter such as water weeds, but especially the stalks, rhizomes and roots of aquatic plants. The swan is often seen upending, using the long neck to reach submerged food. Young birds, frogs, toads and small mammals are sometimes killed, but not often eaten. The bird's great bulk is needed to break down and digest food of relatively low nutritive value in order to obtain sufficient energy. It has exploited a grazing niche in the freshwater habitat.

The mute swan population should have increased at a time when many new waters (chiefly flooded gravel pits and reservoirs) are being created, even allowing for the fact that it takes some time for vegetation to establish. But sadly, mute swans have declined in numbers by 5–13% over the last 30 years and are now down to about 18,900 in Britain. Lead poisoning is thought to be the biggest single killer. An estimated 3,370–4,190 swans die in England each year, almost all having ingested anglers' lead weights (split shot or leger weight). Voluntary measures to substitute non-toxic weights were unpopular so the Government recently decided to ban the import and sale of lead weights.

Mute swans are not long-lived anyway. A third live for less than a year and less than half longer than two years. Females breed at three and males at four. The average lifespan is three years but the oldest birds may last to 15. They usually mate for life.

Despite their name, mute swans have several calls. Adults snore, snort and whistle, trumpet quietly and hiss menacingly at all intruders.

Large numbers of **whooper swans** winter in Britain, but after their long migrations and at that time of year are unlikely to approach the weight of resident mute swans. **Bewick's swans** are considerably smaller.

Britain's heaviest flying bird, the mute swan needs a good, clear stretch of water for its cumbersome take-off. (Laurie Campbell/ RSPB)

The wandering albatross has the greatest wingspan of any living bird, enabling it to soar across the world's oceans with minimal effort. This pair are seen displaying in South Georgia. (M.P. Harris, Nature Photographers Ltd)

THE GREATEST WINGSPAN IN THE WORLD

WANDERING ALBATROSS – up to 3.63 m (11 ft 11 in)

This fabled traveller (*Diomedea exulans*) of the southern oceans, once thought to bring sailors bad luck, undoubtedly has the greatest average wingspan of any living bird. As only a tiny percentage of the population has been measured it is likely that the largest reliably and accurately measured specimen so far (3.63 m/11 ft 11 in) will one day be beaten for size. Over the last 200 years there have been many claims of larger individuals up to 518 cm (17 ft) but it is now considered unlikely that any will have a wingspan greater than about 4 m (13 ft). Many individuals are much smaller and females average less than males. The older birds are generally whiter and the 3.63 m individual was almost pure white.

Like all long-winged birds, albatrosses have evolved elongated inner wing bones with extra secondary feathers attached. The wandering albatross has 88 wing feathers – more than any other species. Its long, narrow wings are used for dynamic soaring over the ocean. Aerodynamically it is very efficient and can fly great distances without flapping because it has a high wing aspect ratio – the figure obtained by dividing a wing's length by its average width. Soaring birds such as eagles have low aspect ratios but can get maximum lift through their broad, strongly cambered wings with the help of rising air currents, thus holding flapping energy in reserve.

The wandering albatross exploits the fact that winds blowing over the surface of the sea are slowed by wave action at the surface and gradually increase in velocity with altitude. Such a relatively heavy bird, with the high aspect ratio needed for control and stability, can gain speed high in the fastest air (usually to about 15 m/50 ft) before plunging downwind. On reaching the surface and the slowest air it uses its momentum to head up again, simultaneously turning into the wind, which blows it back aloft. All this without a single flap. Calculations suggest that dynamic soaring on the wind gradient alone is unlikely to lift the albatross more than 3 m (10 ft) so extra impetus probably comes from energy gathered through slope soaring along a wave.

Though impressive in the air, the albatross has difficulty in landing and almost always arrives at the nest with a thump unless there is sufficient wind to let it float down gently. Take-off is awkward too,

The world's longest wings belong to the sea-going wandering albatross (bottom), but the Andean condor (second bottom) and marabou stork (second top) have the greatest wingspan among landbirds. The white-tailed sea eagle is almost dwarfed in comparison yet has the greatest wingspan of any British bird. (Suzanne Alexander)

and the short legs, on which they balance well, are used to run into the wind.

The wandering albatross feeds largely on cuttlefish, octopuses and squid, probably mostly at night when prey is caught or found disabled at the surface. But they can dive to take fish and other marine animals.

THE GREATEST WINGSPAN OF ANY LANDBIRD

There are two rivals for this distinction – the **Andean condor** (*Vultur gryphus*) of South America and the **marabou stork** (*Leptoptilus crumeniferus*) of Africa, individuals of both species having wingspans up to 3.2 m (10.5 ft). Both have long, broad wings with fingered primaries adapted for soaring over land. Larger individuals have been claimed for both species, but are open to doubt. Notable among these is the 4.06 m (13 ft 4 in) marabou taken by Col. Meinertzhagen in 1934. He was a good ornithologist, so, even allowing for exaggeration through over-stretching the wings, this might well have been a bird of a 4 m (13.5 ft)

wingspan. Average wingspans are well below 3 m (9.75 ft) for both species.

Condors routinely soar for many tens of kilometres in search of carrion and *Vultur gryphus* is the world's heaviest bird of prey, weighing up to 14 kg (31 lb). It can take on considerable weight in one meal. So can the marabou, which also seeks out carrion, often at great heights, and can even drive vultures away from a carcass.

In complete contrast are the **kiwis**, whose wings are so small they are concealed by the body feathers, and whose flight muscles have atrophied, giving the birds a pear-shaped outline.

THE GREATEST WINGSPAN IN BRITAIN
WHITE-TAILED SEA EAGLE – 2.4 m (7.87 ft)

This fourth-largest eagle in the world is back on the British breeding list thanks to a good recent reintroduction programme following its national extinction in 1916 (see page 59). Individuals with wingspans approaching 3 m (9.75 ft) have been claimed but the normal range is 2–2.4 m (6.5–7.87 ft), females being slightly larger than males, with average weights of 5.5 kg (12.25 lb) and 4 kg (8.75 lb) respectively. Body length is 68–90 cm (27–36 in). The wingspans of the **mute swan** and **golden eagle** are usually a centimetre or two less than that of the sea eagle.

While the golden eagle is related to hawks and buzzards, the sea eagle (*Haliaeetus albicilla*) is of the line which includes the Old World vultures. The genus *Haliaeetus* includes the African fish eagle and the well-known bald eagle, national symbol of the USA, a bird whose habits are very similar to those of the sea eagle.

The sea eagle has a massive, vulture-like silhouette but it is not as cumbersome as it appears. Diving birds such as eider ducks, auks and shags are harried to exhaustion but the sea eagle can also easily catch birds in level flight

such as fulmars, gulls and crows. It is equally at home on fresh or salt water and catches stranded, dying or surface-feeding fish, though it does not use the spectacular plunge-dive of the osprey. The very long, broad wings are also useful in soaring around in search of carrion, which becomes increasingly important in winter.

THE SMALLEST BIRD IN THE WORLD
BEE HUMMINGBIRD – 5.7 cm (2.24 in), 1.6 g (0.056 oz)

At a mere 5.7 cm (2.24 in) long and weighing just 1.6 g (0.056 oz), the male **bee hummingbird** (*Calypte helenae*) of Cuba and the Isle of Pines can store very little energy in its diminutive, but comparatively heavy, vertebrate body. Females are slightly larger. It is thought that a bird any smaller could probably not eat enough to find the energy

Male Andean condor over Peru. Its record wingspan enables it to soar for many kilometres in search of carrion. (G. Ziesler, Bruce Caleman Ltd)

needed to feed. As it is, these tiny birds must feed almost constantly in order to maintain basic metabolism.

Reports of even smaller individual hummingbirds are to be doubted because the majority of measurements have been taken from skins which have dried and shrunk.

With the possible exception of the shrews, hummingbirds have the highest metabolism of any warm-blooded vertebrate – **Anna's hummingbird** (*Calypte anna*) has the highest of all studied so far. Wing-beats among the family's 315 species vary between 22 and 78 per second, with the highest rate in the smaller species. It is this phenomenal rate of activity combined with small size and high blood temperature – 39–42°C (102–108°F) – which burns up energy so rapidly. But hummingbirds have evolved a way to exploit the high-energy value of droplets of nectar in flowers and, despite the energy-expensive hovering manoueuvre to obtain this, the result is worthwhile. But energy-balance considerations also seem to have placed an upper limit on hummingbird size and even the largest of the family – the **giant hummingbird** (*Patagona gigas*) at 21.7 cm (8.5 in) long – weighs only 20 g (0.7 oz).

Despite their size, hummingbirds are extremely pugnacious birds and will attempt to drive off large animals such as cats and even humans which venture too near their nests. An astonishing speed of some 45 km/h (28 mph) is attained in forward level flight. But, uniquely, hummingbirds can also fly in reverse. This agility is made possible by a wing which consists mainly of 'hand bones' to which the flight feathers are attached, the whole wing rotating as a wrist. The wings are long and narrow and powered by highly developed flight muscles which take up to a third of the total body weight. Yet oddly, the rate of wingbeat is *slower* than those of most birds when measured in relation to body weight.

'Hummers' (named after the noise of their wings) remain stationary in front of flowers while their very thin and pointed bills probe blossoms for nectar. Their tongues are very long, extensible and grooved, becoming tubular towards the tip, which has a 'brush'. The nectar is not sucked up as through a drinking straw but 'pumped' along the tongue with the aid of capillary action. Some hummers have evolved very specialized bills to exploit certain plants.

Hummingbirds are confined to the Americas where the breeding season is closely tied to the flowering season of certain food plants, but all species also eat some insects, mostly taken on the wing, and spiders plucked from their webs. Insufficient food may occasionally induce torpidity at night but this is usually brought on by low temperatures. Food intake varies with temperature and overall activity, but generally a hummer needs to take in half its body weight in food per day.

Today habitat destruction is the major threat to most hummers, but in the 19th century vast numbers were killed and stuffed for decoration on ladies' hats. As many as 400,000 skins were imported in a single year by one London dealer. Many others went into collections and today some six species are known only from these museum-pieces. However, they are not necessarily extinct as 'new' species of hummingbird have been found within the last few years.

BRITAIN'S SMALLEST BIRDS
GOLDCREST AND FIRECREST –
9 cm (3.54 in)
Not easy to distinguish in the field, these two members of the warbler family are particularly susceptible to severe cold, the average body-weight being only about 3.8–4.5g (0.134–0.159 oz) Britain's third smallest regular breeder, the **common wren**, measures only 9.5 cm (3.74 in) but is about twice as heavy as the *Regulus* species.

After a run of mild winters the **goldcrest** (*Regulus regulus*) may

The goldcrest, one of Britain's and Europe's smallest birds, is particularly susceptible to cold winters and needs to have large broods – up to 10 chicks – to maintain its population level. (David A. Gowans)

number 1½ million pairs and will then spread from its coniferous woodland stronghold into deciduous woodland. After the winter of 1970/71 there was a massive 48% increase. But a very cold and frosty winter can decimate the goldcrest population: in the winter of 1978/79 some 40% died, yet within just one season the population was nearly back to full strength. Like the hummingbirds, when breeding it compensates for its tiny size in being extremely pugnacious and will defend its territory vigorously. Males have been known to fight to the death over a hen.

In winter goldcrests range over conifer plantations with tits, searching for insect eggs and pupae hidden under bark.

Common throughout Eurasia, the goldcrest is widespread in Britain, though rare in Orkney, Shetland and the Outer Hebrides. The **firecrest** (*Regulus ignicapillus*), on the other hand, has been known as a British breeder only since 1962, following steady range extension westwards through Europe. Previously it was known only as a regular autumn migrant and scarce winter visitor to south-west England. Now very small numbers nest regularly in southern England, though the colonization remains tenuous. It is not known whether these British breeders are generally resident.

The recent spread of coniferous forestry is thought to have encouraged the firecrest in Britain, but the species is less restricted to conifers than the goldcrest.

THE SMALLEST FLIGHTLESS
BIRD IN THE WORLD
INACCESSIBLE ISLAND RAIL –
12.5 cm (5 in), 34.7 g (1.2 oz)
One of a number of rails restricted to single, remote islands, the **Inaccessible Island rail** (*Atlantisia rogersi*) fortunately remains common. No larger than a newly-hatched domestic chick, it has dark, degenerate, hair-like plumage and lives among the tussock grass which covers the island.

There is no flightless bird still living in Britain. The last was the **great auk** (*Pinguinus impennis*), which became extinct in about 1844.

The black-winged stilt's extremely long legs enable it to feed in water too deep for other waders. (W. Wisniewski, Frank Lane Picture Agency)

THE LONGEST LEGS IN THE WORLD
BLACK-WINGED STILT—60% of body length

Though there are very many taller birds and species which have longer legs, the **black-winged stilt** (*Himanoptus himanoptus*) has the longest legs relative to body length. In fact they appear so long as to be freakish, but they allow this specialist to feed in water where other waders cannot venture. Much of the food is taken from the surface of the water, and includes aquatic insects and the seeds of sedges and other marsh plants, but molluscs and worms are also taken from underwater.

This 38 cm (15 in) black-and-white bird is very obvious and in flight its long, reddish-pink legs extend 17.5 cm (7 in) beyond its tail, acting as a useful counterbalance to the outstretched long neck and bill.

On dry land the bird has to bend the knees to feed and brooding birds look most peculiar with their long legs forming a large V on either side.

Himanoptus is a widespread species in southern Europe, Asia and central Africa, but is local and a colonial nester. It has been recorded breeding in Britain just once – in 1945 when three pairs fledged a few young at Nottingham Sewage Farm. Others quite regularly nest in the Netherlands, having overshot their normal breeding range in southern Europe. Otherwise it is only a rare occasional visitor to Britain.

Stilts are in the same family as the **avocets** (*Recurvirostridae*), *Recurvirostra avosetta* – having the longest legs relative to body length of any regular British breeder.

The world's five species of flamingo also have extremely long legs, both in terms of actual length and relative to overall body length. The **greater flamingo** (*Phoenicopterus ruber*) of the Atlantic, Central and South America and the West Indies is the tallest with a height of some 145 cm (57 in) to the top of the head, but much of the overall length is taken up by the neck.

Flamingos also occur in Europe, Asia and Africa but are confined to shallow soda lakes and salt lagoons with a high pH value (up to 10.5) and usually barren of vegetation. They are specialist filter feeders and may well live for over 50 years in the wild, usually congregating in spectacular numbers.

All these long-legged waders are able to exploit the food supplies of relatively deep water without wetting their plumage. Long legs are also a feature of fast-running birds such as the ostrich, but the **secretary bird** (*Saggitarius serpentarius*) is a hawk-like species which finds them useful for evading the snakes on which it preys by springing in the air.

Most birds stand on their toes and the raised ankle is often mistaken for a knee (the real knee is concealed in the plumage), though it bends in the reverse direction.

THE SHORTEST LEGS IN THE WORLD

There are several bird families with very short legs, but the shortest of all are found among the species of true **swifts** (*Apodidae*), spread through Eurasia, Africa and the Americas. *Apodidae* means 'lacking legs'. Their legs are virtually non-existent and superfluous as the family has become so well adapted to aerial existence (see page 117) and in some species only the feet are visible outside the plumage.

Yet the claws are strong, being used for grasping vertical surfaces when breeding or sometimes for roosting. Swifts do not have need to walk at all. The *Apodidae* have just four toes, but the grasping motion is lateral inward, not front to back as in most birds. This adaptation is to hold on to nest materials. When not grasping, their toes lie together, giving rise to the common misconception that swifts have all four toes permanently pointed forward.

Many **kingfishers** also have extremely short legs, but their feet are very weak and syndactyl – the 2nd, 3rd and 4th toes being united at the base and the 3rd and 4th for much of their length. Some **bee-eaters** have short legs too, yet are able to dig with these tiny digits by leaning on their wings.

THE LONGEST TOES IN THE WORLD

The seven species of **jacana** (*Jacanidae*), widespread freshwater birds of the marshes, rice fields and freshwater margins of the Tropics, have by far the longest toes and claws relative to body length. Their toes often span 10 cm (4in) while body length is 16.5–53 cm (6.5–21 in). The adult **northern jacana** (*Jacana spinosa*) of Central America and the Greater Antilles weighs only 80–170 g (2.8–6 oz) but its feet cover an area as large as 12 × 14 cm (4.7 × 5.5 in). All the toes and claws are very long but the rear claw is even longer than the toe to which it is attached.

The very wide feet disperse the birds' weight so that they are able to walk over floating vegetation such as lily-pads where they gather chiefly aquatic insects from the surface. But they also take small frogs and fish, molluscs and aquatic vegetation. When they come to an open stretch of water they jump over with a flick of the wings. This behaviour has given rise to the popular name 'lily trotter'. All jacanas have a spur on the carpal joint ('wrist') of the wing. Usually this is short and blunt, but in the northern jacana it is sharp and 16 mm (0.63 in) long.

In all species except the **smaller jacana** (*Microparra capensis*) the female is larger and polyandrous. Mating with more than one male is commonplace, but the northern jacana is the only bird in which the female is known to maintain several males simultaneously.

Other exceptional jacana characteristics include that of the **pheasant-tailed jacana** (*Hydrophasianus chirurgus*) which is reported to incubate two eggs under each wing well away from the water. Some species are said to pick up the young chicks between the wings and the body to shelter them from heavy rain or to move them. And both adults and young of the **African jacana** (*Actophilornis africana*) are reported to hide from predators by submerging, leaving only the bills and nostrils above water.

THE LONGEST BILLS IN THE WORLD

If we take the length of the bill relative to overall body length the longest is that of the **sword-billed hummingbird** (*Ensifera ensifera*) of Venezuela, Colombia and Bolivia, whose 10.5 cm (4.13 in) bill is longer than the rest of the body. This 12–13 g (0.42–0.46 oz) hummer has a high degree of co-evolution with the climbing passion flower which has a corolla tube of 11.4 cm (4.5 in) and produces up to 500 ml (0.88 pt) of nectar per day.

When such a hummingbird inserts its bill into the flower's corolla its forehead, beak and chin may become well dusted with pollen, some of which will be transferred to neighbouring flowers of the same species, thus effecting cross-pollination. For the plant this is better than insect pollination because hummingbirds are relatively long-lived and can fly long distances in all weather conditions. Thus the plants have evolved to make insect pollinating difficult with an absence of an insect landing platform. And the flowers are situated well away from leaves and entangling vegetation so that the feeding hummingbird can hover freely at the appropriate angle. Also such flowers are usually coloured red or orange so that hummingbirds, but not insects, can distinguish them.

If we take the actual bill size irrespective of body length then the longest is that of the **Australian pelican** (*Pelicanus conspicillatus*), which measures 34–47 cm (13.38–18.5 in) and has evolved to catch fish. This massive bill is hooked at the tip and there are no external nostril openings. From near the end of the lower mandible to the base of the throat is suspended a large, extensible pouch of skin capable of holding at least three gallons of water – several times 'more than its belly can'. This acts as a scoop to take in fish to over 0.5 kg (1.1 lb) and 30 cm (1 ft) long, plus the water, when the bird's head is submerged. But only the brown pelican actually dives into the water to feed; the other six species either feed individually from the surface or communally by herding schools of fish and then synchronously scooping them up. When the bird's head is lifted the water drains out of the sides of the gape – this may take up to a minute – leaving the fish behind.

The fish may be swallowed immediately or temporarily stored in the oesophagus, but it must be passed to the stomach prior to flight so that the bird can maintain balance in the air.

The pouch becomes brighter prior to the breeding season and serves both to attract a mate and indicate sexual readiness. Males are generally larger, noticeably in weight (up to 15 kg/33 lb) and bill length. But the long bill is a handicap in display. Pelicans are among the largest flying birds with a length in *P.conspicillatus* of up to 180 cm (6 ft) and a wingspan of up to 2.8 m (9.2 ft).

Other exceptionally large bills are found among the **storks, hornbills** and **toucans**.

THE LONGEST BILL IN BRITAIN
CURLEW – 15 cm (*6 in*)
Europe's largest wader, the **curlew** (*Numenius arquata*), has evolved this very long downcurved bill primarily to probe in the mud for food items which other waders cannot reach, thus reducing competition. On the seashore prey includes tiny crabs, marine worms, crustaceans, small fish and even seaweed, but inland and on the breeding grounds insects, insect larvae, berries, weed seeds and grain are eaten.

The bill of this 55–60 cm (22–24 in) widespread and abun-

Nightjars (left) have some of the shortest bills in the world, but their enormous gapes and rictal bristles act as efficient insect traps. New Zealand's wrybill plover (right) is unique in having a sideways-curving bill. The Eurasian curlew (bottom) has the longest bill of any British bird and uses it mostly to probe for food in the mud. (Suzanne Alexander)

dant wader can reach 15 cm (6 in), the larger being that of the female, which may weigh 1 kg (2.2 lb). It can be thrust into the mud for two-thirds of its length but the bird is able to grasp prey because it has the ability to open the tip of the bill while the rest remains closed. Movement of bones in the front of the skull pushes the bone that runs the length of the upper mandible forward, causing the flexible tip to bend upwards.

The bill of the **long-billed curlew** (*Numenius americanus*) of North and Central America is even longer at 22 cm (8.75 in). Such specialized bills do not develop in the early nestling stage so that the parents may feed the young easily.

THE SHORTEST BILLS IN THE WORLD

We cannot say with great confidence which are the absolute shortest bills, but the shortest relative to body length are among the very wide-gaped species which pursue insects on the wing – the **nightjars** (goatsuckers) (*Caprimulgidae*) and **swifts** (*Apodidae*).

In the 72 species of nightjar the weak bill opens to reveal an enormous gape which, with the aid of rictal bristles at the sides of the mouth, helps to catch the prey. But nightjars do not merely fly along with the mouth wide open: they pursue individual insects, chiefly at dusk and by night with the help of keen eyesight. Hunting by chance would be a waste of time and energy. However, not all nightjars have the rictal bristles, which are modified feathers, and it has been suggested that their prime function is to guard the eyes.

Swifts have equally small bills and, as some species are significantly smaller than the nightjars, they probably also have the shortest bills in absolute length. Many of the larger species have only a few millimetres of exposed bill so those of the smallest species, such as the 10.5 cm (4.1 in) 7 g (0.015 oz) **glossy swiftlet** (*Collocalia esculenta*) must be very small indeed.

THE ONLY SIDEWAYS-CURVING BILL
THE WRYBILL PLOVER'S

New Zealand's **wrybill plover** (*Anarhynchus frontalis*) is the only bird in the world which has a side-ways-curving bill, the end quarter being turned to the right by 12°. The bird, which breeds on South Island and migrates to North Island, uses its unique bill to probe for insects under stones on beaches, though it is not clear what benefit is gained.

THE LONGEST FEATHERS IN THE WORLD
PHOENIX FOWL (ONAGADORI) – up to 10.59 m (34.75 ft)

The **onagadori**, a strain of the red jungle fowl (*Gallus gallus*), has been bred in Japan for over 300 years and is one of several types of chicken kept there for ornamental and exhibition purposes. Prize-winning birds are jealously guarded and the fantastic tails have to be coiled round and round in special boxes when taken to shows. The very longest feathers are actually the tail coverts of the roosters, which grow for six years or so without moulting. The longest, 10.59 m (34.75 ft), were from a specimen owned by Masasha Kubota of Kōchi in 1972.

Innumerable varieties of the red jungle fowl have been developed and introduced worldwide, chiefly as a table bird, but its natural home is in south-east Asia, where it is widespread. The tail length of the wild bird is only to 27.5 cm (10.8 in) in the male and up to 15.5 cm (6.1 in) in the female.

THE LONGEST AND LARGEST TAIL FEATHERS
CRESTED ARGUS PHEASANT – up to 173 cm (5.7 ft) × 13 cm (5.1 in)

This species not only has the longest true tail feathers in the world, but also the largest feathers of any wild bird as the central rectrices (tail feathers) of the male regularly reach 173 cm (5.7 ft) long and are 13 cm (5.1 in) wide. Those of the subspecies *Rheinhartia ocellata ocellata* are slightly longer than those of *R.o.nigrescens*, the latter reaching 162 cm (5.3 ft). Those of the females reach 43 cm (16.9 in) and 40 cm (15.7 in) respectively.

This bird of Indochina, from Vietnam to the Malay Peninsula, is now extremely rare and probably endangered through increased tree-felling and protracted disturbance, including warfare, throughout its range. It is restricted to areas of heavy forest where the males use their spectacular tails in display, when they are often held nearly vertically. It takes three years to get the nuptial plumage but the tail continues to grow for several years thereafter and no doubt exceptional feathers beyond the average maximum length are not unusual.

The central tail feathers of **Reeves' pheasant** (*Syrmaticus reevesii*) are said exceptionally to have reached 2.4 m (8 ft) but the normal maximum for males is 160 cm (5.24 ft) and for females 45 cm (17.7 in). This bird has been extensively hunted and trapped in its natural range in northern and central China where the people value its flesh and ornamental feathers. But its very fast flight, sporting potential and ornamental aspect have also attracted western landowners and it has been widely introduced thoughout the world. In addition to sporting introductions there have also been escapes from bird collections and a feral population has become established in Britain, which even a series of hard winters has failed to eliminate. The tail is used in display and as a very effective brake for stopping and abrupt turning when thrown up in the air or to the side in woodland.

It is often thought that **peafowl** have the longest tail feathers, but it is only the male's tail *coverts* which have evolved to spectacular proportions for display purposes. In both the **Indian peafowl** (*Pavo cristatus*) and the **green peafowl** (*P. muticus*) these reach 160 cm (5.24 ft) whereas the tail feathers proper attain lengths of only 45 cm (17.7 in) and 47.5 cm (18.7 in) respectively.

Many smaller birds have exceptionally long feathers relative to body length. Probably the most spectacular are the two second primaries (main flight feathers) of the **pennant-winged nightjar** (*Sem-*

eiophorus vexillarius) of southern Africa. During the breeding season the male of this largest African nightjar grows two pennants – white streamers almost 60 cm (2 ft) long – as part of his display. The seventh and eighth primaries also become elongated at that time. This bird of the savannahs is more likely to be seen by day than most nightjars. The pennants are rapidly discarded at the end of the breeding season.

Among the longest tails relative to body length are those of some of the tyrant flycatchers such as the **fork-tailed flycatcher** (*Muscivora tyrannus*) of Central and South America, whose 27 cm (10.75 in) tail represents 77% of the 35.5 cm (14 in) body length. **Mousebirds** (*Coliidae*) may have 25 cm (10 in) tails on 35.5 cm (14in) bodies but the **resplendent quetzal** (*Pharomachrus mocinno*) of Central America has a tail at least 60 cm (24 in) long – over twice its body length. Some of the **hummingbirds** also have greatly elongated tails, notably the **marvellous spatuletail** (*Loddigesia mirabilis*) in which the two outer tail feathers carry 'racquets' at the end of long, wire-like shafts that cross over and are almost three times the body length.

In complete contrast are the **kiwis, cassowaries, emus** and **rheas** which are practically tailless, no special tail feathers being recognizably different from the general plumage covering the hind parts.

THE LONGEST TAILS IN BRITAIN

Apart from the Reeves's pheasant (see page 91), which is only tenuously established in the wild, the longest tails among regularly occurring British birds are those of the **swallow** (*Hirundo rustica*) – up to 67% of 19 cm (7.5 in) body length if the two streamers are included, **long-tailed tit** (*Aegithalos caudatus*) – 64% of 14 cm (5.5 in) body length, **kite** (*Milvus milvus*) – up to 62% of 61 cm (24 in) body length in female, **magpie** (*Pica pica*) – up to 55% of 46 cm (18 in) body length, **common**

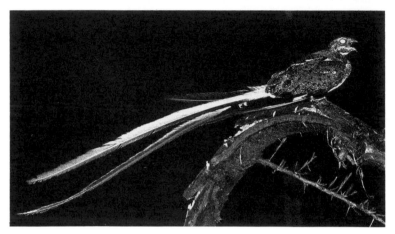

pheasant (*Phasianus colchicus*) – up to 54% of 84 cm (33 in) body length, **cuckoo** (*Cuculus canorus*) – 50% of 33 cm (13 in) body length and **grey wagtail** (*Motacilla cinerea*) – 50% of 20 cm (8 in) body length.

THE KEENEST EYESIGHT

Keenness is too vague a term to be applied to the highly complicated subject of avian vision and must be qualified by dealing with several aspects of eyesight separately. In addition, recent scientific studies have shown many of the old claims about acuteness of bird vision to have been exaggerated.

All birds' eyes are proportionately big compared with man's (for example, a starling's are 15 times as large relative to body size) and they often weigh more than the brain because the bird is more dependent on eyesight than other vertebrates. Some predatory species have eyes which are actually larger than man's and the 5 cm (2 in) diameter eye of

The male pennant-winged nightjar of southern Africa (above and below) grows a 60cm (2ft) long pennant on each wing specially for the display season. (A.S. Weaving, Ardea London)

the ostrich may be the largest of any land animal. Yet we cannot assume that great size implies keen eyesight. On the contrary, some birds, notably passerines, have inferior sight to ours.

When it comes to the ability of birds to see detail – visual acuity or 'resolving power' ('keenness') – this appears to be best developed in species which need to see tiny, moving or distant prey, for example **flycatchers** or **hawks** respectively. But it is now thought that the old claim of diurnal (day-hunting) birds of prey having visual acuity 8–10 times greater than man's is widely exaggerated. Biologists have found that the foveae (parts of the retinas) of raptors have about 1 million cones per square millimetre compared with a mere 200,000 in man. Thus the eyesight of raptors is probably at best five times 'sharper' than man's, but three times is more likely. That of other birds varies from three times poorer to one times better than man's.

Doubt about the visual acuity of diurnal raptors was first raised in 1983 when it was found that the eyesight of the small **American kestrel** (*Falco sparverius*) was only just equal to that of man's. A more recent study discovered that the **wedge-tailed eagle's** (*Aquila audax*) ability to see into the distance was at best twice that of man's and varied with both the contrast and brightness of stimuli. Examination of the eagle's eye revealed structures approaching theoretical limits and as the eye of the wedge-tailed eagle is, in absolute terms, among the largest known, it is unlikely that maximum spatial resolution (ability to pick out detail at extreme distance) in any other bird eye will be much greater.

The study also showed that the eagle's eye is specialized for vision at the highest natural light levels. Once these start to fall the eagle's spatial resolution deteriorates more rapidly than that of man. This also explains why few raptors hunt at or after twilight. There are exceptions, including the **letter-winged kite** (*Elanus scriptus*) of central Australia which hunts mice by moonlight. No doubt there are surprising examples of day-flying raptors spotting tiny prey at great distances but it now seems that the extreme cases have been exaggerated.

How well a bird can see at night is determined by light-gathering ability or 'visual sensitivity' and this is obviously greater in nocturnal hunters, notably **owls** (*Strigidae*). Yet many bird species have greater visual sensitivity than man.

Most owls rely heavily on acute hearing (see page 94) as well as sight in prey location, but controlled experiments have shown that they can spot dead (and therefore silent) prey 1.82 m (6 ft) away at a light intensity as little as one hundredth of what we would require. But owls cannot see prey in total darkness and by night their resolving power is often only slightly better than that of man.

Owl eyes are large and pearshaped with comparatively wide corneal and lens surfaces which allow a maximum amount of light to reach the retina. Concentration of light-sensitive rods is very high, but cones are proportionately few so that owls have low visual acuity compared with the day-flying raptors.

Owls are certainly not 'blind' by day as was once popularly thought. On the contrary, some species have greater visual acuity than man both by day and night. But there are disadvantages for nocturnal hunters. Night vision in birds, though generally superior to that of humans, usually takes longer to 'switch on' – perhaps an hour compared with about 10 minutes in man. And because owl eyes are so large and tubular they cannot turn in their sockets as ours do, so the birds have exceptionally flexible necks and can turn their heads through 360° – a full circle.

Behavioural studies have shown that in the eye of the **tawny owl** (*Strix aluco*) (which has been studied more than any other owl species) both absolute visual sensitivity and maximum spatial resolution at low light levels are close to theoretical limits.

Less than 250 species (circa 3%) of birds are regularly active outside daylight hours and the majority of these are best regarded as crepuscular (active at twilight) rather than strictly nocturnal in activity. **Potoos** (*Nyctibiidae*) of Central and South America, relatives of the nightjars (most of which are chiefly crepuscular), have very large eyes which they use to hunt flying insects at night. **Cave swiftlets** (*Collocallia*) and the **oilbird** (*Steatornis caripensis*) use echolocation to find their nests in pitch-dark caves (though these are structurally simple environments compared with woods), but the latter uses its large eyes to find fruit when feeding at night. It plucks the fruit in flight, as do **bellbirds** and **trogons.**

THE BIRDS WITH THE MOST AND LEAST FEATHERS

The old tongue-twister 'Thirty thousand feathers on a thrush's throat' seems to be based on exaggeration as the highest number of feathers so far counted on any bird is 25,216 on a **whistling swan** (*Cygnus columbianus*), even though 80% of these were on the head and long neck. And it has been found that generally (though not always) larger birds have more feathers than small species, the lowest number recorded so far being 940 for a **ruby-throated hummingbird** (*Archilochus colubris*). However, small birds have more feathers relative to body surface area and weight. About a third of a landbird's feathers are on its head.

Very little work has been done in this field (none in Britain) and most studies deal with contour feathers only (as in above quoted figures), and do not include the semi-plume downy feathers. The contour feathers comprise almost all the visible feathers, including the relatively large, stiff wing and tail feathers and the smaller, softer feathers which give a bird its smooth outline. All these have a rachis (main shaft) and in most the barbs are closely 'zippered' together to form a unified surface or vane on either side of the rachis.

No marked difference has been found in feather numbers between individuals of the same sex and species living in the same area in the same season. But more feathers have been found on a bird in the winter when greater protection against cold is required. For example, **house sparrows** (*Passer domesticus*) were found to have 11.5% less contour feathers in summer and there was a progressive seasonal change from about 3,500 to 3,000. Gradual loss of feathers during the breeding season could be a moulting of the bird's extra winter insulation in warm weather.

In most species feathers constitute 15–20% of the body weight. For example, a **bald eagle** of 4.08 kg (9 lb) had 677 g (1.5 lb) of feathers – 16.6% of the total.

THE MOST SENSITIVE HEARING

As birds hear at frequencies varying from each other and often from

Eighty per cent of the whistling swan's record number of feathers are on its head and long neck. (©Philippa Scott)

man, it is not possible to say absolutely which species have the most acute hearing. However, there is no doubt that many birds have remarkable hearing, ranging from the **great grey owl** (*Strix nebulosa*) pinpointing the faint sounds of mice under the snow to the **American robin** (*Turdus migratorius*) listening for worms underground. It is not surprising that birds should possess acute hearing for they are among the most vocal of animals. Song is used extensively in courtship, proclamation of territory, signalling between parents and young, raising alarm, threat and communication within a flock.

Birds do not have the fleshy external ears so prominent in mammals: their ear holes are totally concealed under the feathers called ear coverts. But some owls have a flap of skin called an operculum or concha along the front edge of the ear hole, which can be closed over the opening or raised to catch sounds from behind. These are nothing to do with the display tufts on the top of the head of the so-called **long-eared owl** (*Asio otus*) and some other species. To minimize obstruction of sounds, birds' ear coverts lack barbules and can be erected from the sides of the head, though this is rarely witnessed.

Sound is measured at the rate at which sound vibrations pass through the air – cycles per second (cps), and the more cycles per second the higher the frequency or pitch. Although collectively birds hear a much greater range of frequencies than man the range of any individual bird species is significantly less than ours: we hear about nine octaves, but birds average only about five. As a group birds hear best in the frequency range 1–5 kHz (1–5,000 cycles per second) and within this range sensitivity approaches the levels reported for man. But above this range sensitivity declines rapidly and most birds show a high-frequency hearing limit of about 10 kHz. Bird species tend to hear

about the same range of sounds they can produce. For example, many small songbirds can sing and hear sounds of frequencies too high for us to hear, but these same species miss several lower octaves which we hear easily, and commonly do not pick up the conversation of birdwatchers. Also, some birds hear 'faster' than we can: only slowing down a recording reveals what we have missed.

It is in prey location that the extreme sensitivity of some birds' hearing has become apparent. Most spectacular is that of owls, which have a high-frequency hearing limit around 12 kHz. Experiments have shown that owls can catch prey in the total absence of light, using sound only. In such conditions, **barn owls** (*Tyto alba*) were able to strike at rodents to within an accuracy of 1°, but if frequencies above 5 kHz were filtered out the birds refused to attack. Infra-red photography showed how an attack in darkness involved moving the head from side to side to enable a three-dimensional 'audio pattern' to be built up.

Owls' ears are unique among birds. Not only are the holes of different size and shape on each side of the head, but also they are in different positions. Owls' heads are relatively wide so that the sounds reach one ear a tiny fraction of a second before the other. Coupled with the symmetry of the ears, this permits precise location of sound source.

Nonetheless, location of prey through hearing is dependent on that prey moving to emit sounds. And as with vision, high performance of owl hearing seems to be linked to familiarity with the local environment. This helps to explain the great territoriality and sedentary behaviour of owls.

Sensitivity of hearing is also well developed in species which must reach nests or roosts in very dark places such as deep caves. Species which echolocate thus utilize signals in the frequency region of 2–8 kHz. Sensitivity decreases gradually below 1 kHz but it has been shown that **domestic pigeons** and **rock doves** (*Columba livia*) can detect 'infrasounds' such as the vibrations from meteorological disturbances or movements in the earth's crust thousands of miles away. This may be of use in navigation.

THE MOST PRIMITIVE BIRDS ALIVE TODAY

'Primitive' applies to the retention of characteristics belonging to an ancestral form, but it is not safe to assume that the most primitive-looking birds are from the oldest bird families alive today. We must go chiefly by the fossil record, but that from the late Jurassic period of the extinct Archaeopteryx and the following Cretaceous period is very sparse indeed. Most named birds of the Cretaceous era (135–60 million years ago) are of indeterminable systematic affinities because of the incomplete and undiagnostic nature of the fossils upon which they were based. Of these, *Gallornis* of the Neocomian of France, *Parascaniornis* of the Campanian of Sweden and *Torotix* of the Lancian of Wyoming have been regarded as early flamingos, and *Elopteryx* of the Maestrichtian of Romania as an early Pelecaniform. And another flamingo-like bird – *Palaeolodus* – is represented in the Miocene of Europe from 26–27 million years ago.

The **flamingos** (*Phoenicopteridae*) have relatively primitive and specialized bills and seem to have been firmly established in the Tertiary period. But in former times they were not confined to shallow saline or alkaline lakes mainly in the tropics, as they are today. They were once widespread in Europe, North America and Australia as well as in areas where they are found today. This relict group is often considered to be a link between the *Ciconiiformes* (storks, herons etc) and the *Anseriformes* (ducks, geese, swans).

A single bone of a primitive **owl** (*Strigidae*) is known from the late Paleocene of Colorado, from 54–57 million years ago, and **penguins** (*Spheniscidae*) are known from the late Eocene of some 45 million years ago from several areas within their modern range. An early **frigate-bird** (*Limnofregata*) dates from the early Eocene of North America.

The **hoatzin** (*Opisthocomus hoatzin*) has often been regarded as the most primitive bird and closely related to Archaeopteryx, but the classification puzzle of this fascinating bird remains unsolved. It is now suggested that its unique characteristics have been evolved relatively recently to suit its life in the flooded, forested borders of quiet streams in Amazonia.

Traditionally aligned with the *Galliformes* – 'fowl-like' birds whose inter-relationships are not fully understood – the hoatzin has been called a 'living fossil', but this seems far from reality. Recent biochemical investigations suggest that the species is closer to the cuckoos than any other group of living birds.

The hoatzin is the only tree-living bird which feeds its young on foliage to any great extent. It is one of the strictest avian vegetarians and its plant-crushing crop has evolved to very large size – about one third of body-weight! In other vegetarian birds the food is broken up by the gizzard. It is also the only arboreal species in which the chicks habitually leave the nest soon after hatching. The lightly-muscled body has little strength to balance on swaying branches but tiny claws (not present in the adult), worked by special muscles, on the 'elbows' of the unfeathered wings help the young to clamber about. A few other species which live precarious lives over water also have this adaptation. And like Archaeopteryx, the hoatzin has a long and broad tail for balance. The development of the flight feathers is retarded and as the young grow they lose both their wing-claws and the ability to swim and dive, but use their relatively large and weak (owing to reduced flight muscles) wings to help them about the branches, often breaking

New Zealand's **takahe** (left) was rediscovered in 1948 after having gone unnoticed since 1898. (New Zealand Wildlife Sevices)

The **echo parakeet** (above) of Mauritius is the rarest member of the parrot family. (D.V. Merton, New Zealand Wildlife Sevice)

The **kakapo** (below) of New Zealand is the only entirely flightless parrot. (G.J.H. Moon, Frank Lane Picture Agency)

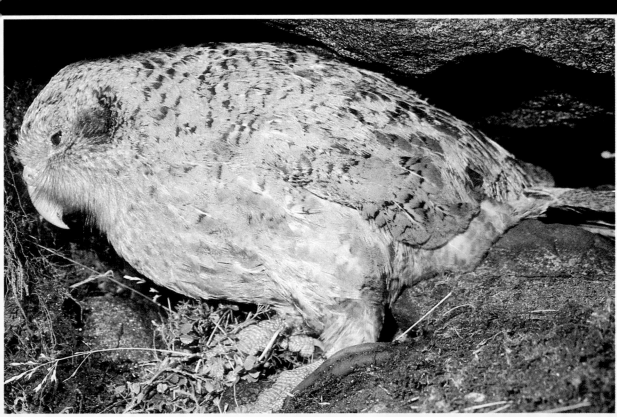

The beautiful **snowy owl** (inset) was first found breeding in Britain in 1967. (B. Hawkes, Aquila Photographics)

Perhaps better known for changing the colour of its plumage to match each season, the winter-white **ptarmigan's** (right) feathered feet are said to help the bird walk on snow as well as keep warm. (M. Newman, Frank Lane Picture Agency)

The **O-o-aa** (above) is one of several honeyeaters which have been exterminated or driven almost to extinction in Hawaii. (P. Barruel, Bruce Coleman Ltd)

The **ivory-billed woodpecker** was rediscovered in Cuba in 1986, after having been considered extinct, and is now probably the world's rarest species. (P. Barruel, Bruce Coleman Ltd)

British **starlings** (this page) perform spectacular aerial displays prior to settling down in roosts of up to a million birds. (Dr C.J. Feare)

It has been estimated that some **sooty tern** island breeding colonies (inset left) contain 1–10 million pairs. This colony is on Desnoeufs Island, Seychelles. (Dr C.J. Feare).

Over a million **lesser flamingos** (right) feed together on Lake Nakuru in Kenya. (M. P. Kahl, Bruce Coleman Ltd)

Australian **budgerigars** (inset right) may congregate in flocks of over a million. (C.M. Perrins, Oxford Scientific Films)

One of the world's two most southerly breeding species, the **snow petrel** *rarely ranges beyond the pack ice of Antarctica. (D. Allen, Oxford Scientific Films)*

Penguins, *such as these adélies, can increase their swimming speed and save energy by 'porpoising'. (F. Erize, Bruce Coleman Ltd)*

The **jacanas**, such as this African, have by far the longest toes and claws relative to body length. (Eric Hosking)

The **hoatzin** (inset) is often regarded as the most primitive living bird. (A. Warren, Ardea London)

*The **emperor penguin** is superbly adapted for life in the coldest season on earth – the Antarctic winter. (D.G. Allan, British Antarctic Survey)*

their primaries in the process. The size and weight of the hoatzin makes it top-heavy and unstable among the branches, but it manages to keep its balance by leaning on its breastbone, which is covered by a specially developed callosity (abnormally hard and thick skin). And such is the size of the crop that the bird has to maintain equilibrium by spreading its wings and flapping its tail when jumping from branch to branch. The adults' feet do not provide sufficient grip on the branches but the feet and bill of the young grip well, an excellent adaptation to life in the mangrove swamp. If threatened, the chicks let themselves fall into the water, where they dive and swim off, using both feet and wings, climbing out again when safe.

THE MOST ACUTE SENSE OF SMELL

Although relatively little work has been done on the avian sense of smell, it is already apparent that this sense is important in the lives of only a few species, and in all (except perhaps the kiwis) it is probably much less important than vision and hearing. Compared with the size of the forebrain the size of the olfactory bulbs in the brain is extremely variable between species. They are largest in the *Apterygiformes* – kiwis; *Procellariiformes* – albatrosses, petrels, shearwaters; *Podicipediformes* – grebes; *Caprimulgi-*

Kiwis are unique in using nostrils at the tip of the bill to locate food such as earthworms in the ground. (Guinness Book of Records)

formes – nightjars etc; and *Gruiformes* – cranes, bustards etc; and it could be that this indicates a highly developed sense of smell in these species.

Kiwis are the only birds known to use the sense of smell for finding food in the ground. Earthworms are the principal item of diet and are apparently located via nostrils which open at the tip of the long, slightly down-curved bill. But whether they use scent for other purposes is not known. In most long-billed birds the nostrils are at the base of the bill. Kiwis are adapted for nocturnal life in which, presumably, sight is less important, but much remains to be discovered about these widespread but secretive birds. The food is picked up by the tip of the bill and thrown back to the throat with a series of quick jerks.

The **turkey vultures** (*Cathartes aura*) of the Americas appear to have the ability to home in on carrion using their sense of smell over considerable distances, whereas other vultures apparently concentrate on visual signs. Like the **oilbird** (*Steatornis caripensis*) and the **albatrosses** (*Diomedea immutabilis* and *D. nigripes*), turkey vultures have large nerve-rich nasal organs. They have been seen to gather above up-currents of the chemical ethyl mercaptan released from hidden sites in a canyon. This heightened sense of smell has enabled these vultures to exploit the forest habitat, vultures of open plains habitat having concentrated on visual acuity. Other vulture species have also been able to feed in forests through observation of turkey vultures.

Honeyguides (*Indicatoridae*) of Africa and Asia appear to be able to trace bee-hives through smelling the wax, which they are uniquely capable of digesting. As early as 1569 a Portuguese missionary in Africa reported how honeyguides flew into his church when he burnt beeswax candles and this was subsequently proved through experiments.

Twelve species of honeyguides are insect-eaters related to the barbets and woodpeckers, but they also eat bees and their larvae as well as the wax. Their tough skin gives some immunity to the stings and they carry special bacteria in the gut to aid digestion of the wax. The **black-throated honeyguide** (*Indicator indicator*) and **scaly-throated honeyguide** (*Indicator variegatus*) entice other animals to open the tough fabric of the bees' nests. Having located a suitable nest, these honeyguides find a honey badger and attract its attention by calling insistently and leading it on, always a few metres ahead. Knowing what to expect, the badger follows, tears open the bees' nest and feeds on the honey and grubs. When it has finished the honeyguide feeds on the remaining grubs and the wax of the comb. Once these birds also followed tribesmen who went in search of wild honey, but now this is done only in very few remote areas of Africa far from the influence of civilization.

Scent odour also seems to play a part in nest location. In experiment, **Leach's petrels** (*Oceanodroma leucorhoa*) in a Y-maze chose an air current coming from their own nest material in preference to one from similar materials collected from the forest floor. In the wild they walk upwind to their nest burrows. Birds taken from their burrows did not return for a week if their nostrils were plugged or their olfactory nerves cut. **Petrels** and **shearwaters** have also been found to respond to airborne odour trails from sponges soaked in cod liver oil, and it has been suggested that olfaction plays a part in helping **pigeons** find their way back to their lofts. It could be that the olfactory system serves a wider function than simply processing information about odorous stimuli. For example, after removal of their olfactory bulbs, pigeons lost the ability to detect X-rays, which they had gained through simple training, and they were generally considerably slower to adapt to new situations.

Endurance & Performance

The great diversity of birds on this planet is testimony to the highly successful manner in which they have exploited every available niche in every habitat from pole to pole, from sea level to mountain top, from swimming deep in the oceans to flying effortlessly from one continent to another. Some are sedentary and have evolved to find food on their 'home patches' in every season while others have developed tremendous stamina to migrate great distances and exploit seasonal food abundances all around the globe. Many endure in the harshest environments, where no man could survive without artificial support, and all live with the constant threat of predation.

In this section we look at those remarkable species whose adaptations in behaviour and life history have been most extreme; whose performance in the field and exceptional endurance seem to approach theoretical limits.

THE WORLD'S FASTEST-
MOVING BIRD
*PEREGRINE FALCON – up to
180 km/h (112 mph) in a dive*
It was discussion about the speed of gamebirds which gave rise to the idea for the *Guinness Book of Records* and this has long been a subject at which men have marvelled. But because admiration of natural ability has always led to exaggeration and bird speed has been extremely difficult to monitor, a great deal of uncertainty remains. Bird flight speed is mostly very erratic and many species are capable of level, short-lived bursts at enhanced speed while others can 'stoop' or plunge-dive after prey at speeds which greatly exceed those of any species in level flight.

Flight is chiefly a very successful method of locomotion which has enabled birds to exploit changing food sources most rapidly, though it is also useful in display and finding a mate and place to breed. But an individual species' flight performance – speed and energy expended – must be governed by the potential energy value of the chosen food. Powered or flapping flight demands much energy and is minimized by every bird so that the net energy gain is maximized. Therefore the optimum flight speed of a species is largely determined by the main food sources. This in turn has partly determined body shape. The two main features traditionally associated with very rapid flight are long, narrow wings, swept back to reduce turbulence, and a torpedo-shaped body. These appear to reach perfection in the swifts, but contrary to popular opinion, swifts are among the slowest of birds so far reliably measured in level flight. In fact this is consistent with the expected performance of long, narrow wings, whose prime function is to permit sustained, energy-saving flight rather than facilitate great speed. In roosting on the wing and being an aerial insectivore, the swift is not particularly concerned with speed. Level-flight speeds of the **common swift** (*Apus apus*) in foraging are around 6.5 m/s or 23 km/h (14 mph). In migration it flies at about 11 m/s or 40 km/h (25 mph). Thus, even allowing for error through mixing up air and ground speeds, claims that the **white-throated spinetailed swift** (*Hirundapus caudacutus*) can feed at 113 km/h (70 mph) and may reach air speeds of up to 170 km/h (105 mph) in courtship display are now doubted. Similar claims for other swifts, such as the **alpine** (*Apus melba*), have also been called into question. In feeding, great speed would be a hindrance, but much higher speeds are no doubt reached in display.

It is the larger birds with streamlined bodies plus powerful flight muscles which fly the fastest in steady flight. The fastest reliably clocked so far is the **eider duck** (*Somateria mollissima*) at 21 m/s or 76 km/h (47.2 mph). This bird also has the highest recorded wing-loading – the smallest wing area relative to body weight. The swifts' low wing-loading is an adaptation for soaring – gliding at low air speed with a low rate of sink. Powerful flight is an obvious asset for the eider duck, which is a coastal bird spending much of its time battling against strong headwinds. Flight speed rises with both mass and wing-loading since higher speeds become necessary if lift is to be sufficient to support weight.

The fastest-moving bird of all is probably the **peregrine falcon** (*Falco peregrinus*) when stooping after prey, but no very accurate determination of speed has been made and the maximum is probably no more than about 50 m/s or 180 km/h (112 mph). Air speedometers have been fitted to trained peregrines and these recorded a maximum speed of 132 km/h (82 mph). The male, or tiercel, is the better flyer and may reach far greater speeds in a display dive, but the accuracy of dives measured to 360 km/h (224 mph) at steep angles has been questioned. There are many variables to be considered, including the speed of the bird before entering the dive and the speed of any head-, tail- or cross-wind. Mathematical theory has suggested an even higher dive speed is possible, but even at the lower figures it is baffling how the peregrine can pull out of such a dive and avoid blacking out.

Cosmopolitan in distribution, with 17 races, the 36–48 cm (14–19 in) peregrine has long been the falconer's choice *par excellence*. Sadly, this has led to many birds being taken illegally from the wild and sold – mostly to Arab enthusiasts for very large sums of money. In the 1950s and 60s its population was much reduced throughout

most of its range by DDT and other organochlorine pesticides, which resulted in direct poisoning through the food chain, loss of fertility and unsuccessful breeding attempts through eggshell thinning and breakage. Many of these chemicals are now banned and the position is much improved in many western countries.

The peregrine's victim is sometimes hit with a glancing blow from the claws, striking it dead in mid-air, but predator and prey may also 'bind' together and both tumble to the ground. A strike lasts only one tenth of a second or less and the feet are lowered and thrown forward at the last moment to increase greatly the impact. Simultaneously the tail may be fanned and the wings thrown up to maximize braking. The bird is such a skilful flyer that its path may be altered even just a few milliseconds before impact. Usually there is a characteristic trail of scattered feathers leading to the remains of the prey with the breast-bone picked clean of meat. Despite the great speed, many stoops fail and the hunt often continues as a direct chase. Sometimes, in a desperate attempt to save itself, the hunted bird may fold its wings and allow itself to fall to the ground as the falcon usually gives up if it cannot hunt the prey in flight.

Male peregrines average 700–850 g (24½–30 oz) and females 1,100–1,500 g (38½–53 oz). Prey varies considerably according to location and ranges in size from 10 g (0.35 oz) passerines to geese and herons weighing over 2,000 g (4 lb), the heavier female peregrines generally taking the larger prey. Over 132 bird species have been recorded in the diet of British peregrines and over 200 seems likely for North American birds. Mammals, reptiles, amphibians and even fish are also sometimes taken.

Really severe peregrine strikes can dismember a wing or sever the head of the prey but a mere stun is more likely. The peregrine's normal cruising speed is probably in the region of 65 km/h (40 mph).

Although it is able to catch very fast-flying birds such as pigeons and shorebirds, in level flight under its own muscle-power it can seldom catch up with a good homing pigeon. A maximum level flight speed of 110 km/h (65–68 mph) in short bursts is suggested.

The maximum flight speed of **racing pigeons** is no more easy to determine than that of wild birds. The **woodpigeon** (*Columba palumbus*) has been reliably clocked at 61 km/h (38 mph) in steady, level flight but trained and specially bred racing pigeons can do better. The highest race speed recorded averaged 117.14 km/h (110.07 mph) in the East Anglian Federation race from East Croydon on 8 May 1965 when 1,428 birds were backed by a powerful south/south-west wind. But in level flight in calm conditions it is doubtful if even a champion racing pigeon can exceed 96 km/h (60 mph). Most birds fly much more slowly without the assistance of wind.

THE WORLD'S SLOWEST-FLYING BIRD
AMERICAN WOODCOCK –
8 km/h (5 mph)
All birds vary their flight speed, either deliberately according to whether hunting, courting etc, or reluctantly in response to wind strength, but few regularly flap very slowly by choice. Those birds which routinely travel great distances in search of food – for example, vultures after carrion and albatrosses after seafood – concentrate on soaring to conserve energy. Slow wing-flapping is not widely used in food-seeking, though there are exceptions, such as the **barn owl** (*Tyto alba*), but it is useful in display flight. And it is in the courtship of the **American woodcock** (*Scolopax minor*) that the slowest powered bird flight of 8 km/h (5 mph) has been measured.

Like all species of woodcock, *Scolopax minor* feeds chiefly on earthworms and in searching for these there is negligible advantage in slow flight. But the slow court-

Opposite: In level flight the peregrine falcon is not the fastest of all birds so it resorts to a very steep dive known as a 'stoop' in order to develop the extra speed required to overhaul and sometimes instantly strike dead prey in the air. (Suzanne Alexander)

Hummingbirds have special 'arm' bones and wing joints which enable them to turn their wings through 180°, tracing a figure of eight, beating their wings as rapidly as 90 times per second in order to maintain station. (Suzanne Alexander)

ship (roding) flights enable sitting females to see their suitors more easily, especially as most of this display takes place in the gloom of dusk. Most feeding is done at night and then slow flight is also an advantage in navigating the edges of the wet woodland habitat. Woodcock have excellent vision with an almost full-circle field of view and eyes placed high on the head, which enables them to remain alert to predators while probing with their long bills for worms in the soft soil.

Very few birds can truly hover, remaining stationary in still air, and those that can are all very small indeed, the most well known being the **hummingbirds** (*Trochilidae*) which specialize in feeding on the nectar of flowers (see page 84), using very fast wingbeats.

Birds such as the **common kestrel** (*Falco tinnunculus*) and **rough-legged buzzard** (*Buteo lagopus*) are commonly thought to hover but they cannot sustain the high power output this would entail. To remain stationary relative to the ground, where potential prey lurks, they must fly into a moderate wind at the same speed as they are being blown back. Generally, slow flight speed is difficult for large birds to achieve, even briefly as in approach to landing, because, just as in an aircraft, a minimum speed is needed for flight generation. And also, like an aeroplane, a long run-up is often needed to build up sufficient air speed.

Some of the very large raptors, such as **vultures** (*Vulturidae*), have flapping rates as low as one beat per second but some, notably the **condors,** may cruise on air currents without flapping their wings at all for up to 100 km (60 miles). They utilize the up-drafts generated by warm air currents and flapping is of only secondary importance in keeping them aloft.

THE FASTEST AND SLOWEST WINGBEATS
HUMMINGBIRDS—at least 90 per second

In evolving unique anatomy and physiology to master the skills of true hovering, the hummingbirds have achieved by far the fastest wingbeats. Few species in this large family have so far been measured, but already rates as high as 90 per second for the **amethyst woodstar** (*Calliphlox amethystina*) have been recorded. Up to 200 per second were reported for the **ruby-throated hummingbird** (*Archilochus colubris*) and the **rufous hummingbird** (*Selasphorus rufus*) during courtship flights, but these incredible rates were for the narrow tips of the primaries only rather than the complete wing.

Such rapid action appears as a blur to the human eye and can be measured only by a stroboscope or similar sophisticated equipment. Generally wings beat faster in smaller birds, but more specifically the frequency increases as the size of the wing decreases relative to body weight.

The hummingbird's energy-demanding flight depends on a highly efficient system for obtaining oxygen and a digestive system capable of quickly processing large amounts of food. These in turn rely upon a unique anatomy which allows the hummingbird to remain stationary in the air, move backwards or forwards, right or left, up or down, and even turn upside down – all to obtain nectar from the chosen food plants. Equally astounding is the speed with which a hummingbird can stop in flight and how quickly it can accelerate to reach maximum speed from the moment of take-off.

To achieve this the hummingbird's flight feathers take up almost the entire wing and the area which corresponds with our hand is extremely developed, while the 'arm' area is greatly reduced even when compared to other birds. That 'hand' secures 10 primaries (main flight feathers) – the same number as in the soaring albatross, but whereas the latter has some 40 secondary feathers attached to the 'arm', the hummingbird has just six or seven. Also the arm bones and shoulder joints are specially adapted so that the wing can turn through 180°.

No less impressive is the large breastbone to which are anchored the mighty flight muscles, which make up some 30% of the body weight – the largest relative to body size of any known bird. Two sets of muscles operate bird wings – the depressors, which power the downstroke, and the elevators which lift the wings. Most elevators are 5–10% of the weight of the depressors, but in hummingbirds this ratio rises to almost 50% and accounts for much of their excep-

tional flight control. With other species only the downstroke provides lift, but the hummingbird can convert even the downstroke into power for both lift and propulsion by means of the very large elevator muscles which enable the wings to twist and rotate at exceptional angles.

When the hummingbird hovers in still air its wings move rapidly backwards and forwards rather than up and down, the tips tracing a figure of eight. Every time the beat changes direction (reverses) the wings are turned through 180° so that their front edges always lead, and on the backstroke it is always the undersides of the wings which are on top. In this way, although both forward and backstrokes produce lift, the two cancel each other out, leaving the bird on station to feed. Precise manoeuvres are achieved with the aid of the broad tail.

Among slower species are vultures with flapping rates as low as one beat per second; the **rook** (*Corvus frugilegus*) with an average of 2.3 wingbeats per second and the **herring gull** (*Larus argentatus*) with 2.8, while the **woodpigeon** (*Columba palumbus*) has 4.

THE HIGHEST-FLYING BIRD IN THE WORLD
RÜPPELL'S GRIFFON VULTURE – 11,274 m (37,000 ft/7 miles)

On 29 November 1973 a **Rüppell's griffon vulture** (*Gyps rueppellii*) collided with a commercial aircraft at 11,274 m (37,000 ft) over Abidjan, Ivory Coast, western Africa. The altitude was recorded by the pilot shortly after impact, which damaged one of the aircraft's engines, causing it to be shut down. But the plane landed safely at Abidjan without further incident. Sufficient feather remains of the bird were recovered to enable their positive identification by the US Museum of Natural History. This was by far the greatest altitude at which a bird has been positively identified, though it is not a normal height for this species.

No bird has ever been found flying higher than the Rüppell's griffon vulture at 11,274m (37,000ft). The species is a high-level soarer which watches for the activity of other vultures to lead it to carcasses.
(A. Christiansen, Frank Lane Picture Agency)

Rüppell's griffon is chiefly a bird of the drier parts of Africa, from Eritrea and Sudan, south to Tanganyika and west to Guinea in desert and open plains, but also frequently in mountainous districts. They are high-level soarers which react to the behaviour of other vultures or scavengers such as hyenas: thus they tend to fly higher than those vultures which concentrate on spotting the carcasses direct. The 7.55 kg (16.6 lb) bird feeds exclusively on carrion, often putrid.

It is a sociable species roosting, feeding and breeding in consider-able numbers. Like other large vultures, it is on the wing about two hours after sunrise and spends much time, especially during the middle of the day, soaring around the hills on which it breeds, though it is also seen flying around singly. In some areas they breed in large numbers on cliffs exposed to the prevailing winds, which provide a continually rising airflow. This gives them some independence of thermals, especially early and late in the day, and they are thus able to remain airborne for extended periods, a great advantage when seeking the migratory herds of wildebeeste, which may be up to 120 km (75 miles) from the cliffs.

Rüppell's vultures have long, naked necks which they thrust deep into a carcass, and they may even climb right inside to rasp off pieces of soft flesh with tongues which are set with backward-facing spines. Their task is made easier by the low-flying, more powerful vultures – the white-headed (*Aegypius occipitalis*) and lappet-faced (*Torgos tracheliotus*) – which arrive at the carcasses earlier. These have bills strong enough to tear the tough carcass skins open.

It is said that vultures sometimes soar to great heights, where temperatures are lower, in order to cool off, and there may be some truth in this. The body temperature of flying birds is generally above that of resting birds so keeping cool is a special problem for birds flying long distances, such as when on migration. Although vultures specialize in soaring and would not therefore generate the blood-heat rise of a steady-flapping species, they do have the problem of keeping a large body cool in a hot climate. Heat can be lost directly from the surface of the flight muscles and underwings or through evaporative cooling through the respiratory system and mouth. It has even been suggested that water availability rather than the size of energy reserves limits the flight range, but proof is lacking.

Altitude selection is also particularly important for migrants or long-distance scavengers in taking advantage of wind speed and direction. It is assumed that a bird is made aware of its altitude through its ear sensing atmospheric pressure changes, but other possibilities include use of flight calls – either by producing a Doppler effect (variations in frequency according to distance) through echoes from the ground or by communicating ideal flight levels to other migrants in a flock.

It is also suggested that high flight paths are selected because stronger, following upper winds

and thinner air allow faster flight without the expenditure of additional energy. Fortunately vultures have few physiological problems with regard to breathing at high altitudes as the blood flow of a bird enables oxygen to be extracted from air with a far greater efficiency than that of any other vertebrate. Man requires additional oxygen supplies above about 4,000–5,000 m (13,000–16,500 ft). Neither do the very low temperatures found at great heights seem to be a problem if flight is in cloudless air. For example, **lapwings** have been recorded at −10°C (+18°F), **starlings** at −12°C (+10.4°F) and **whooper swans** at −48°C (−54.4°F). But sometimes it is necessary for a bird to go below or rise above cloud with a high water content to avoid its plumage icing up. The higher the air temperature the more water vapour it is able to hold, so generally, at a constant relative humidity and atmospheric pressure, the rate of water loss of a bird by evaporation decreases with air temperature at greater altitude – a very important factor in the dry environments used by vultures.

Direct observation, radar and birdstrikes (birds colliding with planes – see page 179) clearly demonstrate that most birds generally fly below 150 m (500 ft), and even in migration, when altitude selection is very important to take advantage of strong, following winds, most passerines fly at altitudes of less than 1,500 m (5,000 ft). In a detailed analysis, the United States Air Force has found that over 70% of bird strikes on aircraft occurred below 900 m (3,000 ft) and consequently recommends that aircraft remain above that level for as long as possible prior to landing.

Some birds begin their flight from very high ground, so their effort is less notable, but others must fly over mountain ranges because their limited energy reserves do not afford them the luxury of flying around major obstacles. **Bar-headed geese** (*Anser indicus*), for example, have been seen flying over the

Like all swans, the whooper has difficulty in taking off, but once airborne its heavy body is helpful in pushing through strong, adverse winds. (Heather Angel, Biofotos) The slipstream effect, derived through flying in V-formation, also saves energy, as does cruising on high winds at great altitude: one group came into Britain at a record height of over 8,230m (27,000ft). (A. Christiansen, Frank Lane Picture Agency)

Himalayas at altitudes approaching 9,000 m (29,500 ft). Mountain ridges also provide updrafts to assist soaring birds on migration.

Among those species which live permanently at great altitude is the **alpine** or **yellow-billed chough** (*Pyrrhocorax graculus*) which is found mostly at 3,500–6,250 m (11,500–20,000 ft) in the Himalayas. One party was observed as high as 8,235 m (27,017 ft) when they followed a British Everest expedition. These crows readily become tame if encouraged. They feed by digging for insects and sometimes descend to lower levels according to the severity of the weather.

Britain's highest-nesting bird is the **dotterel** (*Eudromias morinellus*), which has been found breeding at 1,300 m (4,265 ft).

THE HIGHEST-FLYING BRITISH BIRD
WHOOPER SWAN – 8,230 m (27,000 ft)

On 9 December 1967 about 30 swans, probably **whoopers** (*Cygnus cygnus*), were spotted by the pilot of a civilian transport aircraft over the Inner Hebrides at a height of just over 8,230 m (27,000 ft). They were flying south and the altitude was confirmed by a radar controller in Northern Ireland. He reported that they were moving at a ground speed of about 75 knots – 139 km/h (86 mph). It is thought that these birds took off from a coastal lagoon at sea level in Iceland, in a ridge of high pressure at dawn, for a ride on the strong winds of the jet stream of the lower stratosphere. The temperature at that altitude was later calculated at lower than −48°C (−54.4°F) and upper wind data suggested a flight time of seven hours.

Whooper swans breed in Iceland, Scandinavia and northern Russia and each autumn migrate to the Atlantic seaboard of western Europe to overwinter. Most Icelandic birds go to the British Isles, chiefly to Ireland and western Scotland, but a few do not migrate.

In complete contrast, some birds live below sea level. Perhaps the most extreme case was that of three **house sparrows** (*Passer domesticus*), which managed to live 640 m (2,100 ft) down in Frickley Colliery, Yorkshire, from summer, 1975 to spring, 1978. One pair even nested and raised three young but they died. It is likely that the sparrows first entered the mine as naive juveniles.

THE WORLD'S FASTEST-RUNNING BIRD
OSTRICH – at least 72 km/h (45 mph)

The world's largest and tallest living bird, the **ostrich** (*Struthio camelus*) is also the fastest-running, with speeds reputed to reach as high as 96.5 km/h (60 mph) in short bursts. The species also has considerable stamina – particularly important for a flightless bird in escaping predators. It can travel at 45–48 km/h (28–30 mph) for 15–20 minutes without showing significant signs of fatigue.

As in fast-running mammals, the ostrich has a reduced number of toes, only two remaining, which is advantageous as this reduces surface contact with the ground. One toe takes much of the bird's weight and has a flat nail, while the other is much smaller and without a nail.

Tendon elasticity seems to save a lot of energy for fast-running ostriches, in the manner of a bouncing ball. When the bird is moving most slowly the centre of its body mass is lowest so that kinetic (of motion) and potential (latent) energy have their lowest values at the same time. Then the force on the foot is largest and tendons in the leg are stretched, storing elastic strain energy. As a leg swings forward and touches the ground, kinetic and potential energy are converted to elastic strain energy but restored by elastic recoil when the other leg swings back, and momentarily there is no contact with the ground as the path of the centre of mass undulates. This is most effective at high speed, when the feet are on the ground for only a small fraction

of the stride and the forces on them are increased.

Ostriches also have a much greater proportion of leg muscle than flying birds, enabling them to run a little faster than most antelopes, whereas most birds are slow runners. It is the most graceful running species which have the greatest speed and stamina and they have evolved to make best use of their oxygen supply. Birds which move clumsily, such as penguins and geese, use oxygen up to three times as quickly as the more elegant species. Birds trained to run on a conveyor belt, so that they remain stationary while the belt moves, show that ostriches use oxygen at about the same rate as ponies of the same weight, also graceful and fast runners.

THE WORLD'S FASTEST-RUNNING FLYING BIRD
GREATER ROADRUNNER – at least 42 km/h (26 mph)

This familiar bird (*Geococcyx californianus*) of scrub deserts in south-western North America, a member of the cuckoo family, has been clocked at 42 km/h (26 mph) when chased by a car, but under normal conditions the maximum is about 24 km/h (15 mph). This exceptional speed and agility enables it to capture fast-running snakes, lizards and rodents, but it can even out-manoeuvre dogs, using its long tail to steer and balance, with straightened neck and slightly extended wings acting as very efficient stabilizers.

This 60 cm (24 in) bird is remarkable in other ways too. Being a desert species, it must supplement the water intake in the chicks' food.

To do this it holds an insect, fruit or other food in the tip of its bill and when the nestling goes to receive it the adult regurgitates water into the nestling's mouth before letting go of the food.

A non-parasitic bird, the greater roadrunner nests in trees, shrubs or cacti (rarely on the ground), and has a most unusual physiology for a bird – it is to some extent cold-blooded! Desert air temperatures become very low at night, and in such conditions most birds increase their metabolism to maintain a constant temperature, which means burning precious energy reserves. To avoid this the roadrunner allows its body temperature to fall slightly, thus saving on the costs of 'central heating'. The slight torpor means that the bird may be slow to respond to danger, but the species has few predators and the slight

Above: the flightless ostrich needs its record running speed – up to 72km/h (45 mph) or more – to escape from predators. (C. Haagner, Ardea London)

Above left: The large ostrich foot (here compared with a human hand) has only two toes in order to reduce surface contact with the ground and facilitate high speed. (Guinness Book of Records)

Opposite: The greater roadrunner uses its speed to catch swift-running snakes, lizards and rodents. (J. Van Coevering, Frank Lane Picture Agency)

disadvantage appears to be fairly unimportant.

Also very unusual is the way in which the semi-torpid roadrunner warms up in the morning. On the skin of its back, just between the wings, it has special darkly pigmented areas which absorb the sun's energy more quickly, warming the skin and underlying blood vessels. The bird also fluffs up the feathers covering the patches so that the process is hastened. Without this mechanism the roadrunner would use up to 50% more energy in reaching a 'working temperature'.

Finally, the species has an exceptionally wide vocal repertoire, including an assortment of crowing and whining noises as well as cuckoo-like staccato hoots and clucks.

The **wild turkey** (*Meleagris gallopavo*) of North America is said to reach 48 km/h (30 mph) in occasional short bursts (it regularly travels at 24 km/h (15 mph) on foot), and the widely introduced **common pheasant** (*Phasianus colchicus*) can sprint at 34 km/h (21 mph) to avoid a wide variety of predators.

THE LONGEST MIGRATION
ARCTIC TERN – at least 18,056 km (11,222 miles)

The longest bird journeys are those undertaken through seasonal migration to exploit regional food supplies. The greatest of all migrants is the **arctic tern** (*Sterna paradisaea*), members of the western population frequently travelling 17,700 km (11,000 miles) each way between northern breeding grounds and the winter range near the Antarctic Circle. Among these, the greatest distance recorded so far is the 18,056 km (11,222 miles) travelled by a bird ringed at Valley, Anglesey, North Wales on 26 or 28 June 1966 and recovered near Bega, New South Wales on 31 December 1966. The ring or band number was CK51037. This distance is calculated using the British Trust for Ornithology's current computer program, whereas the Australian Bird and Bat Banding Scheme gives the distance as 17,308 km (10,757 miles) using a different method.

The Australian authorities have no knowledge of another arctic tern which was ringed as a nestling on 5 July 1955 in the Kandalaksha Sanctuary on the White Sea coast, about 200 km (125 miles) from Murmansk, European USSR, and said to have been captured alive by a fisherman 13 km (8 miles) south of Fremantle, Western Australia on 16 May 1956. But if correct, the bird had travelled 22,530 km (14,000 miles) according to the method of calculation at the time. It had flown south across the Atlantic Ocean and then circled Africa before crossing the Indian Ocean, though it did not survive to make the return trip. Unfortunately there is no one place where all ringing recoveries are gathered together so that comprehensive comparisons can be made, and there is a strong possibility that the last record has been well beaten by a Greenland arctic tern travelling to Australasia.

During its migration, the arctic tern enjoys more daylight than any other creature on earth, journeying from one polar summer to the other. The graceful 33–38 cm (13–15 in) bird breeds from the arctic coasts of Alaska, Greenland, Canada, Europe and Siberia and winters in extreme southern continental latitudes, reaching the Antarctic ice edge. The summer of the high arctic is very short and virtually nightless, and arctic terns breed as far north as 82°. Those wintering in Antarctic waters must cover a minimum of 12,800 km (7,955 miles) each way, while the round trip for some, deviating to exploit favourable winds, must entail 35,000 km (21,750 miles). Arctic terns have been known to nest within 720 km (450 miles) of the North Pole and some birds may literally circumnavigate the globe, covering 40,200 km (25,000 miles) between breeding seasons. They arrive in Britain from late April.

Arctic terns raise their young on the short-lived summer abundance of insects and fish in the north, but in the winter of the south Antarctic Ocean they have the benefit of almost perpetual daylight and enjoy an immensely rich food supply of small fish and plankton. One bird was seen aboard a whaling ship just off the pack ice, and the oldest known lived for 26 years, so that in travelling from pole to pole each year it must have travelled several million kilometres in its lifetime.

OTHER REMARKABLE TRAVELLERS

A **common tern** (*Sterna hirundo*) has travelled 17,639 km (10,963 miles) north to south, a **short-tailed shearwater** (*Puffinus teuir tenuirostris*) 33,800 km (21,000 miles) on a figure-of-eight course from South Australia to the north Pacific and back again, and a **sooty albatross** (*Phoenetria fisca*) 30,600 km (19,000 miles) in some 80 days while flying around the world at latitude 40° south.

The westernmost recovery of a British-ringed bird is of a **mallard** (*Anas platyrhynchos*) recovered in the prairie provinces of Canada at the foot of the Rockies at a longitude of 120°W. Also from Britain, a **knot** (*Calidris canutus*) was recovered on its Baffin Island breeding grounds (northern Canada) and both **knot** and **turnstone** (*Arenaria interpres*) on the north-west coast of Greenland.

The easternmost recovery of a British-ringed bird is of a **ruff** (*Philomachus pugnax*) just south of the Arctic Circle, at a longitude of about 130°E, approximately the same easting as North Korea in a line from Britain. A **pochard** (*Aythya ferina*) recovered on the shores of the Sea of Okhotsk, almost as far as the Kamchatka Peninsula, in the far eastern USSR, was at about 150°E.

But great distance is not the sole criterion for calling a bird journey remarkable. The most outstanding feats of endurance are made by birds which, in migration, fly non-stop over hostile environments. The most efficient migrators are medium-sized birds weighing up to 800 g (1¾ lb) without fat, and include the larger, fast-flying waders. It seems incredible that a bird can carry enough fuel to cross an ocean or desert, but flight range does not depend on the absolute amount of fat and energy reserves carried: it is the proportion of fuel to body weight which matters. **Warblers**, for example, burn up 0.5% of body weight during an hour's flying and, as they double their weight before migrating, they will have the capacity for the longest required flights of 2,000 km (1,200 miles) or so, yet retain sufficient reserves to cope with adverse wind and weather.

Large birds cannot carry proportionately large fat reserves because of the difficulty in generating enough power to get the extra weight airborne. For example, a swan or goose could not possibly carry 50% extra weight. But to compensate, their weight and greater momentum provide increased resistance to adverse weather, and they can continue into headwinds which would halt smaller species. Also, their optimum flight speed is greater.

The longest of any uninterrupted flights is probably made by the **American** or **lesser golden plover** (*Pluvialis dominica*), which may travel up to 4,000 km (2,486 miles) over the ocean from Alaska to Hawaii and mid-Pacific islands or from north-eastern Canada to the West Indies. The species has been known to fly non-stop from the Aleutians to Hawaii, a distance of 3,300 km (2,050 miles) in only 35 hours. It also makes some of the longest journeys among landbirds. In loop migration between northern Canada and Argentina it can cover 24,100–27,400 km (15,000–17,000 miles).

The **bristle-thighed curlew** (*Numenius tahitiensis*) of western Alaska has to fly 10,000 km (6,000 miles) across the Pacific Ocean to reach its winter home in the Polynesian islands. For much of the journey it cannot rest or feed and the longest non-stop stretch is over 3,000 km (1,800 miles).

One of the most surprising long-distance flights is made by a **hummingbird** – the **ruby-throated** (*Archilochus colubris*), which travels 1,000 km (622 miles) or more in a non-stop hop across the Gulf of Mexico. Yet this is just one stage in its routine autumn migration of up to 3,200 km (2,000 miles) from the eastern USA to wintering grounds in Central America. A remarkable feat for a 3 g (0.11 oz) bird with a high metabolic rate and limited food reserves.

Homing pigeons too can perform remarkable feats of endurance – for example, 1,887 km (1,173 miles) in 15 days into Britain. Others have journeyed over 1,600 km (1,000 miles) on four occasions. Perhaps the most outstanding was the 1st Duke of Wellington's bird which is said to have flown a direct route of 8,700 km (5,400 miles), but in fact flew some 11,250 km (7,000 miles) to avoid the Sahara desert. It was released on 8 April 1845, from a sailing ship off the Ichabo Islands, West Africa, and dropped dead 55 days later on 1 June – only a mile from its loft at Nine Elms, Wandsworth, London.

But the bird navigation feat of all time was performed by a **manx shearwater** (*Puffinus puffinus*) ringed on the island of Skokholm, off South Wales. She was placed in a transit box and flown to Boston, USA, almost some 5,000 km (3,100 miles) away and far from any regular shearwater haunts. She was released and took just 12½ days to find her way back to her nesting burrow. In so doing she beat the airmail letter from America, giving details of the release, by a short head!

THE SHORTEST MIGRATIONS
These are vertical or altitudinal movements made up and down mountains to take advantage of seasonal food sources when weather permits. For example, the North American **blue** or **dusky grouse** (*Dendragapus obscurus*) spends the winter in mountain pine forests and descends just 300 m (1,000 ft) or so to nest in deciduous woodland where there is an early crop of fresh leaves and seeds. Many sedentary species, especially within the grouse family, make such movements, the actual distances involved depending on the temperature, vegetation, exposure and chill factor, and the precise timing of these migrations will vary with the severity of the seasons.

In countries such as Britain, where the weather is more variable than that of continental land masses, birds such as the **ptarmigan** (*Lagopus mutus*) and **red grouse** (*Lagopus lagopus scoticus*) need make only temporary altitudinal movements, generally returning to high ground whenever the snows relent. Unusually, the red grouse may actually move to higher ground during periods of heavy snowfall, for on the tops the wind is more likely to have drifted the snow and thus exposed the important heather food.

Relief from winter cold is also afforded by migration towards salt-water. For example, in Africa the **mangrove kingfisher** (*Ceyx pusillus*) migrates regularly from mountain streams to coastal mangrove swamps. But in Britain the **common kingfisher** (*Alcedo atthis*) makes only exceptional cold-weather movements towards the coast when persistent, severe frost locks up the fish food supply. Similarly, some species hop back and forth across the English Channel according to the severity of weather. Such temporary movements are not true migrations.

THE FASTEST-SWIMMING BIRDS
PENGUINS

Because they appear so sleek and swift underwater there has been a general tendency to exaggerate the swimming speed of **penguins** (*Spheniscidae*). Earlier claims of up to 60 km/h (37 mph) are now disregarded by leading authorities who suggest that the maximum is probably in the region of 27 km/h (17 mph), but even then only for short bursts. All accurate measurements of normal swimming for emperor, adélie, jackass and gentoo penguins, timed between ice holes, have recorded speeds of only 5–10 km/h (3–6 mph). It is likely that the fastest swimmers are the larger penguins as these are the strongest and deepest divers.

However, these surprisingly low speeds may be surpassed when penguins 'porpoise'. This energy-saving method is usually employed for sustained journeys and involves repeatedly leaping out of the water and plunging back. When a penguin swims just below the surface it meets resistance caused by the surface wave that its own movement is creating, and the faster it swims the greater the resistance. Eventually a point is reached when resistance exceeds the energy needed to leap clear of the water and then porpoising becomes the economical way to travel. Surface drag could be avoided by swimming at greater depths but the penguin must come up to breathe, so porpoising is more efficient. It may also confuse predators.

To facilitate underwater swimming, penguin wings have evolved to become rigid, sabre-thin paddles with very flat bones, and the 'wing-beat' is different from that of flying birds. The entire flipper twists in much the same way as a single flight feather on a flying bird, with the trailing edge forced up on the downstroke so that water is deflected downwards and backwards. On the upstroke this is reversed so that thrust is produced throughout the cycle.

No bird uses both wings and feet for propulsion underwater. Most wing-propelled birds are marine, like the penguins, whereas foot-propulsion predominates among freshwater divers, the **divers** or **loons** (*Gaviidae*) being the most specialized.

THE DEEPEST DIVER AND LONGEST DIVES
THE EMPEROR PENGUIN – 265 m (869 ft), 18 minutes

In a small, but carefully controlled, series of experiments using an isolated ice-hole and depth-recorders attached to the backs of the birds' necks, **emperor penguins** (*Aptenodytes forsteri*) dived as deep as 265 m (869 ft) and stayed submerged for up to 18 minutes. Diving was usually preceded by a few rapid breaths and then a deep inhalation, and the birds were never seen to exhale under water. Seals, whales and other marine mammals can dive for much longer, but they do not inhale specially before each dive. Other diving birds have been able to stay alive for as much as 15 minutes when forcibly held under water.

To be a good diver a bird must have a specific gravity which approaches that of water (normally it is much less) in order to minimize the energy used simply to stay submerged. Diving birds such as the penguins need inhale less than other birds owing to the decreased air-holding capacity (pneumaticity)

of their bones and to a corresponding simplification of the airsac system. Diving birds reduce their specific gravity immediately before diving by compressing their body plumage to force out most of the air normally trapped within it. Some are said to swallow stones to reduce their buoyancy, just as a human diver uses lead weights.

Divers have to make important physiological adaptations to achieve such deep dives. As insufficient oxygen is held in the lungs further supplies are derived from the red blood corpuscles (oxyhaemoglobin) and oxymyoglobin stored in the muscles, the latter being particularly high in penguins. Secondly, the birds can obtain energy from anaerobic (not using free, chemically-bound oxygen in the air), as well as the usual aerobic breakdown of glycogen. Thirdly, penguins can regulate the flow of blood to different parts of the body. Supply to the muscles, and perhaps

to other organs, is greatly reduced, the main flow, and therefore extra oxygen, being reserved for the central nervous system and heart. Furthermore, body temperature control is important during deep, long dives in icy waters, so heat loss from the limbs to water is reduced by cooling the blood entering the limbs. This is done through blood vessels in which arterial blood to the limbs gives off heat to the cooler venous blood returning to the body.

Emperor penguins probably generally dive only to about 100 m (328 ft). And while even the smaller penguins can reach this depth and stay down for six minutes, typical dives are usually much less than these. Through each species having its own depth range penguins have evolved an effective method of 'sharing out' the food sources of the sea around their generally huge colonies in order to minimize potentially harmful competition between each other.

Penguins, such as these adélies, are the world's most efficient diving birds with special physiological adaptations to regulate body temperature and oxygen supply in very cold waters. (Christiana Carvalho, Frank Lane Picture Agency)

Crustaceans, fish and squid are the main prey of penguins.

THE DEEPEST-DIVING FLYING BIRDS

Very little accurate experimental work has been done in measuring the dives of flying birds, which are obviously more difficult to monitor than the flightless penguins. There appears to have been considerable exaggeration and many estimates have been based on birds trapped in deep-sea fishing nets, even though it is not clear whether the birds were enmeshed at the nets' maximum depths or while they were being taken up. Nonetheless, it is likely that the **great northern diver** (*Gavia immer*) (the common loon), the **oldsquaw duck** (*Clangula hyemalis*) and the **common guillemot** (*Uria aalge*) commonly make dives in excess of 50 m (164 ft). Reports of birds caught in fishing nets include one of a great northern diver at 81 m (265 ft), an oldsquaw duck at 61 m (200 ft) and a guillemot at 73 m (240 ft).

Other species of loon and auk are also excellent divers and there is one report of a **razorbill** going down to 137 m (450 ft). If correct, this is Britain's record bird dive.

Over 390 species of bird swim regularly and many others can do so. Of the habitual swimmers about two-fifths seek their food by diving, the remainder either feeding on the surface, up-ending in shallow water or plunge-diving from the air. Of the plunge-divers, the greatest exponents are the *Sulidae* – **gannets** and **boobies**. Gannets often plunge from 30 m (100 ft) or more above the water, but 100 m (330 ft) dives have been estimated for the **masked, blue-faced** or **white booby** (*Sula dactylatra*). Yet these birds are carried only a few metres below the surface. The plunge is very carefully controlled by the wings, tail and feet, which keep the bird on target. Only at the last moment are the wings swept back to avoid injury and minimize drag. Most of the impact is taken on the head, but this is protected by a specially strengthened skull and air sacs under the skin. The stout, conical bill also reduces the force of impact in streamlining entry. As in the cormorants, the nostrils are permanently blocked to prevent water being forced inside, and breathing is through the corner of the mouth. A water-entry speed of some 100 km/h (60 mph) is estimated.

For most diving birds waterlogging is a special problem, which is largely overcome through liberal application of water-resistant oil from special glands on 'close-knit' feathers. But **cormorants** have an unusually large gap between the feather barbs so that they can become waterlogged more easily. They too feed in deep water and find it easier to stay down when the plumage is soaked – thus forcing out air pockets to reduce buoyancy – and before a cormorant starts fishing it raises its feathers to let water in. But the disadvantage is that on returning to the surface the feathers must be dried before flight is possible. This is why cormorants are commonly seen with their wings outstretched, and because they may also be warming themselves in the sun as waterlogging destroys the main insulation.

Whereas penguins, auks, shearwaters and diving petrels use their wings to 'fly' underwater (the feet being used, with the tail, as a rudder) divers, ducks, cormorants and grebes are propelled by large feet set well back on the body. Unfortunately this makes them clumsy on land and most of them can only shuffle to their nests at the water's edge. The guillemot has largely overcome this problem by standing upright when on land.

Landing, too, is a problem for divers and they almost always alight on water. The four species of loon are beautifully suited to underwater life with streamlined and slender bodies, stiff tails and webbed feet. Yet their narrow wings permit powerful flight. They are similar to, and perhaps descended from, one of the earliest bird forms – **Hesperornis**.

Divers such as **puffins**, with feet well back and very small wings, take off only with difficulty, and must launch themselves from cliffs. But underwater they are in their element and the 'sea parrots' even have specially strengthened rib-cages to withstand the pressure at great depth.

Long dives are not necessarily deep dives: for example a **western grebe** (*Aechmophorus occidentalis*) was seen to remain submerged for 63 seconds in only 1.7 cm (5½ ft) of water. Birds will not generally exceed the depths at which their preferred foods are obtained most easily, unless of course they have been chased or shot at and wounded.

THE MOST AERIAL OF ALL BIRDS
SOOTY TERN – 3–10 years aloft
There is no reason to suppose that a **sooty tern** (*Sterna fuscata*) could not stay aloft indefinitely so long as food is available. Any halt in flying is casual and incidental, rather than necessitated by fatigue. Either rest as we conceive of it is not of great concern in the creature's economy or, physiologically, sufficient rest can be obtained while flying, possibly during intervals of gliding or thermal soaring. Sooty terns fly strongly, but beyond that they possess no special anatomical characteristics for the life they lead.

The sooty tern's only real need to visit land is to breed. Even moulting is undertaken while airborne. Detailed studies have shown the period of immaturity and sub-adulthood to be a minimum of three years and perhaps as long as 8–10 years, during which time there is no known reason why the species must land.

The sooty tern is altogether pelagic and not known to frequent shores or near-shore waters at any place in its immense range. Indeed, of all oceanic birds (and particularly within the Tropics) it is by far the one most often seen at very great distances – 2,000 km (1,250 miles) or more – from any land.

Sooty terns obtain their food, primarily fish or squid, either by picking it from near the surface while hovering or by seizing in mid-air prey such as flying fish or fish that jump to escape attacks by aquatic predators. Unlike most terns, they do not plunge-dive and they rarely surface-dive. Thus, in feeding, their contact with water is minimal.

In contrast to almost all other water birds, the sooty tern's plumage is readily wettable, evidently because of a deficiency in the secretions of the oil, or preen, gland. Placed in the water, juveniles swim, albeit rather clumsily, and can cover distances of up to about 100 m (330 ft) before they become waterlogged. Adults appear unable to progress by paddling and, in similar situations, they merely sink in place. After, at most, about half an hour, the weight of water taken up by the feathers prevents the bird from rising off the water unassisted. It is thus quite possible for a sooty tern to rest for a few minutes on the surface of a reasonably calm sea, but very few have been observed doing so.

Sooty terns readily land on any floating objects that provide a relatively flat surface – bits of lumber, branches or trunks of trees, boxes, crab traps, even surfaced sea

The sooty tern's only real need to visit land is to breed: it does not even have to settle in order to feed. (Frank Lane Picture Agency)

turtles. They seem much less adept at perching on narrow or rounded surfaces such as those of marker buoys or rigging wires of ships. But in normal health away from the breeding grounds they appear to have no need to rest on anything.

It is not inconceivable that sooty terns could doze while aloft, holding their posture, altitude and course by sub-conscious perception and control. Biologists have no reason to doubt their incredible aerial performance. But just how long an individual has actually remained aloft without resting on anything whatsoever during the potential years of immaturity and sub-adulthood no one is ever likely to know.

The species nests in hundreds (perhaps thousands) of colonies in a pan-tropical belt between 30°N and 30°S. It is arguably one of the most abundant birds, with a world population in the range of 400–1,000 million, despite very extensive predation on its eggs. In the mid-1950s the bird was yielding over 1 million eggs annually – far more than any other species.

Other terns are also among the most aerial of species. **Noddies** may be unique in their family in that, if forced to do so, they can sit on the water for hours without becoming waterlogged. But they too have hardly ever been seen to rest at sea, except when standing on floating objects. Also arctic terns have rarely been seen resting during their long oceanic migrations.

THE MOST AERIAL LANDBIRD
COMMON SWIFT – up to 3 years aloft

Were it not for the fact that it reaches breeding age slightly more quickly (2–3 years) than the sooty tern, the **European** or **common swift** (*Apus apus*) could, in many respects, be called the most aerial of all birds – it certainly spends more time aloft than any other landbird in the world. It is now proved beyond any doubt that this bird sleeps, eats, drinks and even mates on the wing, though the latter also

takes place in the nest. It may be two or three summers before the young birds first breed and the species has many remarkable adaptations to sustain such protracted periods in the sky.

One of the main reasons for the swift's long adolescence is the species' relatively high survival rate (frequently above 80–85% per year) and good life expectancy for a small bird. It has few predators, only some small falcons occasionally taking significant numbers. Thus traditional colonies tend to be stable and new sites are only gradually occupied. There is no need for rapid breeding.

The swift's body is superbly shaped for aerial life, being torpedo-like, with the eyes almost flush with the body contours, rather like a sports car's headlights. Much of the wing is taken up by the primaries, which give propulsion; the secondary feathers, which provide lift, being relatively small. But speed is only sufficient to compensate for a wing with relatively poor lift: it maintains just enough to remain airborne in order to conserve energy. Despite appearances to the contrary, swifts are not particularly swift and they have very short legs and weak feet, but there is no truth in the story that they are unable to get airborne again if they land on the ground.

In constant pursuit of insects, the swift's bill has become reduced to little more than a rim surrounding a wide mouth which engulfs the prey more easily. But like the nightjars, they do not gape for food at random: that would be inefficient. The chief food items are insects, but ballooning spiders are also taken and day-to-day variability is great.

When feeding young, a swift returns to the nest with a food ball sometimes containing several hundred food items glued together with saliva. This can be seen bulging the bottom of the mouth. Because of this specialist aerial feeding the swift is particularly susceptible to food shortages brought on by the variable and often inclement weather encountered in the west and north of its summer range in Europe. But several adaptations have helped to overcome this.

Firstly, the interval between egg-laying – usually two days – is lengthened to three when food is short. Secondly, although the parents normally relieve each other in incubation, when food is very scarce the eggs may be left unbrooded as they are exceptionally resistant to chilling. The nestlings, too, are unusually hardy. While those of other species would quickly chill and die if left unbrooded, even naked young swifts can reduce their body metabolism: heartbeat and respiration rates drop and their body temperature slowly falls. In other words, the chicks become torpid in a short-lived hibernation (aestivation).

Swift nestlings are left to fend for themselves when the parents must depart in search of better feeding while adverse weather moves through the nest area. In western Europe such journeys may last several days and then swifts swarm together in large numbers. Once 27,000 passed the island of Öland in Sweden on one day. But when the weather improves and the parents return to provide both food and warmth, the chicks soon recover – just like reptiles. This remarkable adaptation sometimes shows in the feather growth of young swifts, reflecting the weather pattern. When food intake is low in poor weather, feather proteins are laid down more erratically than in good weather and holding a feather to the light before the first moult reveals a banded appearance similar to the growth rings in trees.

Because the food supply is so variable, the swift's nestling period is exceptionally long and variable – 5–8 weeks – and the incubation period too is unusually long for a small bird, being 19–20 days, but in keeping with other species which spend much of their adulthood on the wing.

Adult swifts, which are themselves capable of clumping together in semi-torpidity, gather nest materials while on the wing. Feathers, dried grasses, scraps of paper and other ephemera found floating around in the air are bound together with saliva from glands which increase in size for the breeding season. To build the shallow nest in a roof, cliff or tree hole, the saliva is dribbled out in threads and the material worked into a cup with the feet before it sets like mortar.

For many years biologists doubted the swift's capacity to spend night after night on the wing, cruising around in the upper air, where presumably they occasionally doze. But now the phenomenon is accepted and the maximum height is thought to be around 2,000 m (6,500 ft).

Perhaps the only penalty the swift has to pay for this exceptionally aerial life is increased susceptibility to parasites of a wide variety, some confined to these birds, the most obvious being the flightless hippoboscid louse fly (*Crataerina*). As many as 12 may be found on a young bird and over 20 on an adult, but these bloodsuckers seldom cause the death of the host to whose life cycle they have become superbly adapted.

THE GREATEST G FORCE

Obvious candidates for the maximum g force (acceleration due to gravity) are the world's 169 species of true **woodpeckers** (*Picinae*). So far little work has been done, but American scientific experiments have revealed that the beak of the **red-headed woodpecker** (*Melanerpes erythrocephalus*) of Canada and the USA hits the bark of a tree with an impact velocity of 20.9 km/h (13 mph). When the bird's head snaps back the brain is subject to a deceleration of about 10 g. But how this compares with the g force among most other woodpeckers is yet to be established.

The red-headed woodpecker is omnivorous, eating acorns as well as insects etc, but other species are more dependent on excavating for food and it is likely that those which do most excavation in living and hardwood trees, rather than rotten or softwood trees, will exert the highest g force. But the skulls of woodpeckers are specially strengthened to cope with this lifestyle, the brain being cradled and cushioned to withstand the repeated shocks. Even the stiff tail – primarily adapted for vertical climbing – helps in providing a good, relaxed posture to cushion the body. And this is certainly needed as, for example, in the **black woodpecker** (*Dryocopus martius*), which pecks some 8–12,000 times a day.

The most specialized excavating woodpeckers have a straight, broad-based bill with a chisel tip. The nostrils are partly or fully covered by feathers and are often elongated and slit-like to protect the nasal chambers from flying woodchips as the bird drills.

Other remarkable adaptations to the problems of g force include those of the plunge-diving **masked booby** (*Sula dactylatra*), which is said to hit the water at 100 km/h (60 mph) and the **peregrine falcon** (*Falco peregrinus*), which must pull out of stoops onto prey made at speeds of probably at least 180 km/h (112 mph).

THE WORLD CHAMPION AT KEEPING WARM
EMPEROR PENGUIN – breeding in temperatures down to −50°C (−58°F)
The amazing **emperor penguin** (*Aptenodytes forsteri*) is the only bird which has truly mastered the coldest season on earth, the Antarctic winter, when temperatures in the colonies may drop to −50°C (−58°F) and the winds gust to 300 km/h (186 mph) while the males are incubating. But in order to survive and prosper in this habitat the species has had to adapt its anatomy, physiology and behaviour in many remarkable and unique ways. No other bird has learnt to breed in such extreme cold, not even any of the other species of penguin, and all to ensure that the chicks reach independence when food resources peak in Antarctic midsummer.

The emperor has a body mass of 20–40 kg (44–88 lb) and its height is around 1 m (3.28 ft), though this varies from 0.8 m (2.6 ft) for a bird standing in the cold on its heels to 1.3 m (4.26 ft) for a walking bird with neck extended.

The colonies are all situated between 66°S (Wiles Land) and 77°S (the coast of the Ross Sea), and most are on the sea-ice along the coasts of the Antarctic continent, where the mean temperature is higher (the lowest temperature ever recorded anywhere, −88.3°C/ −126.9°F), was inland on the high plateau). No breeding colonies, and few individuals, are found north of 60°S. About 30 colonies are known and the entire population is estimated at 300,000–350,000. Some probably remain to be discovered.

The rookeries are established on sea-ice that is particularly strong and well-anchored, in areas usually located between the coast of the Antarctic continent and small, offshore rock islands. Although such breeding grounds are a precaution against storms that might destroy more exposed sea-ice, and with it the eggs and chicks, the disadvantage is that the rookeries may be far from the open sea. Emperors may have to cross hundreds of kilometres of unbroken sea-ice before reaching the open sea, their only source of food. Since the ice on which the colonies are established disappears during the summer months, the birds must have a breeding cycle that is synchronized with the sea-ice cycle.

Compared with other birds, the emperor's moult is very short – just one month – and takes place between November and January when air temperatures range between about −5°C (23°F) and +1°C (33.8°F). The new feathers are well grown before the old are shed. During this time the body mass decreases from about 35 kg (77 lb) to 20 kg (44 lb) as besides the additional energy needs associated with decreased feather insulation, extra energy is required for the synthesis of new feathers.

During the austral summer, from January to March, and after moulting, emperors feed well in the open sea, accumulating body fat and proteins. By the end of March the sea is entirely covered by ice and then the penguins march inland to the colonies in a single file, often as far as 50–120 km (30–75 miles). When they arrive they weigh 30–40 kg (66–88 lb). After a fast of 40–50 days, through the time when she lays the egg, the female has lost about 25% of her initial body mass. From the beginning of May to mid-July, about 65 days, the male incubates the single egg on the upper surfaces of his feet, without a nest. Later in the winter, the incubating males usually remain huddled together in one giant mass. Sometimes birds leave the huddle, especially on calm days, to eat fresh snow, the only external source of water. It is during the severe weather conditions encountered during the

mid-winter pre-incubation and incubation that the males must endure a fast lasting on average 115 days. During this period their body weight is reduced by about 40%, to 10–15 kg (22–33 lb) from an initial 34–40 kg (75–88 lb).

The chicks hatch about mid-July

The emperor penguin chick is supported by dad's feet. Essential warmth is provided by the adult's pouch-like fold of abdominal skin. (D.G. Allan, British Antarctic Survey)

when most of the females return to the rookery and locate their mates by means of a vocal search. A most striking finding was that if the egg hatched before the female's return, the long-fasting male was still capable of feeding the chick its first meals with an esophageal secretion similar to pigeon milk. But if the male's weight falls to about 22 kg (48 lb) before the female has come back he will abandon the egg or chick and return to sea. If the egg is not hatched when the female returns she will continue incubation and also brood the chick for several days, alternating with the male.

The emperor's fat store is obviously important – of a 37.5 kg (83 lb) body weight about 10 kg (22 lb) is fat – as it is the primary source of fuel during the fast, and enough energy must be saved to enable the bird to return to the sea afterwards, about 1.5 kg (3.3 lb) being needed for a 200 km (125-mile) walk. But fat is only part of the story.

The emperor is able to maintain its body temperature without increasing its metabolic rate in temperatures as low as −10°C (14°F) – the lowest critical temperature known among birds, except perhaps that of the Arctic gull. But this is not entirely due to the species' thermal insulation (a combination of plumage, subcutaneous fat, blood flow at the surface of the body and air movement around the bird). Body shape and behaviour are critical too. The emperor's large body mass has the advantage of requiring a much lower metabolic rate per gram of body mass than a smaller animal. The rate of the emperor is about 20 times lower than that of the hummingbird. Therefore the penguin has a low rate of energy expenditure per unit of body mass, and thus it is capable of fasting much longer than a small bird, yet maintaining its metabolic rate. (Hummingbirds cannot fast more than a few days, even in optimum conditions.) Also the sizes of the bill, flippers and feet of the emperor are not in the same proportion to its body mass as are those of other penguin species and thus greatly reduce heat loss through them by minimizing the body surface/volume ratio.

The emperor's feathers are dense, rigid and short so that they cannot be moved by the wind and are able to maintain an isolating air-bed between the atmosphere and the air. There is a special system of heat exchange between artery and veins of the relatively poorly insulated flipper to minimize heat loss. Similar systems operate in the head, notably in the nasal passages, and the feet. Yet these remarkable systems of energy conservation can be 'reversed' when it is necessary to avoid over-heating.

But the Antarctic winter is so harsh all these adaptations together are insufficient without behavioural specialization as well. First, activity in the rookery is kept to an absolute minimum to conserve energy. Second, birds minimize contact with the ice by leaning on their heels and tail so that the soles are lifted off the ground and the toes covered by the long lower abdominal feathers. The head is pulled in and the flippers held close to the body. To save energy under more severe conditions, individual isolated emperors (even with egg or chick resting on the feet) often lie down to minimize heat loss to high-velocity winds.

The famous huddle, which can reduce individual heat loss by 25–50%, is the most obvious device for keeping warm and may include 6,000 birds with about 10 per square metre. The temperature around the birds in the centre of a huddle is raised by up to 11°C (20°F). But these gatherings are not motionless: movement is extremely slow, but continuous. It is urged along by the wind, the rear-flank birds, those most exposed to the wind, advancing slowly along the sides of the huddle, gradually working their way inwards to gain protection. Thus all have their turn in the centre. During an ice-storm that blew continuously for almost 48 hours a huddle was seen to move 100–200 m (330–660 ft). But huddling is only possible because the emperor has learnt to modify otherwise aggressive penguin behaviour and because it is possible to shunt around while still incubating the egg on the feet which is covered with a pouch-like fold of abdominal skin providing essential warmth.

It is certainly a tribute to the dedication of ornithologists that emperor penguins have been studied so closely in such an inhospitable environment. But the colony of Pointe Géologie, located near the French station Dumont D'Urville, is the only one which is studied throughout the breeding cycle, i.e. with visits by biologists in the colony almost every day since the study was started in 1961. But their hard work has produced many statistics of the aptly named emperor. For example, incubation period 62 days; fledging period 170 days; food 95% fish, 2% crustaceans (krill) and 3% squid; sexual maturity is usually reached at 5 years by females and 6 years by males, though 3 years is possible; 70% keep the mate from the previous year. Some of the studied birds are at least 25 years old. Annual chick losses vary between 4 and 90%, according to weather, and only 19% of fledglings survive their first year of life.

OTHER REMARKABLE LOW-TEMPERATURE SURVIVORS
FINCHES – up to −70°C (−94°F) in experiment
Winter-acclimatized **goldfinches** (*Carduelis carduelis*), **purple finches** (*Carpodacus purpureus*) and **pine siskins** (*Carduelis pinus*) were able to adjust their metabolism and sustain themselves at −70°C (−94°F) in experiment, yet their normal distribution does not encompass such low temperatures. It is not a simple matter to say which is the lowest temperature which any species could endure in the wild, as it depends on length of exposure and size of bird. There is no reason why even a healthy human could not

run out into a temperature of, say, −100°C (−148°F) for a minute or so before returning indoors, but if we tried to sleep with such exposure we would die. But the finches studied could sustain their normal body temperatures at −70°C (−94°F) as long as they had enough stored food energy. Also, in the wild, birds are expert at finding holes and crevices which may be warmer than the outside temperature, bearing in mind the avoidance of windchill and possible gains from solar radiation.

In natural conditions **crossbill** (*Loxia*) nestlings can survive air temperatures down to −35°C (−31°F). When the adults are away foraging the chicks become torpid, but quickly recover when brooded. Under the parent the temperature may be as much as 56°C (100°F) higher than the bitter outside temperature.

THE MOST REMARKABLE BIRD HIBERNATOR
NORTH AMERICAN POORWILL
In the 18th century, before migration was verified, it was generally thought that swallows and other summer visitors hibernated. It was suggested that they slept through the cold in hollow trees and crevices, and even Gilbert White, the famous naturalist, thought they might be found in the mud at the bottom of ponds! When the mystery of migration was unravelled, no one had any reason to suppose that bird hibernation was still necessary, and early accounts of dormancy in swifts and hummingbirds were discounted. But today bird torpidity is well documented, though only some **nightjars** (*Caprimulgidae*) are regarded as habitual hibernators, with prolonged seasonal adjustment in the manner of some mammals. The only other bird groups in which torpidity is verified are the *Apodiformes* – **hummingbirds and swifts**, the *Coliiformes* – **mousebirds**, and *Caprimulgiformes* – **nightjars** and allies.

The most remarkable of the *Capri-*

mulgiformes is the North American **poorwill** (*Phalaenoptilus nuttallii*) which has been regularly found in a torpid condition in the dark, cold days of winter, its heartbeat, breathing and body temperature reduced to a minimum to conserve energy during periods of food shortage. The first hibernating poorwill reported was found in a rock crevice in the Chuckwalla Mountains of the Colorado Desert in California in December 1946. It was ringed and in subsequent winters was found repeatedly in the same spot in a dormant condition with a body temperature of 18–20°C (64.4–68°F). Subsequently only about six other torpid poorwills have been found, though they are very hard to locate. But these and other *Caprimulgids* have been well studied in captivity, where poorwills have remained in torpor for up to four days. It has been calculated that normal fat deposits can sustain a torpid poorwill for 100 days at a body temperature of 10°C (50°F). Others have been found huddled together in the wild with body temperatures down from 41°C (106°F) to 17°C (64°F).

Both adult and young **common swifts** (*Apus apus*) have the ability to become torpid during times of food shortage. The adults may clump together for a few days, reducing temperature and metabolism, but will usually fly off temporarily to find better weather. But nestlings deprived of their food supply have no choice other than to become torpid, and the record period reported so far is of a brood surviving 21 days in 1907. At first, the young swift's body temperature is steady at about 40°C (102°F), but if the air temperature falls below about 18°C (66°F) then the swift's temperature rapidly falls to about 15.5°C (50°F). (Lowering body temperature to below that of the surroundings minimizes heat loss through conduction and saves precious energy.) **Swallows**, too, have been known to become temporarily torpid in their migrations over the Alps.

Because of their extremely high metabolism and inability to store significant food, **hummingbirds** have frequent but very short periods of torpidity. With their typically high avian body temperatures they are never more than a few hours from death by starvation. At night some regularly let their daytime body temperatures of about 40°C (104°F) fall to near ambient, sometimes a decrease of over 30°C (54°F). The ambient temperature at which torpidity is induced varies with the climate and altitude. The **purple-throated carib** (*Eulampis jugularis*), which lives in the mountains of the Lesser Antilles in the Caribbean, where the altitude is mostly less than 1,500 m (4,875 ft), will become torpid at an air temperature of 20°C (68°F). But the ambient temperature must fall to about 7°C (45°F) before the **Andean hillstar** (*Oreotrochilus estella*), which lives at 3,800–4,200 m (12,500–13,800 ft) in the Andes, becomes torpid.

The temperature of most diurnal birds averages 42°C (107°F) (varying between 37.7°C/100°F and 44.4°C/112°F) during the daytime, but will generally drop to an average of 39°C (102°F) at night. The reverse applies in nocturnal species, and varies with degree of activity.

BRITAIN'S CHAMPION AT KEEPING WARM
PTARMIGAN

This beautiful member of the grouse family, *Lagopus mutus*, appears to have slightly regained some of its former British range as the climate has cooled in recent decades, but it is still confined to Scotland. The height at which it is found varies with the latitude, the essential arctic-alpine heath habitat descending to lower levels in north and north-west Scotland than in the Cairngorms and Grampians of the central Highlands. For example, near Cape Wrath in Sutherland it occurs as low as 180–300 m (585–975 ft), but in the Cairngorms the height is 760–1,240 m (2,470–4,030 ft). In many parts of

Ptarmigan burrow into the snow to keep warm at high altitude. (Halle Flygare Photos Ltd, Bruce Coleman Ltd)

this range the temperature remains below freezing for months on end and at the top of the highest peak – Ben Nevis, 1,343 m (4,405 ft) – the mean temperature for the year is only about freezing point. Many of the north-facing gullies contain year-round snow.

Temperatures occasionally sink very low in the Scottish Highlands and the windchill factor can be considerable. Yet the ptarmigan, famous for its camouflaged plumage which changes with the seasons, has learnt to live there throughout the year, getting by through feeding on the sparse vegetation above the tree-line. Bilberry, crowberry and heather form the bulk of the diet, but other mountain plants and a few insects are also taken. Even in a severe winter it is rare for the 'snow birds' to abandon the mountain tops, though they generally seek out the sheltered lower corries if it is stormy and they are fond of basking in the sunshine in the lee of the wind.

Snow is no problem for the ptarmigan: indeed, in its white winter plumage it will congregate on snow patches for optimum camouflage and will burrow through to uncover food plants. Sudden, late snow does not deter birds from incubating and the chicks need only a few minutes per hour foraging to sustain them. But in very low temperatures, wind and ice even this may not be possible and they will then return to the parent for brooding.

Ptarmigan burrow into the snow for shelter in order to conserve energy. But they burrow deeply only in calm weather as such holes would rapidly fill with drifting snow and extra depth is required to avoid the extremely low temperatures at or just below the surface on a calm night. When it is windy they dig shallow holes in exposed places to prevent them being buried and will even move during a blizzard to avoid this. It is all too easy to be trapped by snow which has partially melted at the surface and then frozen over.

In Scotland the depth of snow holes varies with the snow structure, but the ptarmigan always seems to burrow to as high a temperature as possible while minimizing the possibility of being buried. In hard snow their hollows are only 2–3 cm (1–1¼ in) deep, or they may simply shelter behind rocks. In slightly frozen, granular snow the hollows are 5–7 cm (2–2¾ in) deep (sometimes to 20 cm/8 in), but in powder snow they may be 30 cm (12 in) deep. The ptarmigan also has thick feathering on the feet and legs, which reduces heat loss considerably, but may also have some benefit in walking on the snow.

Given the increased difficulty of keeping a small body warm, the **snow bunting** (*Plectrophenax nivalis*) is also remarkable. It too will burrow in the snow, as will other Arctic passerines such as **redpolls** (*Acanthis hornemanni*). In temperatures of −40°C (−40°F) redpolls will forage with flank and belly feathers lowered to cover the legs. But such low temperatures are not encountered in Britain, where this 16.5 cm (6.5 in) bird is mostly a winter visitor, breeding only in very small numbers.

British **snow buntings** mostly winter on the coast, where the temperature is considerably higher, but in the Scottish breeding season proximity to snowfields is beneficial, even crucial. Thermals from adjacent valleys carry many insects aloft and strand them on the snow surfaces, where they are easily spotted. Also, the constant supply of moisture at the edges of the melting snow attracts many emerging insects on which the buntings feed.

GREATEST HEAT ENDURANCE

For birds which live in very hot habitats, such as deserts, keeping cool is very important as death results when the body temperature reaches 46–48°C (115–118°F), only a few degrees above the average maximum. Yet many species of bird are able to live and breed in air temperatures approaching these values through use of a few physical and physiological tricks. For example, there are many **larks** (*Alaudidae*) and **wheatears** (*Oenanthe*) in the Saharan and Arabian Deserts which must regularly endure air temperatures above 44–45°C (111–113°F), without letting their brain temperatures approach that fatal level.

It is not possible to say which are the very highest temperatures which any bird has to nest in because the values supplied by geographers for any region can vary greatly from those where individual birds are sitting in micro-habitats which have been carefully chosen. It also very much depends on whether the figures quoted are ground or air temperatures and on the direct effects of solar radiation.

The problem is greater for small birds because they heat up more quickly. **Gray's lark** (*Ammomanes grayi*) of the Namib Desert in Africa overcomes this by building an elaborate, well-insulated nest within the shade of a rock or tuft of grass. And it gets sufficient water from the insects in its diet.

Availability of drinking water is crucial to the survival of many species in hot places as birds must evaporate a considerable amount to cool off. Birds have no sweat glands in the skin and must expel much of the water through the mouth after it has been vaporized in the lungs and internal air sacs. The rate of evaporation is greatly increased by panting or by fluttering the throat pouch, as in cormorants, pelicans and boobies. A panting **budgerigar** (*Melopsittacus undulatus*) can raise its breathing rate from around 100 to as much as 300 breaths per minute, greatly increasing its capacity to keep cool. Other birds have learnt to soak their belly and leg feathers in water before flying back to their nests in arid areas where they are then able to lose extra heat by evaporation and keep eggs or chicks cool. The **namaqua sandgrouse** (*Pterocles namaqua*) of the Namib Desert and other parts of Africa sometimes gather by the thousand to drink and soak their breasts at the widely scattered pools. The males crouch in the water and carry the drops back to the chicks: their breast feathers have barbules which are not hooked together so that the water-shedding properties are lost and the feathers act as a sponge. Thus, despite often long journeys, enough water usually remains for the young to drink by sucking the feathers.

The **African skimmer** (*Rynchops flavirostris*) probably endures temperatures as high as any other bird while nesting. On some of its breeding beaches, notably Lake Rudolf in Kenya, the ground surface temperature may reach 60°C (140°F) and the air temperature just above ground may reach 40°C (104°F) through intense solar radiation. But this species has a unique method of belly soaking – from the air the feet are lowered to splash water onto the belly before returning to the chicks or eggs. The skimmer is used to skimming the water as it catches fish by flying along with its specially elongated, knife-like lower mandible immersed. This helps to get the bird's 'undercarriage' wet too.

While in cold weather birds fluff up their feathers to increase insulation and keep warm, in high temperatures they will compress their plumage so that heat is more easily lost through conduction. But their feet and legs are more important to heat loss and many species are capable of shunting blood to the legs in order to cool off. Others extend their legs one at a time, or both together in flight. Some wade in water and those with proportionately long legs will get the most benefit. The **turkey vulture** (*Cathartes aura*), **wood stork** (*Mycteria americana*) and some **gannets** and **boobies** even squirt excrement onto their legs and feet to help cool down!

Other cooling devices are more obvious; for example, standing with the back to the wind with feathers raised or shielding young with outstretched wings. But others are more subtle. Incubating **fairy terns** (*Gygis alba*) can produce less heat by slowing the heartbeat and reducing the metabolic rate. Yet others, particularly desert species such as the American **mourning dove** (*Zenaidura macroura*), allow their body temperature to rise above normal to around 45°C (113°F) (this would kill many species) so that they are hotter than their surroundings, enabling further heat to be lost through conduction and radiation.

The **ostrich** (*Struthio camelus*) too has a special way of cooling off

when there is no shade available during the hottest part of the day. It faces the sun with the wings held out so that the long loose plumes shade the body. This also exposes those huge, naked flanks so that they can radiate heat more rapidly.

But even with such controllable adaptations birds could not live in hostile, hot environments without the basic physiological ability to lose water at a very slow rate in everyday living. High blood temperature reduces the *general* need to evaporate water to keep cool and they excrete uric acid in their urine instead of urea, as in mammals. The acid is excreted in a highly concentrated form and bird urine is that thick, white liquid which is deposited with the droppings.

Finally, even the bird's colour can help it to keep cool. White or pale plumages reflect greater amounts of solar radiation and reduce the tendency to overheat in hot, arid environments.

THE MOST 'INTELLIGENT' BIRD IN THE WORLD
THE 'FLY-FISHING' GREEN HERON

Intelligence does not have a precise meaning in the bird world but there are nonetheless some remarkable examples of bird behaviour which appear to us as reasoned thought. But if we define intelligence as the ability to understand and to make deductions from apparent facts then clearly most birds have none at all. Yet birds are capable of what biologists now call 'insight learning'. They are very perceptive of external stimuli, especially sights and sounds, and are easily trained to respond. However, although they might, for example, learn to recognize 1 and 2, they never learn that there is any natural relationship between numbers, that 2 is more than 1, and so on.

It is quite natural for us to view a bird's world from a human angle and to misinterpret mechanical or physiological reaction as intelligence. Birds certainly can learn but different species have different specialized learning abilities and it is hard to tell where innate abilities leave off.

In the past it was generally thought that **crows** (*Corvidae*) and **parrots** (*Psittacidae*) were the intellectual giants of the bird world. But much regard for the 'cleverness' of these species was probably due to their familiarity with man. Most crows have adapted well to the human environment and in some cases have been regarded as competitors – for example, ravens taking newly born lambs – and this is often misconstrued as 'cunning'. Parrots have long been popular cagebirds, and in captivity many live to be very old and are assumed to have gained 'wisdom'. In truth, they have probably merely learnt a few tricks and to respond to certain stimuli. Nonetheless, higher mental faculties are most valuable to opportunist birds such as crows, which succeed through taking advantage of every new opening.

Many birds learn by trial and error: for example, that certain caterpillars and butterflies make them very ill, but they are not aware that this is because the prey contains poisons. It is also thought that many well-known bird tricks have been learnt by accident. For example, when a **gull** (*Laridae*) drops a shellfish onto stones it comes by an otherwise unobtainable meal. And it was many years ago that **tits** (*Paridae*) first learnt to peck through milk bottle tops to get at the cream. It is in copying such practices that birds have succeeded widely. As far as we know, each new generation of birds has to learn such skills from experienced birds, just as young humans watch their parents and learn simple ways, and copying does not require reasoning ability.

It is in the ability of certain birds to use tools that we are most tempted to use the word intelligence, but even here such behaviour is considered to be due to instinct or learning by association. Over 30 species are now recognized as tool users and even tool makers. For example, the **Egyptian vultures** (*Neophron percnopterus*) in some African populations have learnt to break ostrich eggs by dropping rocks on them, but observation of this shows it to be literally a very hit-and-miss affair.

More impressive is the precise way in which the **woodpecker finch** (*Camarhynchus pallidus*) of the Galapagos Islands habitually uses cactus spines to probe for grubs in holes beyond the reach of its bill. They seem to have filled a local niche in the absence of woodpeckers and must use the spines because they do not have the woodpeckers' long tongues. But not all woodpecker finches do this, while individuals of closely related species do, so the habit was probably copied. The original use is thought to have started through frustration and experiment. But while birds first simply picked up any spine to hand, some now snap them off a cactus and even trim the length if necessary. This reaction to a single situation is more difficult to explain.

But perhaps the most remarkable known instance of bird intelligence is that of a few species which use bait in fishing. These include the **sun bittern** (*Eurypyga helias*) of Central and South America and the widespread **lesser pied kingfisher** (*Ceryle rudis*). But the greatest angler of all is the widespread **green heron** or **striated heron** (*Butorides striatus*), which in the USA at least has learnt to use fish-food pellets as bait. Surprisingly, it seems to understand the process well as not only does it retrieve the bait when it floats away but also carries it to new spots to try again. One was even seen to use a feather in this way – the bird world's only 'dry-fly' fisherman!

THE GREATEST WEIGHTS CARRIED BY BIRDS

Folklore abounds with stories of birds carrying fantastic weights, but most are entirely fanciful. They generally involve birds of prey which have always filled man with admiration, and even fear. Yet the largest raptors, the vultures, are primarily carrion feeders and have neither the reason nor the claws for great lifting feats. Thus it is to the eagles that man has turned his attention, and of these the very widespread **golden eagle** (*Aquila chrysaetos*) has been the subject of most stories.

Eagles generally kill their prey before carrying it off and the maximum load for the golden eagle is usually only about 4–5 kg (9–11 lb). But when birds have been disturbed at a kill or sense that a rapid exit is advisable then there is reason to tackle greater loads.

Most tales of human babies, children and even adults being carried off by eagles have, not surprisingly, been disregarded by ornithologists, but there is at least one case which is apparently fully authenticated. In 1932 a four-year-old Norwegian girl is said to have been carried off by a **white-tailed sea eagle** (*Haliaeetus albicilla*) when she was playing in the yard of her parents' farmhouse. The huge bird tried to carry the girl (apparently small for her age) back to its eyrie 224 m (800 ft) up the side of a mountain more than 1.6 km (1 mile) away, but the effort was too great and the poor child was dropped on a narrow ledge about 15 m (50 ft) from the nest. Fortunately, a search party organized by the desperate parents pinpointed the eagle soaring above the eyrie and the girl was found asleep and unharmed save for some scratches and bruises. One theory is that the bird had the advantage of a powerful up-current of air. But whatever the truth, the girl, Svanhild Hansen, grew up happily and kept the little dress she wore that terrible day, with the holes made by the eagle's talons.

The diet of the white-tailed sea eagle in Norway is generally 60% fish and 40% birds but may reach 90% fish in some areas. They sometimes kill arctic foxes and lambs, but mammals are mostly eaten only as carrion. Where fish are too large to lift the bird will tow them to land by 'rowing' with its wings. The largest prey so far seen taken in flight is the greylag goose (*Anser anser*), which rarely has a maximum weight of about 4.25 kg (9.4 lb).

The **harpy** (*Harpia harpyia*) is probably the most aggressive and powerful true eagle. It inhabits the forests of South America, where it kills and carries off monkeys, other mammals and birds. Its short, broad wings help it to lift prey almost vertically and there is a report of a female rising over 18 m (60 ft) with a 5.9 kg (13 lb) sloth in her massive claws.

Other reported great lifts include a **Pallas's sea eagle** (*Haliaeetus leucogaster*) barely managing to fly with a carp of 5.9 kg (13 lb) in India, and an American **bald eagle** (*Haliaeetus leucocephalus*) flying well with a 6.8 kg (15 lb) mule deer in its talons. It is generally assumed that larger individuals among eagles can carry larger weights and it has been suggested that a very large female **Steller's sea eagle** (*Haliaeetus pelagicus*) of 8.6 kg (19 lb) could probably carry a 9.1 kg (20 lb) young seal for several hundred metres.

THE LONGEST-LIVED WILD BIRD

ROYAL ALBATROSS – over 58 years
The longevity record for a free-living wild bird is held by the female **royal albatross** (*Diomedea epomophora sanfordi*) known as 'Blue White', which was banded as a breeding adult in New Zealand by the late Dr Richdale in the 1937/38 season. She laid again in the 1985/86 season when 58 years old and showed no sign of stopping breeding.

'Blue White' lives among the 15 or so pairs of northern royal albatross at Taiaroa Head, Otago, NZ. The northern reaches a length of 1.2 m (3.9 ft), but the southern race *D.e.epomophora* reaches 1.35 m (4.4 ft) and is often regarded as the largest of all albatrosses.

Royal albatrosses spend most of their long lives gliding above the southern oceans, where they hunt mostly for fish, crustaceans and cephalopods such as octopus and

New Zealand's northern royal albatross known as 'Blue White'. In the 1985/86 season she was still breeding at 58 – the greatest age so far recorded for any wild bird. (New Zealand Wildlife Service)

As a proportion of body length, the **sword-billed hummingbird** *has the longest bill in the world. (A.J. Mobbs, Bruce Coleman Ltd)*

The **ruby-throated hummingbird** *(inset) has the lowest number of feathers. (W. Lankinen, Aquila Photographics)*

Australian pelicans *have the longest bills in the world – up to 47cm (18.5in) long – and use them to scoop up fish, often working together around a shoal. (V. Taylor, Ardea London)*

When the **red-headed woodpecker**'s *head snaps back its brain is subject to a deceleration of about 10g. (Leonard Lee Rue, Frank Lane Picture Agency)*

This **green heron** (left) has caught a frog, but the species also displays extraordinary 'intelligence' in using baits and even 'dry-flies' to lure fish within striking distance. (Erwin & Peggy Bauer, Bruce Coleman Ltd)

Britain's smallest nest is made by the **goldcrest**, one of Europe's two smallest birds. (B & M Speake, Aquila Photographics)

Cave swiftlet nests are the main ingredient of the well-known Chinese dish, birds' nest soup. (J. Watson, Bruce Coleman Ltd)

The **common guillemot** varies its egg colour and pattern more than any other bird. (S. Jonasson, Frank Lane Picture Agency)

The **sharp-beaked ground finch** of the Galapagos Islands has learnt to peck holes in the wings and tails of masked boobies to drink their blood. (Dr F. Foster/ Survival Anglia) The inset picture shows that this vampire of the bird world is not averse to the blood of a human researcher, either! (Dr F. Foster/ Survival Anglia)

PLATE XXVI

Extinct Carolina parakeets – one of the hand-coloured illustrations from John Audubon's The Birds of America, *the world's first one million pound bird book.* (Sotheby's)

Carolina Parrot

squid. Birds pair for life and start to return to the colonies in September. The breeding season is very long: from egg-laying to departure of the chick takes an average of 319 days. Because of this, successful breeders nest only every other year and only birds which have lost their chicks or eggs will return in successive seasons. Some chicks return to the colony when four years old, but they do not establish pairs and start breeding till at least nine years old. Thus it was possible to give a minimum age for Blue White when she was first ringed.

No doubt there are and have been many birds which have lived to greater age in the wild but there is no definite way to determine this except by marking individuals and recovering them later. The individuals of only a few species are recognized by plumage variation or bill pattern. Ringing or banding is still in its infancy and no doubt as time goes by the records for longevity for most species will tumble. The system depends on knowing the age of the bird when first ringed. Unfortunately the efforts of many pioneer banders were thwarted because early rings were not so robust as those used today. Nonetheless, it is thought that the absolute record would go to an albatross and it has been suggested that some of the larger species, such as royal and **wandering** (*Diomedea exulans*), may exceed 80 years. Records clearly show that larger birds generally live longer, but extreme age is reached so infrequently in the hazardous wild that quoting the figures can be misleading.

The **laysan albatross** (*Diomedea immutabilis*) is another long-lived species which has been banded. One still alive in 1978 was 53 years old. A **yellow-nosed albatross** (*Diomedea chlororhynchos*) found breeding on Nightingale Island near Tristan da Cunha in 1982 still carried a 1938 ring and its age is likely to have approached that of the royal albatross 'Blue White'. However, its ring was in such poor condition the chances are minimal of finding rings from the other birds which were banded at the same time by a Norwegian expedition. Also, some birds from this colony were eaten in the 1950s and 60s.

The average age of individual birds is related to the species' overall mortality rate (this may even vary between the sexes). For example, in the royal albatross, with annual adult mortality at 3% (i.e. an average of three out of every 100 die each year), the expectation of life for an adult is 32.8 years. These figures fall to 20% and 4–5 years for the **swift** (*Apus apus*), 40% and 2 years for the **woodpigeon** (*Columba palumbus*) and 70% and 9 months for many small passerines.

Among the relatively lightweight species which survive well are **waders** and **terns**. An **oystercatcher** (*Haematopus ostralegus*) has survived to 36 years and an **arctic tern** (*Sterna paradisaea*) to 33.9. Birds which lay large clutches in response to high mortality generally have a low life expectancy. For example, the maximum age recorded for the quail is only 7.6 years.

Other maximum ages recorded so far for free-flying birds include: **osprey** (*Pandion haliaetus*) 31.2; **long-eared owl** (*Asio otus*) 27.7; **fulmar** (*Fulmarus glacialis*) 27; **gannet** (*Morus bassanus*) 24.5; **eider** (*Somateria mollissima*) 22.9; **mute swan** (*Cygnus olor*) 21.7; **swift** (*Apus apus*) 21.1; **mallard** (*Anas platyrhyncos*) 20.9; **blackbird** (*Turdus merula*) 20.3; **starling** (*Sturnus vulgaris*) 20.0; **rook** (*Corvus frugilegus*) 19.9; **red-winged blackbird** (*Agelaius phoeniceus*) 14.2; **robin** (*Erithacus rubecula*) 12.9; **house sparrow** (*Passer domesticus*) 12.0; **peregrine** (*Falco peregrinus*) 9.6; **dunnock** (*Prunella modularis*) 9.0; **goldcrest** (*Regulus regulus*) 7.0 and **house wren** (*Troglodytes aedon*) 6.2. Yet it is estimated that up to 75% of all wild birds die through predation, disease, starvation, bad weather and accidents before they are six months old. One of the shortest-lived species is the robin, with an average life expectancy of only 5–6 months.

'Cocky' the greater sulphur-crested cockatoo which died in London Zoo at the age of 82. No other captive bird is known to have lived longer. (The Zoological Society of London)

THE LONGEST-LIVED WILD BIRD IN BRITAIN
MANX SHEARWATER – nearly 30 years

So far the maximum age recorded for any free-flying wild bird in Britain is 29.82 years for the **manx shearwater** (*Puffinus puffinus*).

A close contender is Lancelot, a **Bewick's swan** (*Cygnus columbianus*) which visited the Wildfowl Trust's Slimbridge reserve for 23 winters but failed to return in the winter of 1986/7. It was estimated to be 26 years old and probably died of old age. However, Lancelot's mate and grandson did return to Slimbridge in 1986.

THE LONGEST-LIVED CAPTIVE BIRD
SULPHUR-CRESTED COCKATOO – at least 80 years

Most longevity records are impossible to verify. Many parrots are said to have been in the same family for a century or more, but hardly any have been documented and it is common for one to have been replaced by another of the same species without other members of the original owner's family being aware. Stories abound of pet parrots reaching ages of 100–140 but the greatest accepted age so far is the 80-plus years for the **sulphur-crested cockatoo** (*Cacatua galerita*) named 'Cocky', which died at London Zoo on 28 October 1982. He was presented to the Zoo in 1925 and was already mature when acquired by Mr R. Stevens at the beginning of the century. London Zoo state that he was certainly over 80 years old and probably at least 82. Little is known about the ages of parrots in the wild, but a ringed New Zealand **kea** (*Nestor notabilis*) has lived 14.1 years.

Another very well-authenticated longevity record is that of a male **Andean condor** (*Vultur gryphus*) named Kuzya, which was in Moscow Zoo from 1892 to 1964, having lived out of doors the whole time. When taken by the zoo it was adult and probably at least 5–6 years old so its age at death is likely to have been at least 77.

Other records of long-lived captive birds include London Zoo's **common caracara** (*Polyborus plancus*), which has been there since 1932; another Andean condor which died aged 71+ in the Menagerie du Jardin des Plantes,

Paris in 1973; a **Siberian white crane** (*Grus leucogeranus*) which died at the National Zoo, Washington in 1967, aged 62+, and a **herring gull** (*Larus argentatus*) which was 44 when it died in the Menagerie du Jardin des Plantes in 1874.

Age reached in captivity is no more than an indication of potential lifespan under ideal conditions. Captive birds are protected from many hazards such as predation, most disease and accident, but on the other hand they can suffer through lack of exercise, artificial diet and even air pollution in city zoos.

THE FIRST CUCKOO

All around the world people look forward to the first migrants as a sign that spring is on the way. In Britain, one bird above all others is looked for with special affection and that is the **European cuckoo** (*Cuculus canorus*). In the old days, when it was thought that swallows spent the cold months in the mud of ponds, it was suggested that cuckoos turned into sparrowhawks for the winter. Not surprisingly then, the dates of the first cuckoo arrivals are noted with care in many diaries. Cuckoos have been recorded in Britain in all months, but the small number of winter sightings are open to suspicion. The earliest thought to have been a genuine spring migrant was the bird seen and heard singing in Surrey on 20 February 1953.

The main arrival dates ('cuckoo days') vary by county and not surprisingly those in the south record the bulk of early sightings. For example, Sussex usually sees the first birds between 12–23 April, but 21–30 April is more likely in Yorkshire and 1–7 May in the extreme north and Scottish islands. Males usually arrive at least a week before the females. The average first arrival date for southern England is 18 April and for northern Britain the last week in April.

It is likely that the late-December sightings of cuckoos are largely due to confusion with the **collared dove** (*Streptopelia decaocto*), which has colonized Britain since the 1950s.

THE GREATEST WILD BIRD MIMIC
MARSH WARBLER

The world champion bird mimic is the **marsh warbler** (*Acrocephalus palustris*) of Europe, Asia and Africa, the average male of which imitates 76 species within a recorded range of 63–84 species. About half the mimicked species are from the warbler's European breeding range while the other half are from its African wintering grounds. A Belgian analysis of sonograms revealed that almost the entire marsh warbler repertoire is made up of mimicry, which is complete within the bird's first year of life, probably shortly after its first arrival in Africa.

Many marsh warblers learn their songs during their youth and on reaching maturity they imitate the songs of their fathers and neighbouring males which they heard as chicks, thus quickly increasing the repertoire to impress the females. Yet the males are still able to recognize each other's song and thus also territories because the mimicry does not appear to be exact, the warbler changing the song it imitates to produce a specific pattern of song elements.

The best natural mimics have the greatest possible number of syringeal (lower larynx) muscles (8–9 pairs), but very few species are good general mimics.

THE MOST FAR-CARRYING SONG

The boom of the Eurasian **bittern** (*Botaurus stellaris*) is both the lowest-pitched and the most far-carrying 'song' of any bird while on the ground. The male's incredible call, which has been likened to bellowing or lowing, is quite distinctive and can be heard over three miles away. A prelude of quite quiet short grunts as well as a long, drawn-in breath precedes each boom. During the grunts the bird's head and neck are horizontal

The marsh warbler is the greatest wild-bird mimic, the average male of which imitates 76 species. (M.C. Wilkes, Aquila Photographics)

and the whole body vibrates, but during the boom the head and neck are raised. A series of three to six booms is normal.

The bittern is a skulking, secretive bird which keeps largely to dense reedbeds and swamp vegetation in which its loud call is a distinct advantage in attracting other bitterns. Most bittern populations have slumped as marshes have been drained, the British breeding stock having fallen to 36–38 pairs.

In flight, the **whooper swan** (*Cygnus cygnus*) probably has the most far-carrying call. The loud, bugle-like note helps to keep the family parties together on their very long migrations with frequently poor visibility, both by day and night.

For its size, the **common wren** (*Troglodytes troglodytes*) utters the loudest song, in Britain at least. Parts are above the range of human hearing but lower-pitched elements can be heard over 500 m (1,640 ft) away.

THE MOST REMARKABLE SONG

The very widespread **reed warbler** (*Acrocephalus scirpaceus*) and **brown thrasher** (*Toxostoma rufum*) of North America can both sing two tunes at once, with different notes coming from each half of the syrinx (song-organ) at precisely the same instant, but no one knows how the brown thrasher utters four sounds at once at one point in its song. Equally mysterious is how the **Gouldian finch** (*Chloebia gouldiae*) of northern Australia maintains a bagpipe-like drone over two independent songs uttered at the same time.

THE MOST ENERGETIC SONGSTER

The **red-eyed vireo** (*Vireo olivaceus*) of North and South America appears to hold the record for the most songs sung per unit of time – 22,197 in 10 hours. The norm for most passerines is probably around 1,000–2,500 per day, higher figures applying to birds in territorial disputes.

THE MAIN CAUSES OF BIRD DESTRUCTION AND ACCIDENTAL DEATH
UNNATURAL

No one can say for sure which factor accounts for the greatest number of 'premature' bird deaths

across the world. But of unnatural causes, impact with motor vehicles may be the most significant. In Britain in the 1960s it was estimated that about 2.5 million birds were killed annually in collisions with automobiles, but since then the number of cars and lorries on the roads has greatly increased and in 1985 a sample survey suggested a figure of 30–70 million. The number of birds killed in the USA and other developed countries with their much more extensive network of highways must be staggering.

Pesticides, PCBs and mercury are the most important toxic chemicals from the ornithological point of view. But nobody knows how many birds are killed either directly or indirectly by herbicides, fungicides, insecticides, rodenticides and growth retardants getting into the food chain. Worldwide the number must be many millions, even for those chemicals used within the law.

Oil pollution has been an increas-ingly serious cause of bird deaths, both through continuing deliberate discharge, in cleaning tanks at sea, and accidental spillage. Mortality from oiling in the Baltic may be the worst. About 30,000 **ducks** mainly **long-tailed** (*Clangula hyemalis*), once died in a single incident off Gotland and when a German ship grounded off the Elbe Estuary in 1955 the release of some 6,000 tons of oil killed 100,000 seabirds. In the winter of 1956, a year in which no major oil spills were reported, 7,500 fatally oiled seabirds were washed up on the beaches of Nantucket Island, Massachusetts alone. It took major incidents, such as the wreck of the Torrey Canyon off Cornwall in 1967 and the leaking oil well which allowed 3.2 billion barrels of crude oil to escape into the Gulf of Mexico in 1979, to focus public attention. Certainly, disasters ('wrecks') involving thousands of seabirds are not unusual and some probably involve tens of thousands. But suggested mortalities of

Dead eider ducks lined up on the beach as a result of oil pollution. Such carnage is often the result of deliberate discharge in cleaning tanks at sea, as well as accidental spills. (M.W. Richards/RSPB)

hundreds of thousands have not been proved.

There have been disastrous spills in freshwater too. In the Detroit River, Michigan, oil once killed 12,000 ducks, mainly the decreasing **canvasback** (*Aythya valisineria*).

Birds are attracted to oil slicks because they appear as areas of calm water, but they inhale the toxic compounds while the oil is fresh or ingest them while preening. Also, oil on the plumage destroys its waterproofing and insulation so that the birds are unable to fly or feed and die through exhaustion, exposure or starvation.

Lead poisoning of birds through discarded or lost anglers' split-shot and shooters' discharged shotgun pellets has caused increasing concern. Particularly susceptible are those species of dabbling duck which feed largely on the hard, round seeds of aquatic plants which resemble pellets. It is said that on one occasion in Illinois, USA 110,000 **mallard** (*Anas platyrhynchos*) succumbed to lead poisoning. One

An oiled gannet. Despite such sickening sights, abuse of the world's oceans and their wildlife continues. (M.W. Richards/RSPB)

estimate is that waterfowl deaths through lead have accounted for 2–3% of the North American population. However, steps have already been taken in the USA and other countries to replace lead split-shot and pellets with non-toxic alloy or steel alternatives.

Very large numbers of birds are also accidentally caught and killed by commercial fishing nets. For example, the Danish gillnet salmon fisheries off West Greenland account for some half-million **Brünnich's guillemots** (*Uria lomvia*) every year, along with a great many **razorbills** (*Alca torda*) and other diving seabirds. And in the 1970s, while it was taking about 50 million salmon, the Japanese North Pacific gillnet fishery was responsible for an annual seabird mortality of 280,000–750,000. Since this salmon fishery began in 1952 the Japanese fishermen have probably destroyed over 5 million seabirds (58% guillemots, 27% shearwaters and 9% puffins). Many other seabirds are killed by lost and discarded sea-nets all over the world. About 18 km (11 miles) of net are thought to be lost every night in the North Pacific alone, where they account for a further half-million or so birds each year.

Even man's buildings and other structures are responsible for many deaths. Birds are frequently killed through colliding with tall office blocks, lighthouses and radio towers, especially while on migration in fog or at night in unfamiliar territory. They are usually attracted by the bright lights and millions are killed each year in the USA alone. On just two nights in early October 1954 over 100,000 migrants were killed in only 25 localities sampled from New York to Georgia. Most flew into skyscrapers and wires.

On top of these long-established, man-made agents of destruction we have the relatively new threat of radioactivity from nuclear incidents such as that at Chernobyl in 1986, which has already been blamed for many bird deaths and lack of fertility. Then there is the more widespread but insidious effect of acid rain. While this may not be directly related to bird deaths it has already been linked with population decrease through reduction in food supplies. Waterways are especially at risk: for example, **dippers** (*Cinclus cinclus*) in Wales appear to have declined through acidification of rivers.

NATURAL

Huge numbers of birds die every year during periods of persistent, severe frost or exceptional drought, but there are also more unusual forms of bird fatalities caused by short-lived weather conditions. For example, sudden wind shifts may complicate bird migration and send thousands to their deaths over hostile environments such as deserts and oceans. **Prairie chickens** (*Tympanuchus cupido*) sometimes die when freezing rain or mist traps them under the snow in which they habitually roost. And prolonged cold rain brings more deaths than dry cold since it soaks the birds enough to chill them.

Violent forms of weather kill many birds too. Tornadoes have killed up to 96% of local breeding-bird populations and the battering force of hail must have killed innumerable birds when stones have been large enough to kill cattle. The hailstorms of central Canada are probably the most destructive of all, especially in July. In 1953 two hailstorms killed an estimated 148,000 wildfowl in Alberta. During the first over 1,800 sq km (1,118.5 sq miles) of parkland were flattened by hailstones as big as golfballs and much vegetation was pulped. The deaths included **songbirds, hawks** (*Accipitridae*), **grouse** (*Tetraonidae*), **coot** (*Fulica americana*), **grebes** (*Podicipedidae*) and **ducks** (*Anatidae*), and the loss of waterfowl was calculated to be 93.4% of the local population.

On another occasion, 1,000 **sandhill cranes** (*Grus canadensis*) were killed in just 30 minutes. Even the large and tough **California condor** (*Gymnogyps californianus*) has suffered fatalities by hailstones. And when ducks on a local feeding movement in Arkansas, USA flew into a thunderstorm in November 1973 they encountered hailstones up to 5 cm (2 in) wide. Many were dashed to the ground, suffering broken bones, gashes, cuts and bruises. At least 18 were found encased in ice, one **mallard** (*Anas platyrhynchos*) having pieces of ice 2 cm (¾ in) across frozen to the tips of feathers on the neck, breast and flanks. The unfortunate birds appear to have been flung high into the sub-zero temperature region of cumulonimbus clouds, where they underwent the same process as a water droplet during its formation into a hailstone. Another four birds were found dead with head feathers singed, apparently by lightning strikes.

Bird deaths through hail and thunderstorms are rarely observed in Britain. Yet, on 3 January 1978 a squall line ahead of a well-marked cold front killed 140 geese over eastern England. They were mainly **pink-footed** (*Anser brachyrhynchus*) but included **Canada** (*Branta canadensis*), **greylag** (*Anser anser*), **brent** (*Branta bernicla*) and **bean** (*Anser fabalis*). The bodies were found along a 50 km (31-mile) strip in Norfolk and post-mortems revealed ruptured livers and haemorrhaging consistent with blast or decompression, and multiple injuries and fractures indicative of a fall from great height. It is thought that the birds were flighting at dawn near the Wash when they were sucked up by intense up-draughts, perhaps even the vortex of a rare tornado.

Breeding

America's bald eagle, symbol of national strength and freedom, as well as builder of the world's largest tree nest. (Karl H. & S. Maslowski, Frank Lane Picture Agency)

In reproducing their kind, birds frequently show great ingenuity, whether it's the blackbird nesting in the garden shed, the stork on the chimney pot or the falcon on a sky-scraper in New York City. Many have adapted well to a world now dominated by man, but millions of years before homo sapiens first walked the earth birds had already learnt to build nests and rear young in virtually every natural niche on earth. Despite the rigours of having to protect fragile eggs in frequently hostile environments, they nest in every continent, from arctic ice to waterless deserts where no man could endure. All lay eggs, but not all make nests. Some are born blind, naked and helpless, but others hatch 'ready to go'. Most are good parents, but others show surprising lack of care and a few parasitic species have learnt to hand the entire business of baby care over to foster parents.

THE LARGEST TREE NEST IN THE WORLD

BALD EAGLE'S – up to 2.9 m (9.5 ft) wide and 6 m (20.0 ft) deep

If we take the popular meaning of nest – a structure made by a bird from natural materials such as twigs

and grasses, and containing a cup or cavity in which eggs are laid or incubated – then the largest are undoubtedly made by some of the birds of prey which use the same site year after year. The very largest of these are generally made by the **bald eagle** (*Haliaeetus leucocephalus*) and the biggest known was 2.9 m (9.5 ft) wide – more than enough for the tallest man in the world to lay across with his arms outstretched – and an incredible 6 m (20 ft) deep. This monstrous fortress at St Petersburg, Florida was almost certainly added to by several pairs, the usual maximum depth for any – even the largest eagle eyrie – being about 3 m (10 ft). The nest weighed more than 3,000 kg (2.9 tons). Another bald eagle nest at Vermilion, Ohio reached 2.59 m (8.5 ft) across and 3.66 m (12 ft) deep after 35 years. Eventually it crashed to the ground during a storm, killing the eaglets inside. It had an estimated weight of 1,814 kg (1.78 tons).

The bald eagle characteristically builds a nest of sticks and twigs high in living trees and usually lays two eggs. Its former range was virtually throughout North America from the tree-line in the north to northern Mexico and Baja, California, in the south. The main reasons for its decline included the widespread use of DDT, which became highly concentrated in the tissues of its preferred fish food. This hampered the bird's breeding success. Also significant were encroachment on habitats through human population growth and some trophy shooting. It is still listed as endangered in some states but there has been a notable recovery since the banning of DDT and the species' position as the USA national emblem has helped its status. Nonetheless its position is still serious. As recently as 1983 US authorities uncovered a smuggling business worth 1 million dollars a year of bald eagle carcasses and plumages used to make replicas of Indian artefacts such as fans, whistles, rattles and head-dresses.

Eighteen other species were also involved.

Most huge bird-of-prey nests occur in remote or inaccessible areas where the birds have nested undisturbed for centuries. Those of the Australian **white-bellied sea eagle** (*Haliaeetus leucogaster*) may be 2–3 m (7–10 ft) across and 4 m (13 ft) deep and traditional nests of the **osprey** along the Red Sea coast are at least 1 m (3.25 ft) across and 2 m (6.5 ft) high. The largest nests in Britain are those of the **golden eagle** (*Aquila chrysaetos*): in 1954 British naturalist Seton Gordon saw one in Scotland which was 4.6 m (15 ft) deep and had been in use for 45 years.

THE WORLD'S LARGEST NEST-MOUNDS
THE MEGAPODES'–to 11 m (36 ft) across and 5 m (16.4 ft) deep

If we take the word nest in its widest possible sense, to mean any place or structure in which eggs are incubated, then the largest are undoubtedly those of the megapodes (*Megapodiidae*), a small family of three ecological groups – the **scrub fowls, brush turkeys** and **mallee fowl**, those of the **common scrub fowl** (*Megapodius freycinet*) sometimes being 11 m (36 ft) across and 5 m (16.4 ft) high. These may have been worked for many years and may be shared by several females, even of different species. It is not known whether these amazingly skilful birds ever acquired the art of brooding or discarded it, but mounds were first reported from the Philippines in 1521. Yet it was not until the 19th century that such reports were authenticated. One mound discovered on an island by John Macgillivray of HMS *Rattlesnake* had a circumference of 45 m (150 ft).

Scrub fowls, big-footed relatives of the pheasants (*Phasianidae*), mate for life and a pair inhabits a large territory. It is mostly the male which works the mound. This begins with the digging of a hole up to 5 m (16 ft) in diameter and 1–1.5 m (3–4.5 ft) deep. The mound may contain 300,000 kg (295 tons)

The huge nest-mound of the Australian mallee fowl, one of the megapodes which lets heat from the sun or from rotting vegetation hatch its eggs. Chicks have special adaptations to dig their way out unaided. (Tom & Pam Gardiner, Frank Lane Picture Agency)

of matter and the birds can move very large objects. A 1 kg (2.2 lb) scrub fowl was once seen to shift a rock of 6.9 kg (15.2 lb). During the winter this hole is filled with vegetation swept up from the ground over a radius of about 45 m (150 ft). When this is moistened by rain the whole is covered by a layer of sandy soil 50 cm (20 in) or more thick. Sealed from the air, the vegetation ferments and generates heat, later supplemented by solar heat. When fermentation heat is too much in the spring the birds need to open the mound frequently to let the heat escape and maintain the ideal incubation temperature of 34°C (93.2°F). In midsummer the sun's heat is most important, but this may be too much and then the thickness of soil has to be increased to prevent 'overcooking'. But by autumn the sun's heat is less and the fermentation heat is exhausted so the birds open and flatten the mound daily to let the sun's rays warm the eggs more easily. In this way the birds achieve precise temperature control over several months.

None of the 12 species of mega-

pode of Australia, New Guinea, Indonesia and Polynesia uses body heat to incubate eggs. The required heat comes from the decomposition of vegetable matter in the mounds, directly from the sun or even from volcanic upwellings. Where the mound temperature is naturally fairly constant some species leave the eggs to hatch on their own, but most megapodes employ great skill in maintaining a remarkably constant incubation temperature so that the eggs are not spoiled through chilling or over-heating. The precise way in which they do this is uncertain, but one suggestion is that they gauge the incubation temperature with ultra-sensitive tongues.

In some areas scrub fowls are regarded as rain-prophets as they start to scratch their mounds together at the approach of rain in spring. But they will also begin work if rain falls in the autumn and will attend to mounds through practically the whole year, raking them over for essential temperature regulation and aeration.

Direct solar heat may be more important for the well-studied

mallee fowl (*Leipoa ocellata*) of southern Australia as it breeds in dry places where, in the absence of rain, rotting of mound material is very slow. But for those species which live in dense, sunless jungles heat from decomposition is crucial. Yet some moisture is important in every mound to prevent the egg shells cracking.

The number of eggs laid varies from 5 to 35, the great variation being not only between females but also in the same individual from year to year. The interval between the laying of eggs depends on the nutritional state of the female but is often several days. They may be laid over several months but each begins the nine-week incubation immediately so that some chicks may leave the mound before the last eggs are laid.

The eggs are laid in tiers and in 1842 John Gilbert discovered that they are stood upright on their smaller apex and that the shell is unusually thin and fragile to help the buried chick escape. In the same year, Sir George Grey, the Governor of South Australia, discovered that each mallee fowl egg laid is completely enveloped in soft sand.

Megapode chicks lack both egg teeth and special hatching muscles, but they are very advanced. In the egg the head remains tucked between the legs and strong movements of the wings and feet crack the shell in several places allowing the chick to break free.

Chicks emerge feet first, the reverse of normal procedure, so that they can scramble up to the surface more easily, and only after the shell has broken away does the head lift. The large feet give the megapode its name.

On hatching, the chicks are also particularly damp and slimy and presumably this helps them in their almost perpendicular surfacing. Once up they can run swiftly within a few hours and fly within 24 hours. They never see their parents and live completely independent and solitary lives.

THE LARGEST SOCIAL NESTS
SOCIABLE WEAVERS'—up to 300 chambers
The weaver family is well known for its 'hanging sock' nests with tubular entrances as long as 70 cm (27.5 in) and as much as 10 cm (4 in) wide. One of the most remarkable is that of the **sociable weaver** (*Philetairus socius*), of south-west Africa which first constructs a roof of coarse straws in a tree or on a telephone pole and then makes as many as 300 nest chambers below. The ensuing mass can dominate an entire large tree and attract other species. The tiny **pygmy falcon** (*Polihierax semitorquatus*) is one guest but, although it feeds on small birds, it does not molest its hosts.

Probably the most remarkable of the social-breeding parrots is the South American **monk parakeet** (*Myiopsitta monachus*) which builds huge colonial twig nests in the tops of trees. Within the main structure each pair has its own nest chamber. In *Birds of La Plata* (1920), Hudson noted that such a clump can 'weigh a quarter of a ton and contain enough material to fill a large cart'.

THE LARGEST ROOFED NEST
HAMMERHEAD STORK'S—up to 2 m (6.5 ft) wide and 2 m (6.5 ft) deep
More popularly known as the hammerkop, the African **hammerhead stork** (*Scopus umbretta*) defies accurate classification and is not closely related to the storks. It prefers to build its huge nest of twigs, grass and mud about 12–15 m (40–50 ft) up in a tree. And although the nests are usually 1–2 m (3.25–6.5 ft) across, often of similar depth and take some two months to make, this industrious bird may make several in one season. No one knows why it goes to such great lengths to raise its young.

First a platform is constructed of sticks cemented with mud. Then the walls are raised and roofed over with a metre of thatch which may be decorated with feathers, bones, snakeskins and other debris. The whole thing may contain over

Sociable weavers build the world's largest bird communes, with up to 300 chambers. (A.S. Weaving, Ardea London)

The hammerhead stork's nest is huge and can support the weight of a man, yet this industrious bird sometimes makes several in one season. No one knows why. (Planet Earth Pictures, J. Scott)

10,000 sticks and easily support the weight of a man. The internal chamber, which is about 30–50 cm (12–20 in) in diameter and height, is very carefully shaped and large enough to house both parents and young. The entrance tunnel is 13–18 cm (5–7 in) wide and 40–60 cm (16–24 in) long and heavily plastered with mud to give it a smooth surface. It faces away from the tree trunk so that predators such as genets and snakes find it very hard to get in. Where trees are scarce the nest may be built on a cliff face or the ground, but man-made structures such as dams are also used.

The three to six young, fed by both parents, spend about seven weeks in the nest before fledging. When both birds feed the young they may leave them for long periods, and presumably the thick nest walls then provide good protection. Even after fledging the young remain near the nest for a month or so, roosting in it at night. Many other species are also attracted to the massive nests, whether occupied or not. During construction some nests have been taken over by **Verreaux's eagle** (*Aquila verreauxii*), and **grey kestrels** (*Falco ardosiaceus*) and **barn owls** (*Tyto alba*) often evict the rightful owners from the finished nests. Many smaller birds such as **weavers, mynahs** and **pigeons** attach their own nests to the main structure. Other hole-nesting species such as the **Egyptian goose** (*Alopochen aegyptiacus*) and **African pygmy goose** (*Nettapus auritus*) soon take over the vacated nests, so overall the hammerkop provides important nest-sites for many birds which might otherwise have to foresake the habitat.

SMALL BUILDERS OF BIG NESTS

The most extraordinary large nests for small birds are made by **oven-birds** (*Furnariidae*) (10–26 cm/4–10 in long) in South America. That of the **rufous-breasted spinetail** (*Synallaxis erythrothorax*) is made from thorns, with tunnels to the nest chamber. It is roughly oblong or retort-shaped and as much as 75 cm (30 in) long by 50 cm (20 in) wide. It has a large platform on the side which leads via a tunnel through a tangle of thorns to a thatched nest-chamber lined with downy leaves. That of the **rufous-throated thornbird** (*Phacellodomus rufifrons*) has further chambers added in subsequent seasons and gives the impression of a large colonial nest. It is unlikely that spare chambers are used other than by non-breeding members of a previous brood. Also voluminous is the thorny nest of the 21 cm (8.3 in) **firewood gatherer** (*Anumbius annumbi*) of Argentina. It measures about 70 cm × 30 cm (28 in × 12 in) and is made of big sticks with a crooked passage at the top leading down to the nest chamber. But the largest in this varied family is probably the huge, thorny nest of the

white-throated cachalote (*Pseudoseisura gutturalis*), being up to 1.5 m (5 ft) in diameter. The enclosed structure has a cavity big enough for an eagle or vulture and strong enough for a man to stand on without damaging it. The **brown cachalote** (*Pseudoseisura lophotes*) of Paraguay, Uruguay and Argentina makes a nest the size of a barrel. Famous naturalist W. H. Hudson noted that he could stand on the nests of some of these species and make no impression. Although these huge nests are a conspicuous feature of open South American countryside little is known about the breeding because of the impenetrability of the structures.

THE LONGEST NEST BURROW
THE RHINOCEROS AUKLET'S – 8 m (26 ft)

Why the 36 cm (14 in) **Rhinoceros auklet** (*Cerorhinca monocerata*) of the North Pacific should excavate such a long burrow is a mystery. This misnamed bird is actually a puffin and its range is from the coast of Kamchatka and the Kuril Islands and from the west coast of Alaska south to Washington. In winter it is found in Japan and lower California. Its single egg hatches after about 40 days and the chick fledges after 40–50 days, having been fed on fish.

Ovenbird nests are among the largest relative to the size of the builders. (F. Erize, Bruce Coleman Ltd)

THE STRANGEST NEST-SITES

There are many fascinating nest-sites across the world, but the strangest must include that of the **violaceous trogon** (*Trogon violaceus*) of Central and South America. This bird takes over a wasp's nest, eats the adult wasps, then digs out the comb to make a nest cavity.

The **water thick-knee** or **dikkop** (*Burhinus vermiculatus*) of Africa is equally unusual in frequently laying its eggs on the dried droppings of large mammals such as the hippopotamus.

THE HIGHEST TREE NEST
THE MARBLED MURRELET'S –
45 m (148 ft)

Kinglets (*Regulus*) and **Lewis's woodpecker** (*Melanerpes lewis*) nest at 30 m (100 ft) up in trees but the highest nest found so far is that of the **marbled murrelet** (*Brachyramphus marmoratus*) at 45 m (148 ft). A very strange situation indeed for a 24–25 cm (9.5–10 in) auklet. The single egg is laid in a small cup, made mainly of guano, on a pad of moss in large coniferous trees in remote areas up to 10 km (6 miles) inland. Only five nests of this common seabird have ever been reported. Whereas other auks breed in colonies, often huge, only the **marbled** and **Kittlitz's murrulet** (*Brachyramphus brevirostris*) nest in solitary pairs. No one had ever seen the nest of this bird until 7 August 1974 when one was found in a Douglas fir in Big Basin State Park, Santa Cruz County, California. Kittlitz's murrulet is also exceptional for an auk in that it lays its egg on bare ground above the tree-line and far from the sea.

North American sequoias are the tallest trees in the world and may exceed 90 m (300 ft), but their tops seem to be avoided by birds and there are no records of any bird nesting at such a height.

THE SMALLEST CUP NEST IN THE WORLD
THE BEE HUMMINGBIRD'S –
thimble-sized

There is no doubt that the tiniest cup-shaped nests are made by hummingbirds. These are mostly fixed to twigs by cobwebs and built by the female alone. The narrowest is the thimble-sized cup of the world's smallest bird – the **bee hummingbird** (*Calypte helenae*) of Cuba and the Isle of Pines. But this is slightly deeper than that of the **vervain hummingbird** (*Mellisuga minima*) of Jamaica and Hispaniola, whose nest of lichen, silk and cotton is only about the size of half a walnut shell.

The female hummingbird alone incubates the eggs and cares for the young. Except in three or four species, male hummingbirds do not even know the whereabouts of the nests. Some, such as the **hermit hummingbirds**, build hanging nests, attached by cobwebs to the undersides of large leaves, such as palms and ferns, so that the leaf forms the inner wall and they are sheltered from tropical downpours. Others, such as **lancebills, metaltails** and **hillstars**, use cobwebs and glue to suspend their nests from the ceilings of caves or rocky overhangs. The deepest hummingbird nest was the only one known of the **blue-fronted lancebill** (*Doryfera johannae*), which was a pendent structure attached by cobwebs to a rocky overhang near the bottom of a 75 m (250 ft) shaft. Many birds make no nest at all and lay their eggs on bare rock or

The fairy tern makes no nest at all, merely laying its single egg on a bare branch, leaf or cliff. (Eric Hosking)

earth, or even in a tree cavity. Some scrape together a few woodchips or merely make a depression in vegetation or shingle. The 25 cm (10 in) **fairy tern** (*Sterna nereis*) of Australasia lays its single egg on the bare branch or leaf of a tree, or on coral boulders and cliffs. In the absence of a nest to contain it, the young has strong claws which enable it to cling tightly and even hang upside down.

Palm swifts also make tiny nests, one of the smallest being that of the 10.5 cm (4 in) **pygmy palm swift** (*Tachornis furcata*) of Colombia and Venezuela. The **Asian palm swift** (*Cypsiurus batasiensis*) and **African palm swift** (*Cypsiurus parvus*) build tiny open nests on the insides of palm leaves (they are restricted to where the fan palm grows). In Africa the minute eggs are glued to the nest with saliva. The nest is made from feathers and fibres and has a small lower rim for the bird to perch on while it incubates vertically.

THE SMALLEST NEST IN BRITAIN
THE GOLDCREST'S

The smallest nest in Britain is, not surprisingly, made by the smallest bird in Britain – the **goldcrest** (*Regulus regulus*). It is about 8–9 cm (3–3.5 in) in diameter and mostly placed underneath and generally near the end of a branch of fir or other tree. The materials used are moss and lichens interwoven with willow down, cocoons, spiders' webs, wool, grasses and a few hairs, spherically shaped and with a deep, tight cup. The well-camouflaged structure is usually 1–5 m (3–17 ft) from the ground and frequently lined with carefully placed feathers.

However, two of Britain's other very small birds – the **common wren** (*Troglodytes troglodytes*) and the **long-tailed tit** (*Aegithalos caudatus*) – make relatively large structures, both domes. In proportion to the size of the bird, the wren probably makes the largest British nest, and the male frequently constructs several 'cock nests' in an attempt to attract a mate (see page 65). The beautiful long-tailed tit's nest, made with mosses, lichens and cobwebs, has the highest number of feathers of any lining: up to 2,000 have been counted.

THE MOST VALUABLE NESTS IN THE WORLD
THE CAVE SWIFTLETS'

Cave swiftlets (*Collocalia*) are best known for providing the Chinese with their esteemed birds' nest soup. While all swifts and swiftlets use saliva to glue their nests together, species of *Collocalia* use saliva as the principle ingredient, though some incorporate feathers, leaves and other materials in varying proportions. Those most prized for soup-making are made of pure saliva, and include the little nests of the **grey-rumped swiftlet** (*Collocalia francica*), which do not require extensive cleaning. The crop of such nests may be both valuable and extensive. In one year alone over 3.5 million nests were exported from Borneo to China. The best sell for about £3 each and it takes two to make a single bowl of soup selling for up to £10 a bowl. The nests have no nutritional value and are tasteless, but are highly regarded as an aphrodisiac.

The colonies in vast Asian caves may contain several hundred thousand individuals whose nests of dried saliva are often stuck to the roofs and walls of caverns in total darkness up to 400 m (1,300 ft) or more from the entrance. Collection of them can be very hazardous, involving ropeways and ladders up to 100 m (330 ft) high. But the swiftlets have no trouble in negotiating the bird-filled blackness because they have developed the faculty of echolocation to a higher degree than any other bird species.

The well-studied **edible-nest swiftlet** (*Collocalia inexpectata*) has two peaks of maximal breeding activity: October–December and February–April, and the nests take about 30–40 days to build. Even without the cropping by humans, breeding success is poor as they can fall prey to cave crickets which eat the eggs and sometimes the young. Many other nestlings fall and are eaten by snakes, while those in houses may be eaten by rats and shrews.

The vast colonies also provide another valuable resource – the droppings (guano) which accumulate on the cave floor and are mined for use as fertilizer. But neither this nor taking the nests endangers the swiftlets' population. Rights to the caves are jealously guarded and nest removal has been carefully controlled for many centuries, even long before the first white man set foot in the area.

THE LARGEST EGG OF ANY LIVING BIRD
THE OSTRICH'S – up to 17.8 cm (7 in) × 14 cm (5.5 in)

The largest egg of any living bird and the biggest single cell in the animal world today is that of the **ostrich** (*Struthio camelus*), the world's largest living bird. There is

Ostrich eggs are the biggest single cells in the animal world today. (H. Miles, Nature Photographers Ltd)

considerable variation among the races but the North African birds generally lay the largest eggs, up to 17.8 cm × 14 cm (7 in × 5.5 in).

As with all species, egg-size is linked to individual female size, heavier individuals producing larger eggs, and is genetically controlled and inherited. Thus exceptional eggs do occur throughout Africa. One from Lake Jipe at the south-west corner of Tsavo (West) National Park in Kenya was 17.1 cm (6.7 in) long, 13.6 cm (5.35 in) across, 49.1 cm (19.3 in) round the long circumference and 43.7 cm (17.2 in) round the short circumference. It weighed 1,974 gm (4.35 lb) fresh weight. This was the largest of 600 eggs weighed and measured in East Africa and considerably larger than any of 100 measured on an ostrich farm at Oudtshoorn in South Africa. Most North African ostrich eggs are about 15.5 cm (6.1 in) long by 13.5 cm (5.3 in) across and weigh about 1.65 kg (3.63 lb).

Ostrich eggs are very strong, with a shell some 1.6 mm (0.063 in) thick, resisting the attentions of most predators, even playful lions, but **Egyptian vultures** (*Neophron percnopterus*) have learnt to crack them with stones (see page 127). One egg is equal in volume to some two dozen hens' eggs and takes about 40 minutes to boil.

Despite its great size, the ostrich egg represents only about 1% of the female's body weight. Other species lay eggs which represent up to 25% of body weight. Smaller specimens are laid by females breeding for the first time, but the oldest birds sometimes revert to laying smaller eggs. Scarcity of food may also restrict the size of eggs and small eggs are less successful at producing strong fledglings.

Large as they are, ostrich eggs are much smaller than preserved eggs of the extinct *Aepyornis maximus* (see page 15).

THE LARGEST BRITISH EGG
THE MUTE SWAN'S – up to 12.2 cm (4.8 in) long
The largest British egg is laid by Britain's largest free-flying bird, the **mute swan** (*Cygnus olor*). The average size is 11.43 cm (4.5 in) long by 7.31 cm (2.88 in) across, but some specimens of up to 12.2 cm

The mute swan lays Britain's largest egg, yet its incubation is not the longest. (E.K. Thompson, Aquila Photographics)

(4.8 in) by 8.8 cm (3.47 in) have been recorded.

Laying begins in the latter part of April. Incubation takes 34–40 days, sometimes 43, and is almost entirely by the female (pen). There is just one brood of 5–7 but 8–17 have been recorded, the larger numbers usually involving more than one female.

THE LARGEST EGG PROPORTIONATE TO THE LAYER
THE LITTLE SPOTTED KIWI'S – 25% of the female's weight

As a proportion of the female's weight, the largest egg is laid by the **little spotted kiwi** (*Apteryx owenii*) of New Zealand (now known on only three offshore islands). The average 35 cm (13.8 in) female has a body weight of about 1.2 kg (2.6 lb), about 20% heavier than the male, and her eggs weigh 275–370 g (9.7–13 oz), with an average of 310 g (10.9 oz) – about 25% of her body weight. Average dimensions are 108.5 × 71 mm (4.27 × 2.79 in). Eggs of the North Island **brown kiwi** (*Apteryx australis*) are larger at 330–520 g (11.6–18.3 oz), with an average weight of 440 g (15.5 oz) (125.5 × 78.5 mm/4.94 × 2.76 in), but represent just 18–22% of the female's body weight.

Eggshell thickness varies considerably between species and this significantly alters the internal volume. The shell of the larger **emu** (*Dromaius novaehollandiae*) egg (635 g/22.3 oz, 525 ml/1.05 pt) is about four times and the shell of the **ostrich** (*Struthio camelus*) egg (1,240 g/43.7 oz, 985 ml/1.97 pt) about eight times the weight of the kiwi eggshell. Total weights, therefore, exaggerate the size differences between the kiwi egg and the eggs of larger ratites, as the weight of the ostrich egg is nearly three times the weight of the kiwi egg, but its internal volume is only about 2½ times as great. The average 53 g (1.86 oz) **domestic chicken** egg and a 435 g (15.3 oz) **kiwi** egg are both laid by birds weighing about 2.4 kg (5.29 lb). Not surprisingly, kiwi eggs take a long time to incubate – 65–85 days, almost entirely by the male.

The little spotted is the smallest of the three species of flightless kiwi. The largest is the Stewart Island race of the brown kiwi (*A.a.lawryi*), which has females of at least 3.5 kg (7.7 lb) and is the only kiwi active by daylight. Kiwis are much smaller than the other ratites because they have no natural predators in New Zealand and therefore size is unimportant in defence. The high-protein diet also makes size unimportant. As well as worms, this includes woodlice, millipedes, centipedes, slugs, snails, spiders and a wide range of insects, as well as seeds and berries – all highly nutritious.

Captive females have laid up to five eggs in a continuous series with an interval of about 33 days between each. In the wild, clutches are usually 1–2 eggs (rarely 3) and the egg is heavily yolked (61%) like those of other species whose chicks hatch active, open-eyed and fully-feathered.

Even though a hen ostrich lays 12–15 of the largest eggs in the world, weighing in total 20–25 kg (44–55 lb), such clutches represent only 20–25% of body weight. **Hummingbirds** lay two eggs, each of which weighs about 13% of the female's body weight, but the proportion is even greater in the smaller species.

In total contrast, the smallest of all clutches as a proportion of body weight is that of the **emperor penguin** (*Aptenodytes forsteri*) whose single-egg clutch represents a mere 1.4% of the female.

THE SMALLEST EGG IN THE WORLD
THE BEE HUMMINGBIRD'S – 6.35 mm (0.25 in) long

In terms of average weight or volume, the question of which hummingbird lays the world's smallest egg is unresolved as comparatively few eggs have been comprehensively and accurately measured, and among these there has been considerable variation. But in terms of length alone the egg of the world's smallest bird – the **bee hummingbird** (*Mellisuga helenae*) of Cuba and the Isle of Pines – is the shortest, varying between 6.35 mm (0.25 in) and 11.4 mm (0.45 in) long. Those of the **vervain hummingbird** (*Mellisuga minima*) of Jamaica and Gonave Island, Hispaniola are generally no smaller than 10 mm (0.39 in) long and 0.365 g (0.0129 oz) in weight.

However, abnormally small hummingbird eggs have also been reported for several species. These 'sports' or 'runts' are fairly common throughout the bird world and are generally thought to have been laid prematurely. One exceptionally small example of the **Costa's hummingbird** (*Calypte costae*) of south-west USA and north-west Mexico measured only 7.36 mm (0.29 in) by 5.33 mm (0.21 in) and contained no yolk. In the same nest at Escondido was a second egg which was slightly incubated and measured 12.7 mm (0.5 in) by 8.4 mm (0.33 in). Amazingly, the finder managed to blow the tiny egg and it is now preserved in the Western Foundation of Vertebrate Zoology at Los Angeles, California. The bird which laid the two eggs was just 8.6 cm (3.4 in) long.

Hummingbirds generally lay two (sometimes one) elongated, white eggs which may be very small to us but represent about 13% of the female's bodyweight. Incubation takes 14–23 days and the nestling period is 18–38 days.

THE SMALLEST EGG IN BRITAIN
THE GOLDCREST'S –
12.2 mm (0.48 in) long
The smallest egg in Britain is laid by Europe's smallest breeding bird – the **goldcrest** (*Regulus regulus*). Average size is in the region of 12.2–14.5 mm (0.48–0.57 in) long by 9.4–10.2 mm (0.37–0.40 in) wide. There are often two broods of 7–11 eggs, sometimes 12. Laying begins in the latter part of April and incubation is by the hen.

The eggs of the **long-tailed tit** (*Aegithalos caudatus*) are almost as small, averaging 14.2 × 11 mm (0.56 × 0.43 in).

THE LARGEST CLUTCH
GREY PARTRIDGE'S – average
15–19 eggs
The largest single clutches are laid by those species with a high mortality and low average life expectancy. This is particularly marked among the ground-nesting partridges, pheasants and grouse, some species of which frequently lay over 20 eggs. The **bobwhite quail** (*Colinus virginianus*) is often said to lay the most eggs, and indeed it produces between 7 and 28, but its average is just 8–15. This is considerably less than the widespread **grey partridge** (*Perdix perdix*), which usually averages at least 15–16, and in Ostrobothia, Finland the average is 19. Within many species clutches become larger with increasing latitude and longer summer days as there is a shorter breeding season with less time for successive broods but more daylight in which to feed a large family. The largest grey partridge clutch to a single hen reported in Britain was 25 in Sussex in 1974. Twenty-four chicks hatched and all were still alive at six weeks. Although it is thought that clutch-size in most species is linked to the physical condition and age of the hen, it now seems that the amount of food the parents can collect for the potential brood is more important. There is also evidence that clutch-size is hereditary and that some individual females are either more experienced or more capable than others in caring for large broods.

Hole-nesting birds often lay more eggs than closely related species in more open sites, presumably because the enclosed eggs and young are safer. For example, the **blue tit** (*Parus caeruleus*), which has adapted so well to the widespread use of nest-boxes, generally has the largest clutch of any nidicolous (having young birds that remain in the nest after hatching) species. An

The grey partridge lays a record number of eggs in a single clutch because the species suffers high mortality. (M.C. Wilkes, Aquila Photographics)

average of 11–12 eggs is normal for good habitats in Europe, but individuals may lay up to 19. In tits and many other species there is also some seasonal variation in clutch-size, the larger clutches generally being laid early to benefit from peak food abundance.

Many supposedly large clutches are due to 'dump-nesting' where two or more females have laid in the same nest. This is particularly common among **gamebirds** and other *Galliformes* as well as **ducks**, and the generally unmanageable nest is usually abandoned. This sometimes happens when females have no nest of their own or occasionally practise parasitism. Incubation is very occasionally attempted, though not when the egg pile reaches intimidating proportions. For example, one North American **redhead** (*Aythya americana*) nest contained 87 eggs! Some redheads are entirely parasitic, making no attempt to build a nest and laying all their eggs in the nests of other duck species. Others are partially parasitic and lay eggs in the nests of other ducks, before settling down to raise their own family. Yet others never practise parasitism at all.

Some species, such as **anis** (*Crotophaga*) nest communally and share the incubation. This is quite distinct from dump-nesting. Up to 29 eggs have been found in one ani nest and the socially dominant pair does most of the breeding. The anis of the Americas are related to the parasitic **cuckoos** (*Cuculidae*).

Ostriches (*Struthionidae*) have a fascinating system of communal nesting. The cock defends a large territory and acquires a mate who lays her eggs in a scrape. A few days later other hens arrive and also lay in the nest. Surprisingly, the first, or major, hen gets off her nest to let them in, but only she and her mate will incubate – up to 40 eggs! But even an ostrich cannot cover so many eggs and some get pushed to the edge. This was once thought to be a way of regulating the temperature of the eggs, but investigation has shown that the outer eggs get overcooked in the sun.

The major hen is able to recognize her own eggs (perhaps by the pore pattern in the plain white shell) and she rolls those of the minor hens to the edge. The 'rejected' eggs form a front-line defence against predators such as jackals and vultures, which can eat only a few eggs or chicks. This reduces the chances of the major hen's eggs being eaten and presumably strengthens the species as the offspring of the dominant major pair are likely to be more successful than those of the minor birds. But the minor hens gain in that although they have failed to get mates it is likely that at least some of their eggs will hatch.

By removing their eggs as they are laid, some birds may be fooled into laying way beyond the normal clutch-size. In this way a hole-nesting **common flicker** (*Colaptes auratus*), a North American member of the woodpecker family, was once induced to lay 71 eggs in 73 days. Also in the woodpecker family, the **wryneck** (*Jynx torquilla*) was made to lay 48 eggs instead of the usual 5–14. A **house sparrow** (*Passer domesticus*) laid 51, **mallards** (*Anas platyrhynchos*) 80–146 and a **bobwhite quail** 128. Such stimulated laying is put to good use among domesticated birds such as the common chicken, which will lay for much of the year. And in protected environments, domesticated birds may be exceptionally successful with unusually large clutches. A **muscovy duck** once hatched 25 ducklings from a clutch of 31.

Many birds with relatively low mortality and high life expectancy lay single eggs. Some of the longest-lived birds, such as the three **great albatrosses** (*Diomedeidae*) and various large raptors, may breed only once in two years. The single egg laid in the summer produces a chick which is fed through the winter to fledge a year later – the lowest reproductive rate of any bird.

The **redlegged partridge** (*Alectoris rufa*), on the other hand, has a most unusual method of attaining high reproductivity. It is unique among British birds at least in that one female may lay two clutches in separate nests – one for her mate to incubate and one for herself so that each will raise a brood at the same time. The average clutch size is 10–15 but up to 28 have been recorded. The high rate of egg production is offset by increased losses, for, unlike the grey partridge, the redleg never covers its eggs when left and many are taken by predators. Surprisingly, clutches left for weeks and eventually incubated by the male are hatched as successfully as those incubated immediately.

THE MOST CLUTCHES, EGGS AND FLEDGLINGS IN ONE YEAR

The number and size of clutches, and of chicks surviving from each brood, are all governed by seasonal abundance of food. Some species, particularly passerines, have a prolonged breeding season and the maximum number of broods raised in the wild is generally six. But there are reports of captive **zebra finches** (*Poephila guttata*) raising as many as 21 consecutive broods. In the wild this finch is an opportunist breeder, laying in dry parts of Australia at irregular intervals after rainstorms and continuing to breed until the weather deteriorates. But adults of all species are restricted by their own survival needs such as moulting and building up fat reserves for winter, and, for most, late broods do not produce as many surviving young as earlier ones.

Because of their semi-wild state and adaptation to the protecting human environment, **feral pigeons** (*Columba livia*) often enjoy a protracted breeding season and may well hold the record for the number of clutches laid in one year by a free-flying bird, in Britain at least. However, many of their eggs do not produce fledged young. Within Britain, older, more experienced **blackbirds** (*Turdus merula*) probably fledge as many young as most other birds – often 17 from four broods of 4–5. Birds such as the **grey** and **redlegged partridges** (*Perdix perdix* and *Alectoris rufa*), which often lay over 20 eggs, generally have only one brood per season and suffer a high mortality rate. Yet the redlegged partridge may occasionally fledge more than the blackbird because it has a unique system whereby the male and female raise broods simultaneously.

Another prolific breeder is the **moorhen** (*Gallinula chloropus*), which commonly raises 2–3 broods of 5–11 and is most expert in their care. Predation is high at the beginning of the season but there are many repeat layings as well as 'dump nesting' (see page 149). Both parents share the incubation and feeding of young. The chicks leave the nest quickly – within 2–3 days – can swim and dive immediately and may even be fed by young of an earlier brood. There may be several special brood nests, depending on the number of young. Some have ramps and are built soon after the chicks hatch.

The moorhen is unusual among monogamous birds in that the female plays a dominant, even aggressive, role. The largest females get the pick of the males, but, rather surprisingly, they prefer small males as these need less food to keep healthy and can put on comparatively more fat. Such males need to spend less time feeding and are better placed to concentrate on incubating so that their mates can start more clutches and replace losses.

Though laid singly in the nests of different hosts, the eggs of parasitic species may produce a larger number in a year. Females of several species of African **cuckoo**, as well as the **European cuckoo** (*Cuculus canorus*), commonly lay as many as 20–24 eggs in a season.

THE FASTEST AND SLOWEST EGG-LAYING
A FEW SECONDS TO 2 HOURS
The actual laying, or voiding, of an egg from the end of the oviduct (vagina) is made possible by wave-like contractions of the vaginal wall and in most birds takes 1–3 minutes. However, some parasitic species such as **cuckoos** (*Cuculidae*), which must lay quickly to minimize chance of detection, can lay in just a few seconds. On the other hand, **turkeys** (*Meleagridinae*) and **geese** (*Anatidae*) may take 1–2 hours.

The interval between the laying of each egg in a clutch also varies. The first egg is often laid as soon as the nest is finished, but some species start before the nest is complete and others delay for a day or two after nest completion. A regular time of day is adhered to for many species. **Songbirds** seem to prefer dawn, but **pigeons** and **doves** (*Columbidae*) like the early afternoon and a few species the evening. Although one egg every 24 hours is common, a three-day interval is not uncommon among **birds of prey** (*Falconiformes*) and **owls** (*Strigiformes*), for whom varying prey supply is linked to survival. When food is short the older and larger birds get the lion's share and are more likely to survive. But even slower is the **masked booby** (*Sula dactylatra*) with a seven-day interval between the two eggs. Where food is in short supply from impoverished waters, the booby brood is often reduced to one by sibling murder.

THE MOST VARIABLY COLOURED/PATTERNED EGG
THE COMMON GUILLEMOT'S
No two birds' eggs are identical in appearance, though shape and size are remarkably similar within most species. Even in colour and pattern there is little significant variation, though in a few species great variety is a distinct advantage. Of these the **common guillemot** (*Uria aalge*) is by far the most notable, with a huge variety of egg shades and patterns. The ground colour ranges from white to creamy yellowish, ochreous, blue or deep blue-green, with the most extraordinary variety of markings, interlacing lines, spots, blotches or uniform masses of colour ranging

from bright red or brown to deep black and greenish black and, occasionally, there are no markings at all. The **Brünnich's guillemot** (*Uria lomvia*) also has a wide variety of shell markings, but the closely related **razorbill** (*Alca torda*) has much less variable eggs.

The guillemot's great egg variation helps to prevent confusion over egg ownership in the species' large, dense colonies on the cliff ledges. It has been clearly shown that guillemots identify their own eggs on the basis of individual combinations of ground colour and marking patterns. **Great-tailed grackles** (*Quiscalus mexicanus*) may also recognize their eggs in this way among the crowded coconut-palm colonies of Central America.

The single guillemot egg is pear-shaped to help prevent it rolling off the cliff ledge, though many still do. Interestingly, the rolling radius changes from 17 cm (7 in) for fresh eggs to 11 cm (4 in) for fully incubated eggs, but this is a fortuitous outcome of a change in the egg's centre of gravity as the embryo develops, rather than a special adaptation. The large egg (12% of female's body weight) is rested across the feet when incubated. Its shell is thicker at the narrow end, where it is in contact with the rocky nest-ledge, and thinner at the broad end, where the chick emerges. Parents find the right chicks in the crowded colonies through voice identification.

Eggshell is secreted in the uterus and consists largely of proteins and minerals, largely calcium carbonate in the form of calcite. Colour is derived from pigments secreted by cells in the wall of the oviduct, particularly of the uterus. The colours are deposited at different depths in the shell according to the position of the egg in the oviduct at the time of secretion. Much of the ground colour is provided by pigments in the spongy layer of the shell and must therefore be secreted at the upper end of the oviduct, while the blotches, speckles and scrawls on the surface are secreted

lower down, shortly before laying. The colours are derived from blood haemaglobin and bile pigments. Some shades are achieved by overlapping of colours. Originally all eggs were probably white as the ancestral reptilian method is to bury them in sand or loose soil. Pale eggs are retained by primitive families such as **cormorants** (*Phalacrocoracidae*), **pelicans** (*Pelecanidae*) and **albatrosses** (*Diomedeidae*) and by more advanced species which nest in holes. Eggs laid away from daylight have no need for cryptic colouring. Hole-nesters, such as **titmice** (*Paridae*), with speckled eggs, may have taken up the habit after a period of nesting out in the open.

Parasitic species also lay a wide variety of eggs to mimic those of their hosts. The **brown-headed cowbird** (*Molothrus ater*) of North America and Mexico is recorded as parasitizing 206 species, some regularly. But the **screaming cowbird** (*Molothrus rufoaxillaris*) of South America parasitizes just one host – the **bay-winged cowbird** (*Molothrus badius*).

Although cuckoo species such as the **European cuckoo** (*Cuculus canorus*) parasitize many different hosts, individual cuckoos generally lay eggs to match just one host and therefore do not produce a wide range of egg patterns and colours. It is believed that a female cuckoo inherits her egg colour exclusively from her mother and that the egg colouration is not affected by the father's genetic input. She chooses the right nests by seeking out the host species that reared her and is probably attracted by the habitat in which she was raised.

THE LONGEST INCUBATION PERIODS
WANDERING ALBATROSS and BROWN KIWI – up to 85 days
Being warm-blooded, bird embryos must be kept at a constant, relatively high temperature when they leave their mother's body. Thus, except for the **megapodes** (*Megapodiidae*), which use incubation

mounds (see page 138), and parasitic species such as **cowbirds** (*Molothrus*) and **cuckoos** (*Cuculidae*), which let other birds incubate their eggs for them, all birds keep their eggs at the proper temperature by covering them so that their body heat is transferred more or less directly to the developing embryos. The incubation period is strictly defined as the time between the laying of the last egg in a clutch to the hatching of that egg, and among species reliably studied so far the longest periods have been up to 85 days for the **brown kiwi** (*Apteryx australis*) and **wandering albatross** (*Diomedea exulans*). But that is an extreme and the incubation ranges of these two species are generally 74–84 and 75–82 days respectively. The **royal albatross** (*Diomedea epomophora*) has a similar range of 75–81 days, with a tendency towards the higher figure. Generally, the heavier the egg of a species, the longer the incubation: each doubling of egg weight increases incubation time by 16% on average.

Most birds develop a special brood patch for incubation. This comprises 1–3 adjacent abdominal areas which are normally relatively free of feathers all year round, but any down which occurs there, and some marginal contour feathers, are shed as the skin thickens slightly and the density of blood vessels increases.

Sometimes birds will sit on the incomplete clutch but not apply full body heat. The required temperature of 34–39°C (93–102°F), depending on species, is achieved only after a warm-up period, the length of which may be related to tightness of sit and time required for the incubation patch to develop. Some 75% of species aim for a constant temperature of 35°C (95°F).

Most birds cover eggs for 60–80% of the incubation period, regulating the egg temperature according to atmospheric conditions. Periods spent sitting vary greatly from under an hour for many passerines such as the European **robin** (*Erithacus rubecula*) to several hours in most seabirds, such as **gulls** and **terns** (*Laridae*). Offshore-feeding seabirds such as **shearwaters** and **storm-petrels** (*Procellariidae*) sit for 2–12 days at a stretch and the **great albatrosses** (*Diomedeidae*) for 2½–3 weeks. But the male **emperor penguin**'s (*Aptenodytes forsteri*) 64-day continuous sitting beats them all. In some species the time spent sitting decreases as the season advances, probably due to rising air temperatures.

Maintenance of correct humidity is also important during incubation, most eggs losing about 15% of their weight before hatching. This is lost through the porous surface, which also allows important ventilation. Turning the eggs, too, is important: some species do this up to 11 times an hour to prevent 'sticking' of membranes and avoid the adverse effects of any temperature gradients in the nest.

In 54% of species sexes share the incubation. For 25% it is the female alone, for just 6% the male alone, and it varies between male, female and both in about 15%. Single birds sit more continuously, but where both sit hatching is not necessarily quicker. Some parents, such as **bushtits** (*Psaltriparus*) of North and Central America, are assisted in the incubation by adults without nests of their own. Others, such as **anis** (*Crotophaga*) and **acorn woodpeckers** (*Melanerpes formicivorus*), have communal nests with several females laying and males and females sharing the incubation. The **waxbills** (*Estrilda*) are the only species in which the male and female incubate side by side on the nest.

The percentage of egg volume taken up by the yolk food supply at the start of incubation depends upon how advanced the chicks need to be at hatching. For most passerines, which hatch blind, naked and helpless, a 12–15-day incubation is normal, with the yolk taking up only about 20% of the egg.

So-called precocial species

Despite a record British incubation period of up to 56 days or more, the fulmar's chick is blind on hatching and has a very long fledging period. (D. Urry, Ardea London)

(hatching young which are soon able to leave the nest) such as **shorebirds**, **ducks** and **gamebirds**, which hatch in 3–7 weeks, require a larger yolk of about 35% total egg volume. Such chicks emerge from the shell with a full coat of protective down and are soon able to fend for themselves.

An embryo consumes the yolk until just before hatching, when the remains of the yolk sac pass into the body of the chick through the umbilical opening and, in some instances, may continue to nourish the bird for several days after hatching, giving the parents or chick time to establish the new feeding routine.

THE LONGEST INCUBATION IN BRITAIN

THE FULMAR'S – up to 56 days

The longest incubation recorded for any bird on the British list is 56 days for the **fulmar** (*Fulmaris glacialis glacialis*), though a period of 52–53 days is more likely in a range said to start at 42 days and perhaps exceed 56. The **manx shearwater** (*Puffinus puffinus*) has a range of 47–55 days, though 52–54 is more likely. Next come the **gannet** (*Morus bassanus*) with 39–45 days, and **white-tailed sea eagle** (*Haliaeetus albicilla*) with 35–45.

Although resembling a gull, the fulmar belongs to the relatively primitive family of **tube-noses** or petrels (*Procellariidae*). It lays just one egg and this is not generally replaced if lost to a predator, bad weather or accident. Despite the long incubation, the chick is hatched blind, but covered in long, thick down. Typical of the family, the fledging period is very long – 3–5 months – varying with the erratic food supply, the chick eventually becoming heavier than the parents. It may take eight years to reach maturity and actual breeding condition, but visits the colonies for a couple of summers before this in order to establish territory and perhaps a pair bond. Many live for 30 years or more so there is no need for a high replacement rate to maintain the population. The fulmar is the only British seabird which stays at its nest-site throughout the winter, when it will continue to defend its cliff territory.

The Atlantic population of fulmars has undergone a dramatic but largely unexplained increase this century. This started in 1872 from the species' single stronghold on the remote island group of St Kilda, off the Outer Hebrides, and they are now found around the entire coastline of Britain, though in smaller numbers in the south-east. The population is about 600,000 pairs, but with young and non-breeders at cliff-sites in winter may be over 1½ million birds. They now even nest at inland quarries, on ledges of large coastal buildings and in sand-dunes, having taken all suitable cliff-faces. The increase has been linked with more food in the form of offal from a growing fishing fleet, but this has not been consistent throughout the bird's range.

The name fulmar probably derives from the word foul, the bird having developed the art of spitting foul-smelling stomach oil at molesters.

THE SHORTEST INCUBATION PERIODS
SMALL PASSERINES – 10 days
Ten days seems to be the shortest possible incubation period for a fairly small number of passerines which lay eggs weighing under 1 g (0.035 oz). These include the **hawfinch** (*Coccothraustes coccothraustes*), **blackcap** (*Sylvia atricapilla*), **lesser whitethroat** (*Sylvia curruca*), **redpoll** (*Acanthis flammea*), **great-spotted woodpecker** (*Picoides major*) and the **black-billed cuckoo** (*Coccyzus erythropthalmus*). But these birds may also incubate for 11 days or even longer, according to how long the egg was in the oviduct and whether or not it was fully formed when laid.

Many more small birds have 12–14-day incubation periods, their young generally hatching from eggs with relatively small yolks. Birds which hatch in a more advanced state are sustained by proportionately larger yolks over longer incubation periods.

THE FASTEST AND SLOWEST HATCHING
30 minutes to 6 days
The actual process of 'escaping' from the egg – hatching – can take anything from 30 minutes or so in small passerines to six days for the larger albatrosses (*Diomedeidae*). But for most small to medium-sized birds it takes from a few hours to most of a day on average. In most clutches the eggs do not hatch together, but in sequence, reflecting the intervals in laying.

Preparation for hatching begins quite early in the incubation. As the embryo's moisture gradually evaporates through the porous eggshell an air pocket gathers at the blunt end of the egg, between the inner and outer shell membranes. The developing chick uses this for breathing over several days prior to hatching, though it still depends on a part of the embryo called the allantois for oxygen exchange.

The actual 'tools' of hatching – the temporary egg tooth on the tip of the upper mandible, and the special hatching muscle – also form early in the incubation, and the eggshell becomes conveniently weaker as it provides minerals for the developing chick's skeleton.

First the embryo realigns its body to lie along the length of the egg, the best position to force its way out from the blunt end. Convulsive thrusting forces the bill against the shell, and with the aid of the horny egg tooth the shell is soon cracked or 'pipped'. After the chick has broken out the hatching muscle withers away and the egg tooth either drops off or is reabsorbed into the bill, according to species. From pipping to full emergence is the hatching period. During this, the chicks of some species are helped by the parents, which may pick at the shell or poke into the cracks. It is said that ostriches crack their eggs with their breastbones and even drag the chicks out with their bills. Some parents will begin bringing food in response to the chick's peeping even from inside the unbroken shell.

QUICKEST TO FLY
CABOT'S TRAGOPAN and MEGAPODES—within 24 hours of hatching
It would not be right to say these species are the fastest at *learning* to fly because they seem to be born able to fly without any training or exercising of flight muscles. Most birds are born with down and are said not to be fledged until they have acquired their first true contour feathers, including the primaries which will propel them in flight. This generally takes at least 10 days and ground-nesting species, whose young leave the nest soon after hatching, are usually much quicker at getting into the air than birds which are born naked and helpless and remain in the nest after hatching. This is taken to the extreme in the **megapodes** (*Mega-podiidae*), whose young hatch in special incubation mounds (see page 138) and must fend for themselves immediately. They never see their parents and instead of the usual down they are born with extremely advanced contour-like feathers which enable them to fly and escape from predators almost at once.

Equally advanced on hatching is **Cabot's tragopan** (*Tragopan caboti*) of China, a member of the pheasant family. Its chicks hatch with a thick coat of coarse, shaggy down, but with primaries so far advanced they are immediately able to flutter up to perches. They also climb well and within a day or two can fly as well as any young passerine. Yet, although incubation is generally long among pheasants, it is not particularly long for this advanced bird, being just 28 days. This species is also unusually arboreal and lives in dense forests with very thick undergrowth which is often saturated. In this habitat a well-developed plumage is a distinct advantage.

Cabot's tragopan is listed as endangered, but reserves have recently been established within its historic range. Only one nest has ever been described from nature and that was 9m (30ft) up in an old squirrel drey.

The **satyr tragopan** (*Tragopan satyr*) is also highly precocial at hatching and within two or three days can fly up to an elevated perch to roost under its mother's wings. It too nests in trees, and is widely hunted and trapped with nooses in Nepal, legal protection being little help.

Temminck's tragopan (*Tragopan temmincki* – the Chinese crimson horned pheasant) of the eastern Himalayas can also fly up to elevated perches within two or three days of hatching. Yet the chicks grow slowly, are sensitive to disease and chilling and do not attain full adult male plumage until the second year, the adult female plumage coming first. This tragopan has a wider range and is more secure, but it too is extensively trapped and shot for its feathers and flesh, and much of its forest habitat is being cut for timber or razed for agriculture.

The shortest fledging time for altricial young – those helpless when hatched – is about eight days for some of the **warblers** (*Sylvinae*) and **finches** (*Fringillidae*).

The corn bunting has the shortest fledging period in Britain – just 9–11 days. (B.Speake, Aquila Photographics)

BRITAIN'S QUICKEST TO FLY
CORN BUNTING and BEARDED TIT – *from 9 days old*

The shortest fledging period in Britain is that of the **corn bunting** (*Emberiza calandra*) at 9–11 days. This is advantageous for a species which breeds late in the season – late May to July – yet usually squeezes in two broods. Its incubation is short too, at 12–13 days. The **cirl bunting** (*Emberiza cirlus*) and **yellow bunting** (yellowhammer) (*Emberiza citrinella*) also breed late and have short fledging periods of 11–13 days.

Bearded tit (*Panurus biarmicus*) chicks also sometimes fledge in 9 days, but may take 12, the shorter time perhaps being linked with the early part of a long breeding season – April to July. They frequently manage more than two broods and the 13-day incubation is by both parents.

Among Britain's ground-nesting species, the **ptarmigan** (*Lagopus mutus*) is the quickest to fledge, at 10 days. Laying takes place May–June, according to variable weather, and the 25-day incubation gives time for the precocial chick to develop as it must leave the nest soon after hatching. It is fed by both parents as quick growth is particularly important during the short summer at high altitude.

SLOWEST TO FLY
GREAT ALBATROSSES – *9–12 months*

The slowest birds to fledge are the **great albatrosses** (*Diomedeidae*), especially the **royal** (*Diomedea epomophora*) and the **wandering** (*Diomedea exulans*), which generally take 9–12 months.

At first the bulky young birds sit very quietly in the nest. They have two successive coats of down and are brooded by a parent for the first three to five weeks, after which they are visited and fed at intervals on regurgitated food. As the time approaches to leave they fidget and flap. Most fly straight from the nest, especially if inland, but they are likely to make abortive flights and land clumsily in unsuitable places. Sometimes they are drawn to village lights, and late-developing young may swim out to sea if they can reach the water. But strong chicks fly well immediately and never see their parents or birthplace again. When fledging is as long as this the parents can breed only once in two years.

Britain's slowest bird to fledge is the **mute swan** (*Cygnus olor*), which leaves the nest after a day or two but does not fly for some four months. The cygnets are tended by both parents.

THE FASTEST TO BREEDING MATURITY
QUAILS–from 5 weeks
The five species of quail in the genus *Coturnix*, including the **common quail** (*Coturnix coturnix*), reach maturity before any other bird – one reason why they have been bred in large numbers for the table. They are able to reproduce from as little as five weeks, though in most quails adult plumage is not attained before 10–12 weeks. Some other bird species are also capable of reproduction while still in immature sub-adult plumage, while others look adult before they are sexually mature.

Most small songbirds breed for the first time when just under one year old, in their second summer, and many others near the end of their second year. But some individuals within a species mature a year earlier than others.

Although physiologically capable of breeding, some species delay breeding for years as they need to develop their food-finding skills before they are capable of feeding themselves and a family. Hunting species in particular rely very much on experience, so young predatory birds continue to depend on their parents while practising their skills. Some manage this in two or three weeks but the **African crowned eagle** (*Stephanoaetus coronatus*) continues to receive food from its parents for up to a year even though it can fly.

THE SLOWEST TO BREEDING MATURITY
ALBATROSSES–from 6–10 years old
Despite the fact that the larger **albatrosses** (*Diomedeidae*) – notably the **royal** (*Diomedea epomophora*) and the **wandering** (*Diomedea exulans*) –

have very long incubation and fledging periods, they still delay for the record period of 6–10 years before breeding for the first time. There are even reports of a first breeding at 12 years old, though the birds are physiologically capable of reproducing before this. And even after all this time, first efforts are frequently unsuccessful.

After fledging, the transequatorial migrants set out on long journeys which must include a period of starvation as they cross the tropics. The early years are spent at sea, and they sometimes gather in nurseries where there is a good food supply. As they get older they return to land for increasing periods wandering in search of new nest-sites, though most return to their birthplaces. Further years are spent displaying and excavating nests before they even attempt to breed.

The wandering albatross chick takes so long to fledge – 9–12 months – the adults can breed only once in two years. (J. Visser, Bruce Coleman Ltd)

The Search for a Meal

Finding enough to eat dominates every day in every wild bird's life and what they choose or find to eat determines their subsequent behaviour and, eventually, shape. Also, the way in which birds have been able to exploit so many different habitats on earth is a reflection of their great variety, versatility and adaptability through food specialization. In finding a meal, their bills in particular have become highly adapted tools, though some species, such as **crows** (*Corvidae*), have been successful in retaining a fairly standard bill for a more general, or omnivorous, diet. The value of food specialization is that it enables closely related species to live side by side with minimal competition. But the greatest drawback for the specialist is that if the food supply disappears rapidly, sometimes through man's impact on the environment, there is an increased risk of extinction.

Nonetheless, in their feeding behaviour birds have never failed to surprise us and frequently react well to sudden, dramatic changes. Who could have foreseen the way in which so many species quickly became tame enough to feed at garden bird tables, or how species such as **tits** (*Paridae*) would even learn to take the cream from our milk? But even without man's help birds are surprisingly resourceful. A **kestrel** (*Falco tinnunculus*), which usually feeds on small birds and rodents, was once seen eating apples during a severe winter.

THE MOST SPECIALIZED DIETS
Over 30 species of bird have learnt to use tools to obtain food, but most of these do not have very specialized diets, and if necessary they can switch to other food supplies. But the greatest specialists, usually those species with highly-adapted and often peculiarly-shaped bills,

are often condemned to rely on very restricted or localized foods.

A textbook case of such food specialization is that of the North American **Everglade kite** (*Rostrhamus sociabilis plumbeus*), which eats only snails of the genus *Pomacea*. The Everglade kite has three races in Cuba, the Isle of Pines, Mexico, Guatemala and South America, where it remains generally abundant in its preferred habitat. But the fourth race – *R.s.plumbeus* of southern Florida – is now down to just 300 individuals through feeding exclusively on the large freshwater 'apple snails' (*Pomacea paludosa*). A bird of marshes and lake-margin rush beds, the 'snail kite' suffered a drastic decline along with the snails when most of the Florida wetlands were drained earlier this century. In 1965 there were only about 10 individuals left, on the shores of Lake Okeechobee, but thankfully this bird is hardy and resilient, and with protection and good management has established stable breeding populations in the Everglades National Park and two other refuges.

The bill and feet of *Rostrhamus* are specially adapted for extraction of snails from their shells. The long toes and claws are ideal for grasping the round, slippery shells and the long, slender, strongly down-curved upper mandible serves to penetrate the columellar muscle by which snails hold on to their shells. In Guyana snail kites (*R.s.major*) have been seen to wait until a captured snail raises its operculum (the plate covering the shell opening where the body emerges) of its own accord, before stabbing their bills into the soft muscle and then waiting for the pierced muscle to relax before shaking the shell free. But in Florida they specialize in inserting the bill under the closed operculum to sever the columellar muscle.

Another specialist raptor is the **lammergeier** or **bearded vulture** (*Gypaetus barbatus*), which feeds on nutritious bone marrow. The carcass bones are too big to swallow whole so the lammergeier has learnt to drop them from great heights to smash them on rocks. It uses the updrafts of air which prevail along the high mountain cliffs of Europe, Asia and Africa to lift it up repeatedly, thus saving precious energy.

The lammergeier swallows dangerously sharp fragments of bone, which its powerful, acidic digestive juices break down to make use of the nutritious bone marrow. (Dr Alan Beaumont)

The lammergeier's long, slim tongue is shaped like a narrow trowel to scoop the marrow from the core of the bone. Dangerously sharp fragments of bone, with marrow attached, can be swallowed safely because the lammergeier has powerful, acidic digestive juices which soon break them down. Tortoises are also sometimes eaten.

Some species have developed total or partial immunity to poisons in butterflies and caterpillars. For example, most species have learnt to avoid the North American monarch butterfly, which derives poison from the leaves of the milk-weed plant. The caterpillars store the poison in their bodies and it is retained when they pupate and then become butterflies. The **black-headed oriole** (*Icterus graduacauda*) has learnt to eat only those parts of the butterfly which contain small amounts of poison. If it ingests too much it is sick. But the **black-headed grosbeak** (*Pheucticus melanocephalus*) can eat the monarch butterflies indiscriminately. How it does this remains a mystery.

Sapsuckers are three species of North American woodpecker in the genus *Sphyrapicus*, which drill horizontal or vertical lines of slightly uptilted round or square holes into a wide variety of coniferous and deciduous trees and shrubs and return later to lap up the sugar-rich sap which has dribbled down. They use the brush-like tips of their extensible tongues. They also eat the green inner bark, called cambium, as well as a wide variety of insects. Other bird species are attracted to the holes, both for the sap and the insects which gather there.

THE MOST BIZARRE FEEDING
Blood-drinking by the SHARP-BEAKED GROUND FINCH
The vampire-like activities of the small **sharp-beaked ground finch** (*Geospiza difficilis*) were not discovered until a television camera team visited the remote Galapagos Islands in the 1980s. To their great surprise, on Wolf Island they found the bird drinking blood from holes which it had pecked in the wings of nesting **masked boobies** (*Sula dactylatra*), which do not seem particularly bothered by this. For their part, the finches not only gain extra food but also valuable moisture in a very arid environment. Normally seed eaters, the finches have also learnt to exploit the boobies by rolling their eggs away so that they crack apart on the rocks and provide further food.

BRITAIN'S MOST SPECIALIZED FEEDER
THE CROSSBILL
The **Scottish crossbill**'s (*Loxia scotica*) crossed bill may look awkward, but it is one of the most efficient natural tools in the world. In fact *scotica* is just one of a number of crossbill species and sub-species which have crossed bills of varying size and strength, which correspond to the heaviness of the preferred conifer cones to be cracked apart for their seed. For example, whereas the massive-billed **parrot crossbill** (*Loxia pytyopsittacus*) of north-east Europe and West Siberia specializes in the toughest of green Scotch pine cones, the relatively delicate-billed **white-winged crossbill** (*Loxia leucoptera*) of Europe, Asia, North America and Hispaniola prefers larch cones.

The precise way in which the crossbill's bill works has been debated for centuries, but it is clear that the bird does not always need to use all the bill's extraordinary functions in cone-seed extraction. In fact it can turn to other foods, such as suet put in bird feeders, insects and seeds of fruit (after slicing the pulp in two with a scissor-like action). The full technique employed by this remarkable bill is used only in opening green, tightly closed, unripe cones. After plucking the growing cone, the crossbill takes it to a horizontal perch where it holds it down firmly with one of its exceptionally large and powerful feet. The tip of the downward-curving, longer upper

Crossbills have evolved extremely specialized bills in order to prise the seed from the cones of coniferous trees. (H. Reinhard, Bruce Coleman Ltd)

mandible is wedged between two of the cone scales so that the curve of the lower mandible rests on the outside of the cone. Then the bird twists its head to force the scales apart. Simultaneously, the two mandibles are moved sideways by special jaw muscles.

When the scales have been parted, the exceptionally large, protrusible tongue reaches in to detach the firmly anchored, unripe seed with the aid of a special cartilaginous cutting edge at the tongue tip. Such power is exerted by the bird when tackling cones in this way that the loud cracking noises can be heard for some distance.

Although the crossbill chick's upper mandible begins to lengthen by the fourteenth day, no crossing takes place for about four weeks so that the parents can continue to feed it. It is only the horny sheath of the bill, not the underlying bones, which is bent and curved.

OTHER REMARKABLE FEEDERS
HAWFINCH and
OYSTERCATCHER

For its size, the **hawfinch** (*Coccothraustes coccothraustes*) has the most powerful bill and jaw muscles of any bird. The 18cm (7in) finch concentrates on the soft seeds of elm and hornbeam in Britain, but it can easily deal with the very hard stones of cherries and olives. Its massive bill has four rounded knobs at the base – two on the inner side of each mandible – and by placing a stone between them the force for cracking it is shared equally by the muscles on each side of the head. To crack an olive stone it has to exert a force of nearly 50kg (110 lb).

The **oystercatcher** (*Haematopus australegus*) is a shellfish specialist with a bill that is laterally flattened towards the tip. This chisel-like tool is inserted into the shells of bivalves such as mussels and oysters and then severs the powerful adductor

For its size the hawfinch has the most powerful bill and jaw muscles of any bird. (R. Siegal, Aquila Photographics)

muscle that holds the shell together. But sometimes a shell closes very tightly on the bill before the muscle is cut. Then, if the shell-fish is still anchored firmly to the seashore, the bird drowns when the tide comes in.

THE LARGEST ITEMS SWALLOWED WHOLE

Irrespective of size, birds can be incredibly ambitious feeders and swallowers of surprising objects. The **ostrich** (*Struthio camelus*), for example, is well known for swallowing inedible objects in captivity, from padlocks to beer bottles. In the wild they must swallow stones to aid digestion of vegetable matter and these are usually fairly small pebbles, but one swallowed a ruby and led to the discovery of a mine.

Much larger, extinct birds, such as **moas**, were also vegetarians which had to swallow stones to aid digestion. Some remains are so well preserved the contents of the gizzards remain untouched in the skeletons. They reveal that the grasses, leaves, berries and twigs were pulped in the gizzard by up to 3 kg (7 lb) of stones!

One species of **imperial pigeon** (*Ducula*) stretches the base of its bill, like a snake swallowing prey, to gorge on whole nutmeg fruits of 5 cm (2 in) diameter – larger than its own head. But whereas most opportunist fruit eaters must regurgitate large stones, specialist birds such as the fruit pigeons can pass nutmeg seeds 2.5 cm (1 in) in diameter through their intestines.

One of the world's 'greediest' birds is the **common cormorant** (*Phalacrocorax carbo*), which sometimes takes salt and freshwater fish of astonishing size, including conger eel 0.76 m (2.5 ft) long. One bird died from exhaustion after trying to swallow an immense mullet.

THE MOST WIDE-RANGING DIET

Crows (*Corvidae*) and **gulls** (*Laridae*) eat a very wide range of plant material, live vertebrates and invertebrates as well as carrion and waste products provided by man. Their medium size and general shape of bill are probably more suited to an omnivorous and opportunist diet than those of any other species. But no one can accuse the North American **ruffed grouse** (*Bonasa umbellus*) of being fussy: it is known to have eaten part of at least 518 species of animal and 414 species of plant!

THE GREATEST APPETITES

The amount of food any bird eats in a day is related to its body weight, metabolism, calorific value of the food and how much energy the bird can store. Although large birds obviously eat more in absolute quantity than small birds do, in general, the smaller the bird the more it eats in proportion to its body weight. Smaller birds generally have a more active lifestyle and higher metabolism which uses up energy more quickly. For example, although an average **pelican** (*Pelicanidae*) might eat 1.8 kg (4 lb) of fish in a day and an average **eagle** (*Accipitridae*) up to 1 kg (2.2 lb) of meat, this constitutes only about a half and a quarter of body weight respectively.

In contrast, **hummingbirds** (*Trochilidae*), which are the smallest of all birds and probably have the highest metabolic rate of any living creature, must consume twice their weight or more in nectar and insects each day, even though this may be less than 15 g (0.5 oz) of food.

But there are exceptions to the general rules, with sedentary birds in warm climates needing far less energy than very active and migratory species who spend at least part of the year in very cold regions. Most fruit eaters live in warm countries where fewer calories are needed, but the calorific value of fruit is generally low so that relatively large quantities must be eaten. For example, **waxwings** (*Bombycilla garrulus*) in northern Europe eat three times their body weight in cotoneaster berries each day. Other gluttonous fruit eaters are sometimes made drunk by the juice of overripe fruits which have fermented.

Birds will also eat very large numbers of single items in one day. A dabbling duck's stomach often contains 50,000–100,000 seeds or plant parts, and 185 blue mussels have been taken from the digestive tract of a **common eider** (*Somateria mollissima*). The stomachs of insectivorous birds may contain over 5,000 small insects such as mosquitoes and ants or several hundred caterpillars – impressive quantities considering that birds can pass food through their digestive tracts in 30–90 minutes and such numbers represent only a fraction of an average day's consumption.

Insectivorous birds take even larger quantities of food when raising a family. **Pied flycatchers** (*Ficedula hypoleeuca*) will visit the nest over 30 times an hour and make a total of 6,000 provisioning journeys to rear the brood. But other hole-nesters with larger broods must make even more trips. Automatic counters set up at nest-boxes show that **tits** (*Paridae*) always make many thousands of visits in rearing a brood, the actual number varying with the size of the main local food items. One pair of **great tits** (*Parus major*) fed their young 10,685 times over 14 days but another pair 'only' 4,655 times before the chicks flew on the 19th day. Even more active was a **wren** (*Troglodytes troglodytes*) which fed her young 1,217 times in a 16-hour day while still having to feed herself.

THE LONGEST FAST
THE EMPEROR PENGUIN'S –
average 115 days

Except during hibernation, no living bird fasts for anything like as long as the male **emperor penguin** (*Aptenodytes forsteri*) of the Antarctic. He begins the fast before incubation starts, and while the female is away at sea feeding he must incubate the single egg for some 64 days despite the very low temperatures of mid-winter. The colonies are often far from the sea (the only source of food) on the pack ice and travelling to and from them extends the fasting period. Thus the average male's fast is 115 days and the longest so far recorded an incredible 134 days. The birds do not all fast at the same time and, overall, they fast during six months of the year.

To endure such a fast in the most hostile climate on earth the average 30 kg (66 lb) male will put on a lot of fat, but many other special adaptations are also necessary (see page 119).

The only other birds which can fast for such long periods are the few species which hibernate and, of these, the most remarkable is the North American **poorwill** (*Phalaenoptilus nuttallii*), a relative of the **nightjars** (*Caprimulgidae*), which can 'sleep' in a torpid condition in rock crevices for some three months.

Birds & Man

This section goes from one extreme to another, looking at those records which reveal how mankind can both love and hate birds at the same time. On the one hand there are a whole clutch of bird-spotting records which demonstrate the extraordinary lengths to which an ever-increasing and adoring army of birdwatchers will go. But on the other we see how certain birds are despised as serious pests, occasionally even causing human death and exhaustion of local food supplies. And for as far back as we can trace, man has shown his admiration for birds through painting them in meticulous detail. Yet at the same time men have hunted, trapped and collected birds and their eggs, sometimes to extinction. Many have been killed quite unnecessarily through superstition, ignorance and fear, but today there is an increasing international awareness of the need to preserve as many life forms as possible.

DOMESTICATED AND CAGE AND AVIARY BIRDS

Man has kept birds for thousands of years, chiefly for their flesh and eggs. But they have also been held captive for sports such as falconry and cockfighting, for sacrifice and for their feathers and bones in ceremony. Others have been prized purely for their companionship as pets and many are extensively bred in ornamental forms purely for show, many strains now showing hardly any resemblance to the original stock from which they came.

Although many cage birds are extensively bred in captivity, interest in them has been so wide this century a black market in wild birds has made a mockery of protective legislation. Huge numbers are exported worldwide, but most of them die in transit and as a result many species remain endangered.

THE EARLIEST DOMESTICATION OF BIRDS

JUNGLE FOWLS – over 5,000 years ago

It is likely that birds were first held in captivity for religious rather than economic reasons but much of the early evidence, based on paintings, is confusing. Domestication of birds for meat and eggs would have been worthwhile and practical for only those peoples who had largely given up the nomadic life of the hunter/gatherer for that of the 'civilized' settler. Very early rock paintings of Australian birds by wandering tribesmen have no link with domestication as we know it; the earliest evidence of real bird domestication, about 3,200 BC, comes from India and is of one or more species of **jungle fowl** (*Gallus gallus*), the ancestors of our common chickens, and in China jungle fowls are known to have been domesticated by 1,400 BC.

In many cases these early paintings are stylized and bear little resemblance to the species we know. The position is particularly vague concerning geese, which were certainly domesticated by the Egyptians well over 4,000 years ago. Some Egyptian frescoes resemble the **greylag goose** (*Anser anser*), the common ancestor of most domestic stock in Europe, but the **Egyptian** or **Nile goose** (*Alopochen aegyptiacus*) was their main domesticated form. It was very common in the Egyptian Old Kingdom, which ended in 2,300 BC. Although its flesh was widely eaten, it was the sacred bird of the god Geb so the eggs, with symbolic power, were never consumed.

The **mallard** (*Anas platyrhynchos*) was also domesticated by the ancient Egyptians and other early civilizations. Domestic pigeons, descended from the **rock dove** (*Columbia livia*), were held sacred in the early culture of the Near East, and Egyptian images of them date to 3,100 BC. These birds were kept as carriers as well as for food.

The **turkey** (*Meleagris gallopavo gallopavo*) was probably first domesticated in Mexico, possibly at a time approximating the Neolithic in Europe. It was probably imported to Britain between 1525 and 1532 by William Strickland of Boynton-on-the-Wold, Yorkshire, as he was allowed to incorporate a turkey cock in his family crest.

THE LONGEST-LIVED DOMESTICATED BIRD
THE GOOSE
Domesticated birds which are of some use to man are not usually kept into old age because then their flesh would be tough and egg-laying capacity much reduced. **Geese** (*Anser anser domesticus*), however, are also kept for their down, which is cropped regularly, and some are maintained as 'watch-dogs' and pets. They frequently live to 25 years and there are many reports of others reaching 50.

Domesticated **ostriches** (*Struthio camelus*) are potentially long-lived but they are rarely kept beyond 15 years for feather production while many die through breaking their legs. Nonetheless, one bird is said to have lived to 62 years 7 months before being killed in the unique ostrich abattoir at Oudtshoorn, South Africa, and another is thought to have been 68.

THE LARGEST DOMESTICATED BIRD
THE OSTRICH
The largest domesticated bird, the **ostrich** (*Struthio camelus*), is also the largest of all living birds. Males can stand over 2.5 m (8 ft) tall and weigh over 150 kg (340 lb). They have always been valued for their meat and feathers, with the result that one sub-species, *Struthio camelus syriacus* of the Syrian and Arabian deserts, is thought to have been hunted to extinction by the 1940s. The other races too have declined dramatically.

Ostriches have been farmed in South Africa since the middle of the 19th century. More recently, they have been introduced to the USA, Australia and Europe, where they are easily bred in captivity. There is no longer any great interest in their plumes for the hat trade, but the bird's skin is still sometimes used to produce a first-rate leather.

Unlike domesticated turkeys, which appear to be the 'dimmest' birds, ostriches seem to be fairly intelligent. There are reports of some African birds being trained to herd sheep and chase bird pests away from crops.

THE LARGEST CAGE AND AVIARY BIRD
THE HYACINTH MACAW–
1 m (3.28 ft) long
The largest of the parrot family's 328 species, the 1 m (3.28 ft) **hyacinth macaw** (*Anodorhynchus hyacinthinus*) of central southern Brazil, is the largest of all pet birds. Males are slightly larger than females, exceptional specimens being slightly in excess of 1 m (3.28 ft). **Blue and yellow macaws** (*Ara ararauna*), **scarlet macaws** (*Ara macao*) and **military macaws** (*Ara militaris*) are almost as big at about 90 cm (3 ft) long.

THE WORLD'S MOST ABUNDANT DOMESTICATED BIRD
THE CHICKEN–over 8,000 million
According to the Food and Agricultural Organization (FAO) of the United Nations, the world's **chicken** population stood at 8,295,760,000 in 1985, having grown steadily from a population of 6,429,077,000 in 1978. Thus the human race is outnumbered by this domesticated form of the wild red jungle fowl (*Gallus gallus*) by about two to one.

Among the largest national chicken populations are those of China (excluding Taiwan) – 1,300 million; the USSR – 1,090 million; the USA – 1,047 million; Brazil – 479 million; Japan – 327 million; Mexico – 200 million; France – 188 million;

India – 161 million; Nigeria – 160 million; Indonesia – 143 million and the UK – 112 million, including minor holdings.

Broilers are by far the most abundant type of chickens in the world. In Britain modern commercial stocks are hybrids of several breeds. The ISA brown probably accounts for over 50% of commercial layers (with a handful of others, including the Hisex Brown and Ross Brown accounting for most of the others) and the Cobb and the Ross together account for over 80% of broilers. In 1985 34.92 million chicks were placed on UK farms for egg production and 487.9 million for table production (mainly broilers). In June 1985 the Ministry of Agriculture Fisheries and Food (MAFF) estimated the British chicken population at 109,610,736 excluding some minor holdings.

Turkeys have become increasingly important in recent years. The FAO-estimated world stock of 170 million in 1978 had grown to about 217 million in 1985. The largest national flocks then were those of the USSR – 66 million, the USA – 53 million, Italy – 21 million, France – 17 million, and the United Kingdom 11 million, including all minor holdings. The MAFF estimate for June 1985 was 7,864,000 including minor holdings in England and Wales only. The number of poults placed on farms for the table was 29.78 million.

THE MOST EGGS PRODUCED
CHICKENS' – over 562,000 million per year
Undoubtedly more chicken eggs are eaten each year than those of any other bird. In 1985 the Food and Agricultural Organization of the United Nations estimated annual world production to be 562,746,880,000, rising from a figure of 462,077,696,000 in 1978. The biggest producer was China with 88,800 million, followed by the USSR with 75,800 million and the USA with 68,245 million. The UK produced 12,228 million.

The UK Ministry of Agriculture Fisheries and Food return for 1985 estimated that 47.58 million layers produced 1,090 million dozen eggs – an average of 258.4 each. Of these, 12,224,400,000 eggs were used for human consumption.

It is unlikely that all these figures are conservative as innumerable fowls are kept for self-sufficiency rather than sale of eggs.

THE MOST ABUNDANT CAGE AND AVIARY BIRDS
No one can yet say with any certainty which is the most commonly kept cagebird across the world as little is known of many remote areas. China, for example, which is only now opening up to the West, has a quarter of all mankind and almost all Chinese hope to own a cagebird, such as the very popular **laughing thrushes** (*Garrulax*) and the **Mongolian lark** (*Melanocorypha mongolica*), all of which are trapped in the wild.

But in western, developed countries at least the most numerous cagebirds are **budgerigars** and **canaries**. The budgerigar (*Melopsittacus undulatus*) is a native of the arid regions of Australia but innumerable varieties have been bred in captivity. There are several species of wild canary, but most caged canaries are derived from the **wild serin** (*Serinus canaria*) of the Canary Islands, the Azores and Madeira and have been chiefly prized for their fine song.

There have been no recent world estimates of caged budgerigar and canary numbers. In Britain, the National Council of Aviculture estimates that there are over 3 million budgerigars – approximately 2 million owned by aviculturists and 1 million as household pets. The Budgerigar Society alone sells over 400,000 rings a year in Britain. The number of canaries is extremely hard to estimate as there are over 20 varieties bred by aviculturists, among whom they are easily the most popular bird. In addition, a huge number are kept as household pets, and many are used in industry, such as in testing for mine gas. The National Council of Aviculture estimates a British population of at least 5 mllllon – 4 million in the care of aviculturists and 1 million as pets.

Parrots (*Psittacidae*) are also extremely popular, though none of the 328 species is anywhere near as numerous in captivity as the budgerigar or canary. In Britain, the Parrot Society has about 4,500 members, many from overseas, and they are breeding species such as **lovebirds** (*Agapornis*) and **cockatiels** (*Nymphicus hollandicus*) in large numbers. The National Council of Aviculture estimates a British population of some 3 million for the wide-ranging parrot family.

Sadly, the larger caged parrots are mostly taken from the wild and over-exploitation of many species such as **cockatoos** (*Cacatuidae*) in Australia, **grey parrots** (*Psittacus erithacus*) in Africa and **Amazona parrots** and **macaws** (*Anodorhynchus*) in Latin America is threatening their future. In the USA alone importation of wild exotics currently runs into millions of birds annually and up to 80% die before reaching their destinations. Even the most endangered species are still being exported, including the **golden-shouldered parrot** (*Psephotus chrysopterygius*) of Australia, one of whose sub-species now numbers under 250. Many of the 17 species of **macaw**, especially the **red-fronted** (*Ara rubrogenys*), **scarlet** (*Ara macao*), **hyacinth** (*Anodorhynchus hyacinthinus*) and **blue-headed** (*Ara couloni*), are particularly endangered by the pet trade. Over 21,000 were exported in the 1970s to the USA alone, and for each macaw eventually sold there it is estimated that eight die in transit.

But the irresponsible trade in wild birds is not confined to parrots. Many third world countries export huge numbers of birds of every description. India, for example, exports on average some 1,345,000 birds per year. The greater the rarity the more it fetches. One of the most valued is the **Bali mynah** or **Rothschild's starling** (*Leucopsar rothschildi*)

of Bali, which is still caught with decoys or birdlime despite its population having fallen to about 250.

Birds are also kept captive for sporting purposes. Of these by far the most numerous are **racing pigeons**. Approximately 10 million are registered worldwide each year and a world population of 40–50 million is estimated. The International Pigeon Racing Federation has about 600,000 affiliated members with an average of 40 pigeons per loft, giving a total of some 24 million birds, possibly half the world population. Britain is thought to have about 250,000 pigeon fanciers with an average of 40 racing birds per loft, giving a total of some 10 million. No total figures are available for the USA, but the American Racing Pigeon Union issues some 1½ million bands a year.

Many pigeons are also kept for showing or simply for fun. The British National Pigeon Association, the governing body of fancy pigeons, sells about 50,000 rings a year, but that does not take into account all the birds bred purely for pleasure, which are not ringed.

THE MOST TALKATIVE CAGEBIRDS

As a species, the most talkative cage and aviary bird is the **hill** or **talking mynah** (*Gracula religiosa*) of India, Sri Lanka and Indonesia. But individual parrots have been taught more words. The champion to date is a male African **grey parrot** (*Psittacus erythacus*) which has a vocabulary of nearly 800 words and won the Best Talking Parrot-like Bird title at the National Cage and Aviary Bird Show for twelve consecutive years – 1965–76. This remarkable bird, named Prudle, was taken from a nest at Jinja, Uganda in 1958 and retired undefeated.

In Victorian Britain, when most species were not protected by law, all manner of wild birds were taken into captivity as pets. Among country folk especially, the most popular talkers were the **jackdaw** (*Corvus monedula*) and **jay** (*Garrulus* *glandarius*), *garrulus* being Latin for talkative. Sadly, many simple people had the mistaken belief that the birds would talk better if their tongues were slit!

THE MOST EXPENSIVE BIRD IN THE WORLD
A RACING PIGEON at £41,000

The highest price ever paid for any bird was £41,000 (equal to 10 times its weight in gold) for the racing pigeon Peter Pau in 1986. The buyer was Mr Louis Massarella who, with his three sons, runs the biggest racing pigeon complex in the world at Hall Farm, Charley, Loughborough, Leicestershire, England.

Although Peter Pau can fly distances of over 600 miles, averaging 72–80 kph (45–50 mph), it will not be racing any more as it was bought for breeding only.

The previous record price for a racing pigeon was £25,000 paid by a Taiwanese fancier. Also, in 1986 it was rumoured that master fancier Andre Van Bruane, who has an outstanding record in international racing, refused an offer of £45,000 for his six-year-old bird Barcelona II.

Most racing pigeons are bought-in for breeding and change hands for an average £150 for a 'squeaker' straight from the nest at about 24 days old. Birds are paired in mid-February and lay after 7–8 days. Both parents sit for about 19 days and the young are fed on both parents' 'milk'. This changes naturally to a minced grain, the squab or squeaker putting its bill into the parent's mouth. Hard food is offered at 22 days and from 24 days the squab feeds alone.

Young birds are discouraged from flying, even though they can manage 300 miles at six months old. They begin with 20-mile release flights in light winds at an average 65 kph (40 mph).

THE MOST EXPENSIVE CAGE AND AVIARY BIRD
A HYACINTH MACAW – at £5,000

According to the National Council of Aviculture, the highest price ever paid for a cagebird was £5,000 for a **hyacinth macaw** (*Anodorhynchus hyacinthinus*), the largest member of the parrot family. This was a private deal between an importer and a zoo in the South of England, though the bird was a particularly fine specimen and other bids may have raised the price to that exceptional level.

It is rumoured that a **budgerigar** (*Melopsittacus undulatus*) of extremely high exhibition quality was sold in England in 1986 for £17,000. Budgerigars commonly change hands for £50–3,000 among private dealers.

THE HEAVIEST AND MOST EXPENSIVE TURKEY
36.75 kg (81 lb 0¼ oz) and £3,600

The heaviest turkey ever weighed 36.75 kg (81 lb 0¼ oz). It was a Big 6 breeding stag reared by British United Turkeys of Chester, England and sold for a world record price of £3,600 on 9 December 1986 to Dewhurst Butchers in auction at London's Smithfield Market. The money raised went to the Save the Children Fund and the bird was donated to the children's ward of St Bartholomew's Hospital, London. The runner-up weighed 35.94 kg (79.25 lb), and was raised by AMS Turkey Breeders.

Such stags (males) are produced by firms specializing in producing breeding stock for poultry farms and are not the result of special breeding programmes. However, they are selected at the end of their breeding season, when they are just one year old, and fattened for a further three months. The secret is to house them in groups of about six birds in a warm building, ensuring that they have as little stress as possible. The weight can never be guaranteed until a bird is killed as the weather plays an important role and birds of this type can put on weight one week and lose it the next. The chief risk for such unnaturally heavy birds is heart failure.

During its 15-month life one of these stags consumes an average

269.3 kg (593.8 lb) of feed – approximately 3,610,300 pellets measuring 22.93 km (14.25 miles) if put end to end. The 1982 record holder of 35.78 kg (78.9 lb) had multiplied its birth weight by 361 times in 24 weeks and by 720 times by the time it was killed.

The **wild turkey** (*Meleagris gallopavo*) of North America, from which all table birds are derived, may stand 1.2 m (4 ft) tall but its maximum weight is about 9 kg (20 lb). It flies well in short bursts and can run very fast (see page 109). Once resident throughout most of North America south of the coniferous forest zone, it was reduced to remnant populations because of its appeal as a table and game bird. But its popularity with sportsmen has led to its artificial re-establishment in many states by fish and game agencies wanting to satisfy shooters.

Whereas the wild turkey is alert and sharp-witted, domesticated strains are sometimes said to be the dimmest birds in the world. They frequently stand in the open during the heaviest downpours and may be drowned because they are not intelligent enough to walk a few metres to their hutches. And many thousands freeze to death on cold nights because they appear too lazy to seek refuge in their warm sleeping quarters. Others are so backward they even have to be persuaded to eat. They are also easily panicked: once 13,000 were trampled to death on a Californian ranch when a low-flying jet flew over. But perhaps the most extreme example of their stupidity was when six birds scrambled into a farmer's empty barrel, one on top of the other, and died of suffocation because none had the sense to get out.

THE EARLIEST BIRD BOOKS

The first printed descriptions of birds appeared in 15th century books covering most aspects of natural history, and sometimes other subjects as well. The earliest of these was **De sermonum propri-etate seu de universo** by **Rabanus (Hrabanus) Maurus**, Abbot of Fulda, later Archbishop of Mainz. Printed in 1467 by Adolf Rusch at Strasbourg, it was a kind of encyclopaedia in 22 books, based on the etymologies of St Isidore of Seville, originally written in the 7th century. The animals are treated in Book VII, in a series of chapters, one of which is entitled *De Avibus*.

Other works with natural history themes soon followed, including **C. von Megenburg's Buch der Natur** in 1475, the GAZA's edition of **Aristotle's Historia animalium** in 1476 and **Albertus Magnus' De Animalibus** book 23 in 1478, all with sections on birds.

The first work ever published which was devoted entirely to birds was by **William Turner**, an Englishman then resident in Germany, whose **Avium Praecipuarum quarum apud Plinium et Aristotelem mentio est brevis & succincta historia** was printed in Latin at Cologne in 1544. Few copies still exist.

Turner was born at Morpeth, Northumberland in about 1500. He was the son of a tanner and went to Pembroke Hall, Cambridge in 1526. Two of his friends were burned at the stake for heresy and his Protestant beliefs forced him to seek refuge on the Continent from religious persecution. While at Cambridge he developed a deep interest in birds, particularly those of the Fens which were then largely undrained and reached near to the town of Cambridge. Then there were huge numbers of birds in the area, including species such as cranes, which no longer breed in Britain.

In *Avium Praecipuarum Historia* Turner made one of the first serious attempts to separate folklore and mythology from reality, and he tried hard to be accurate and introduce order into the naming of birds. Some of the old fallacies were included, but so were his own original and accurate observations. Of some 130 species described 25 were domesticated or foreign to England,

Geese were among the earliest domesticated birds. This painting is from the tomb of Ne-fer-Maat and Itet, circa 2,600 BC. (British Museum)

but at least 15 were mentioned for the first time in a written work. Also in 1544, Turner edited **Dialogue de Avibus**, a bird book written by Gybertus Longolius, who lived in Utrecht but died before its completion. In later life Turner was Dean of Wells and he devoted much of his spare time to his *Herbal* and botany before he died in London in 1568.

The first bird book devoted to birds and written in the English language was **The Ornithology of Francis Willughby**, edited by John Ray and published in London in 1678 (Willughby's notes were published in Latin in 1676). This large book of 460 pages measured about 38 cm (15 in) by 25 cm (10 in) and had 80 engraved plates. The major part of it was by Ray. He and Willughby had collaborated for many years and when Willughby died in 1672 his notes for a book on birds were given to Ray along with a legacy. These notes were largely descriptions of birds' plumages and scant basis for what Ray was to develop into the first genuine bird book to be published in Britain. Ray was well-travelled and made extensive original observations, many of an analytical scientific nature. Species whose existence he doubted were relegated to an appendix and, unlike most of his contemporaries, he omitted fanciful birds such as the harpy, griffin and phoenix. His book is regarded as the basis of scientific ornithology in Britain. However, he had many sources such as Merrett and Charleton, who

published in Latin, and Sir Thomas Browne, whose notes on the birds of Norfolk were not actually published till 1836.

There were several earlier books devoted to falconry. The first in English was **George Turbevile's Book of Faulconrie or Hawking**, published in 1575, but the first real book about birds was by the emperor **Frederick II** and entitled **De Arta Venandi cum Avibus** (the art of hunting with birds). This was written about AD 1240, but existed only in manuscript until it was printed for the first time in 1596. It is a remarkable book, being not just a treatise on falconry, but also a study of birds as a whole based on original observations and surpassing anything written on the subject until Willughby over 400 years later.

THE EARLIEST BIRD ART
PALEOLITHIC CAVE PAINTINGS
–17,000 years ago
Among the oldest known works of art are Paleolithic cave paintings of birds in hunting scenes, from about 17,000 years ago. Some of the species are realistically depicted. Much later, in about 2400 BC, the ancient Egyptians clearly portrayed **kingfishers** (*Alcedinidae*) and **herons** (*Ardeidae*), and one of the treasures of Tutankhamen's tomb (*c.* 1360 BC) is a painted chest showing the young king hunting **bustards** (*Otididae*) and attended by two **griffon vultures** (*Gyps fulvus*). But the earliest Egyptian bird painting is of six geese, from the tomb of Ne-fer-

Maat at Medum, dating from 3000 BC at least.

In mediaeval Europe tiny bird forms were used to decorate the elaborate borders of manuscripts, psalters and breviaries. Early efforts were stylistic and fabulous, but in the 13th century nature was studied more closely and as a result pictures became more realistic and lively.

The first known serious studies of birds were painted by Emperor Frederick II, who wrote his treatise on falconry, *De Arte Venandi cum Avibus* (now in the Vatican) in the middle of the 13th century. His book contained carefully executed marginal illustrations of hawking scenes and bird life. But the first great artist to make detailed studies of birds was Pisanello, about a century later.

The first British bird artist was John White (active 1577–90), who drew and painted the birds of Virginia and Florida on a voyage made with Sir Walter Raleigh.

THE WORLD'S MOST EXPENSIVE BIRD BOOK
AUDUBON'S BIRDS OF AMERICA – £1.1 million

On 1 February 1984 Sotheby's of London sold a copy of **The Birds of America** by **John James Laforest Audubon** (1785–1851) for £1 million (£1.1 million with commission etc) – the highest price ever paid for any bird book. The bidding started at £400,000 and was completed in one minute.

It was a particularly fine example of this massive double elephant folio book, in which Audubon wanted to depict most of the species life-size on 435 engraved aquatint plates, all coloured by hand by a team under his guidance. Approximately 200 sets of four volumes were distributed, each volume measuring about 100 cm (39.5 in) by 75 cm (29½ in) and weighing a mighty 25 kg (56 lb). It was the largest work ever undertaken in the history of book publishing, but even that was insufficient to portray the larger birds comfortably in life-size. Tall species such as the flamingo had to be fitted in by drooping their necks unnaturally.

The son of a prosperous sea captain and a genteel French-Creole, Audubon was born in Haiti. At 15 he started to draw French birds and in 1803 he went to America, to one of his father's plantations in Philadelphia. He led a leisured life but pursued a keen interest in birds. Fortunately for art, he did not have his father's business acumen and his various trading enterprises were failures. For example, when he opened a general store in Kentucky in 1810, he left his partner in full charge while he roamed the countryside. But at that time he struck up a friendship with famous frontiersman Daniel Boone, who is said to have given him tips on how to shoot. Indeed, shooting was very important to Audubon as he was a keen collector of birds. In his book, he frequently refers to the palatability of species – not just owls, loons, cormorants and crows, but also juncos, white-throated sparrows and robins. But far more birds fell to his gun than were ever needed for drawing, research or food. He once said that it was not really a good day unless he shot 100 birds, though later he regretted this, and the loss of his hearing through so much firing of his gun.

There were no binoculars or cameras in Audubon's day so fresh specimens were invaluable to him in drawing natural, relaxed poses before the birds were stuffed for his own museum. Audubon was also keenly interested in bird behaviour, and must have been one of the first persons ever to ring birds: he bound silver threads around the legs of nestlings.

Some of the birds which Audubon painted were on the verge of extinction. His carbonated warbler has never been seen since and the greak auk is gone for ever. So too have the Carolina parakeet and the passenger pigeon which were then very common. He travelled endlessly and extensively in search of new species, but some he

GALLINULA CHLOROPUS.

Moorhens – one of the fine, hand-coloured prints from John Gould's Birds of Great Britain, *which sold for a record £36,000 in 1985. (Sotheby's)*

claimed as new were merely local variants.

The idea for his book came when Alexander Wilson showed him his own work on the birds of America and Audubon rightly surmised that he could do better. But he did have some help with the paintings, notably from Joseph Mason, who was his apprentice, later to become a partner specializing in painting the flowers.

It was not easy to get the book published. Audubon tried to find a publisher in Philadelphia and the eastern USA, but failed and went to England, arriving at Liverpool in July 1826. He proceeded to Edinburgh where he met William Lizars, who agreed to help, but when the workers there went on strike Audubon had to go to Havell in London and he frequently changed the artist's designs.

They planned to publish the plates separately in groups of five because if the work had accompanying text in the eyes of the law it would have been a book

proper and Audubon would then have had to deposit a copy in each of nine copyright libraries at $1,000 each! Thus the text, entitled *Ornithological Biography*, was published separately in 1838, a few months after the last groups of plates was completed and 12 years after the entire massive undertaking was begun.

The cost of the first edition was £28,910 13s 7½d. Only about 134 complete sets are now known: 94 are in the USA, 17 in England and 12 elsewhere. There are also incomplete sets.

The highest price ever obtained for a book on British birds was £36,000 for **John Gould's Birds of Great Britain** 1862–73, a five-volume work auctioned by Sotheby's of London on 8 November 1985. Only 500 sets were produced and the very large hand-coloured plates were works of art in themselves, quality varying with the colourist.

Assisted by several other accomplished artists, including

famous nonsense poet Edward Lear, Gould produced other large bird books with fine hand-coloured plates. On 25 August 1985 Australian auctioneers Kenneth Hince sold a copy of Gould's *Birds of Australia* 1848–69 for a record price of A$215,000. The seven large folio volumes contained 681 plates, compared with just 353 in *Birds of Great Britain*.

John Gould also had the dubious distinction of being the first person known to have made a pet of a budgerigar.

THE MOST EXPENSIVE BIRD PAINTING
$290,000 (£147,959)

The most expensive original painting with birds as the main subject was the *Menagerie* by **Melchior Hondecoeter** (1636–95), which was sold on 6 December 1981 by Christie's of New York for $290,000 (£147,959). It depicts pelican, flamingo, heron, cockatoo, ducks and other birds in a park.

Hondecoeter was the last and best of a family of Dutch painters who specialized in still-life and scenes of birds, many of them exotic, his specialty being the representation of a farmyard or a courtyard containing a great number of different birds. He was the pupil of his father Gysbert (1604–53) and of his uncle J. B. Weenix, and worked at The Hague and Amsterdam. His numerous pictures include examples in the Royal Collection, Amsterdam (Rijksmuseum), Boston, Brussels, Cardiff, Cologne, Derby, Glasgow, The Hague, London's National Gallery and Wallace Collection, Lyons, Munich, New York's Metropolitan Museum, Nottingham, the Louvre in Paris and Amsterdam's Academy.

The record price for a painting by Haiti-born **John James Laforest Audubon** is £56,100 for a study of chaffinch, bullfinch and greenfinch, sold by Sotheby's in March 1980. The record price for a print from Audubon's famous book *Birds of America* is $45,100 for a trumpeter

swan sold by Sotheby's New York in June 1983.

In July 1984 Sotheby's London sold an album of 20 bird watercolours, by the great English landscape artist **Turner**, for £200,000, but individually the paintings of British artist **Archibald Thorburn** (1860–1935) are more expensive. So far the record for a Thorburn is £23,760, paid for the watercolour *A Cock and two Hen Pheasants*, at Christie's of London on 28 April 1986.

THE WORLD'S FIRST RESERVES AND OBSERVATORIES

The first person known to have taken special steps to protect birds on his own land was **Charles Waterton** (1782–1865) of **Yorkshire**, who is generally regarded as the father of nature conservation. He was certainly the first Englishman to establish a wildlife sanctuary simply for its intrinsic value and interest. He built a high wall around his Walton Hall estate, forbade his keepers to shoot vermin there, put up nestboxes and elaborated other nest-sites. Although himself a keen collector of specimens around the world, in Britain he did much to dissuade other landowners from unnecessary slaughter of many birds. But such beginnings were a long way from the public purchase of land specifically for management as bird and nature reserves.

Most of the earliest publicly owned reserves were established for all nature rather than birds only. The earliest to have been set aside primarily for its ornithological interest was probably **Lake Merritt** in **California**. In 1852 Samuel Merritt of Oakland bought land which was then a slough and developed it into a body of water known as Lake Merritt. This was certainly America's first official wildlife refuge, recognized under Californian state law passed in 1870, and the main interest seems to have been in the large numbers of waterfowl found there.

America's first National Park was **Yellowstone** in **Wyoming**, declared in 1872 to be the first wildlife refuge for the nation, where many exciting mammals and species of bird could roam freely without fear of or competition with human activity.

In 1900, **William Dutcher**, the principal founder and first president of America's **National Audubon Society**, hired the first wardens to guard seabird colonies on islands in Maine. By 1904 the Society was financing 34 wardens in ten states and on 8 July 1905 one of them, Guy Bradley, was shot to death while guarding a great rookery of egrets, ibises and roseate spoonbills at **Cape Sable, Florida**, in what is now the **Everglades National Park**.

Mounting concern over slaughter primarily for the plume trade led to President Roosevelt declaring **Pelican Island**, on the Indian River on Florida's east coast, America's first **National Wildlife Refuge** in 1903. Before the Civil War, Pelican Island's four acres were covered by thick mangroves and a colony of herons, ibises and roseate spoonbills splashed the sky with colour. But an over-abundance of nesting birds and a severe frost in 1886 killed the mangroves, and the plume hunters later killed remaining birds. Pelican Island became a treeless mudflat taken over by nesting brown pelicans and it was to protect these that the refuge was set up.

Roosevelt was keenly interested in birds and by the time he left office in 1901 he had created 51 bird reservations on public land.

In Britain, bird conservation really got underway in 1888 when the **Breydon Society** purchased one of the choicest **Norfolk Broads** – **Breydon Water** – famous for its wildfowl. Then in 1899, the **National Trust** began to acquire its first nature reserve, **Wicken Fen** in Cambridgeshire, though there was as much interest in its plants and insects as in its birds. This is generally regarded as **Britain's oldest nature reserve** and covers 605 acres. Its secluded open water is very attractive to migrant and wintering wildfowl, but the reed fringes also support a wide variety of songbirds, including bearded tit (reedling) (*Panurus biarmicus*) and Cetti's warbler (*Cettia cetti*).

The first property acquired by the National Trust primarily for its bird interest was **Blakeney Point**, a strip of land on the north **Norfolk** coast, taken on in 1912, followed by **Scolt Head**, also on the north Norfolk coast, in 1923, and the **Farne Islands** off **Northumberland** in 1925.

The **first British county naturalist trust reserve** was **Cley Marshes**, acquired by the **Norfolk Naturalists Trust** in 1926, where breeding species include avocet (*Recurvirostra avosetta*), bearded tit and Eurasian bittern (*Botaurus stellaris*), and rare visitors include white spoonbill (*Platalea leucorodia*).

The **Royal Society for the Protection of Birds'** first reserve was **Cheyne Court** on Romney Marsh in **Kent**, which was acquired at the end of the 1920s but subsequently sold. **Eastwood** at **Staley Bridge** and **Dungeness** in **Kent** were both acquired at the beginning of the 1930s and are still under RSPB ownership.

Western Europe's first bird observatory was unofficially established at the home of **Heinrich Gätke** on **Heligoland** island, near Germany, where he lived from 1837 till his death in 1897. Gätke coined the term 'bird observatory' though his house at the former British colony (1807–90) did not become a proper observatory till 1910. The **first official European observatory** was set up in 1901 at **Rositten**, then in **Germany** and now **Rybachi** in **Russia**. It is still a bird observatory.

Skokholm Island off **south-west Wales** was **Britain's first bird observatory**. First leased by R. M. Lockley in 1927, it was established in 1933. In 1948 it was leased to the West Wales Field Society and administered by the Field Studies Council till 1969. Since then Skokholm has been in the care of the West Wales Naturalists Trust, but the observatory closed in 1976.

THE LARGEST BIRD-PROTECTION ORGANIZATIONS

The world's major conservation organizations are concerned with all aspects of wildlife welfare and study, not just birds. Of these the largest is the **National Wildlife Federation of the USA**, which is based in Washington and has 4.6 million members and supporters and 51 affiliated organizations nationwide. Founded in 1936, this private, non-profit-making organization is concerned with education, research and liaison with governmental and private conservation bodies.

The **Canadian Wildlife Federation** has over 528,000 members and supporters. Another very important organization is the **National Audubon Society**, based in New York, which has over 550,000 members 'working at international, national, regional, state and local levels towards the preservation and wise use of America's national heritage'. The **World Wildlife Fund** has a worldwide membership of about 1 million and a UK membership of 100,000 subscribers and some 400,000 supporters. World Wildlife Fund US has 172,000 members.

Of organizations concerned mainly with birds, the world's largest is **Ducks Unlimited Inc** of **North America**, with over 600,000 members. Founded in 1937, it is a non-profit-making and non-political corporation.

The **largest bird-protection organization in Europe** is the **Royal Society for the Protection of Birds**, based at Sandy, Bedfordshire, England. In August 1986 it had a membership of 427,570 plus 81,584 in its Young Ornithologists' Club. Founded in 1889, it was originally called the Fur and Feather Group and was started in Didsbury, Manchester by a small group of women protesting at the barbaric trade in plumes for the hat business. By 1960 the membership had reached 10,500, but shot up to 65,677 by 1970 and between 1976 and 1986 it doubled. Now it is Europe's largest voluntary conservation organization and manages 116 reserves throughout the UK, covering over 100 square miles (259 sq km) of some of the country's best bird habitat. Of this area 46% is owned and 17% leased, with the remainder being managed by licence or informal agreement with the landowner. In recent years the Society has also made an enormous contribution towards the international conservation of birds and is certainly the most dynamic force in ornithological circles today.

THE LARGEST BIRD EGG AND SPECIMEN COLLECTION
THE BRITISH MUSEUM'S WITH OVER 2¼ MILLION ITEMS

The world's largest collection of bird specimens of all types is that of the **British Museum of Natural History's** sub-department of Ornithology at **Tring, Hertfordshire**. In 1986 it contained about 1¼ million bird skins, 12,000 fluid-preserved specimens, 6,000 skeletons, 1 million eggs and 2,000 nests.

The **American Museum of Natural History** in **New York** also has a very impressive collection with over 850,000 skins, 50,000 incomplete specimens (skins, wings, feathers, exhibition material etc), 17,000 skeletons, 45,000 eggs, 14,000 fluid-preserved specimens, 12,000 nests and 10,000 uncatalogued specimens. The museum's chairman, Lester Short, believes that this bird collection is 'scientifically the most significant in the world' because of the high percentage of good condition, accurately identified specimens useful to researchers.

The **Western Foundation of Vertebrate Zoology** at **Los Angeles**, California has the second largest egg collection in the world. It houses about 160,000 clutches with full data and approximately 25,000 clutches with insufficient or no data whatsoever. Each clutch averages 3–4 eggs so the entire collection includes some 555,000–740,000 eggs. It has been assembled from some 250 individual collections from all around the world.

Although display and education are chief concerns of the world's great natural history museums, they are primarily research institutions supported by libraries, technical facilities and specialist staff. Many are based on the early accumulations of wealthy collectors who were more interested in numbers and gathered together as many 'curiosities of nature' as they could in the days before photography made them available to everyone. A large number of the birds still in collections were specially shot in the 19th and early 20th centuries. For example, Lord Walsingham bagged many of the hummingbirds now in the British Museum using a special dust shot to minimize damage.

A record £9,000 was paid for this stuffed great auk in 1971. It is now in the Natural History Museum, Reykjavik, Iceland. (Eric Hosking)

THE MOST EXPENSIVE STUFFED BIRD
A GREAT AUK at £9,000

The highest price ever paid for a stuffed bird or bird skin was **£9,000** for a **great auk** (*Pinguinus impennis*) at a Sotheby's London auction in 1971. The bird, in summer plumage, had been collected by the naturalist Count Raben in Iceland in 1821 and it was bought by the director of the Iceland Natural History Museum, who later said that he would have bid up to £23,000 for the extreme rarity.

The now extinct great auk once bred in Norway, Iceland, southern Greenland and down the east coast of North America as far as the St Lawrence, and wintered regularly as far as Cape Cod. It was still abundant in the late 18th century, but by the mid-19th century it had been exterminated by white men for food and commercial gain. The largest North American colony on the Funk Islands off the east coast of Newfoundland was decimated between 1830 and 1841, though there was an unconfirmed sighting near the Grand Bank of Newfoundland in 1852. For generations the species had been traditional food on fishing and other vessels around Britain and Scandinavia. Adults and young were killed and salted down or even kept alive on board as a valuable source of fresh meat. The eggs were collected and the young birds commonly used as fishing bait. They were also a source of oil and their feathers were used for stuffing mattresses.

Collecting the great auk was easy because the bird was flightless, awkward on land and unafraid of man. The sailors simply walked among the colonies clubbing the birds to death. The last positive record is of a bird killed on Eldey Island, Iceland in June 1844. The species probably ceased to breed in Britain long before this, but a bird was captured alive in Waterford Harbour, south-east Ireland, in 1834, and beaten to death by the local people who thought it was a witch.

Today all that remains of the great auk is about 80 stuffed specimens and four skeletons.

In most countries, sale of bird skins is now carefully controlled by law. In Britain, for example, they must be registered, though some are still acquired for the market illegally. But prices are not what they used to be, with a **golden eagle** (*Aquila chrysaetos*) fetching only £600–£800. British taxidermists are now obliged to keep records showing where each item originated from.

THE MOST EXPENSIVE EGG
ONE OF THE EXTINCT AEPYORNIS MAXIMUS AT £1,000
£1,000

There is no way of knowing what large sums have been paid privately and illegally for rare birds' eggs, but the highest price paid in legal auction was **£1,000** for an example of the extinct **Aepyornis maximus**, at Sotheby's London sale in March 1971. *Aepyornis maximus* was one of the heaviest birds that ever lived and laid the largest eggs ever known.

This flightless bird inhabited Madagascar and its egg held more than two gallons – eight times the volume of an ostrich egg. Undamaged eggs are still found after the heavy, seasonal rains have washed them out of the soil in certain parts of the island, the species probably having become extinct about 1,500–2,000 years ago.

Today egg-collecting is illegal in many countries, though sadly a small number of fanatical collectors continue to hound the rarest of birds. In Britain it is now illegal to possess the egg of any wild bird taken after the introduction of the Wildlife and Countryside Act 1981 – that is from September 1982. However, earlier eggs might still be liable for confiscation under the Police (Property) Act 1897. Penalties for offences range from £400 for the majority of species to £2,000 for a species included in Schedule I of the Act, with a separate penalty in respect of each egg.

The rarer the egg, the higher the price it will fetch illegally. In recent years, the nest of one of the first few **Ross's gulls** (*Rhodostethia rosea*) to have bred in Canada was robbed and it is said that the eggs were sold for **$10,000**.

THE MOST FEARED BIRDS
CROWS and OWLS

For as far back as we can trace, **crows** (*Corvidae*) have struck fear into the hearts of superstitious people across the world. The **raven** (*Corvus corax*) in particular, in its 'black as death' plumage, has been thought to spell doom. A long-held superstition is that should the Tower of London lose its ravens then disaster will befall the realm. The **carrion crow** (*Corvus corone*) and the **magpie** (*Pica pica*) are thought to be tricky or clever and are frequently associated with misfortune or mischief. Much of their reputation is no doubt due to their habit of feasting on carrion. It

is believed that a crow striking at the window is summoning a human soul to the grave.

Owls (*Strigidae*) too are frequently associated with doom and disaster. Since ancient times they have been connected with the black arts in both hemispheres, though since the mysteries of their nocturnal lives have been unravelled they have become much more popular.

THE GREATEST BIRD-PEST PROBLEM
AIRCRAFT LOSS and DAMAGE involving human deaths

Quite apart from the occasional associated loss of human life, bird damage to aircraft causes great economic loss every year. Worldwide, this was put at over 1,000 million US dollars in 1976. In North America alone, from 1960 to 1972, losses were calculated to be more than $100 million and in the 1980s US carriers have been suffering damage costing $24–30 million

This United States Airforce chart shows how the number of bird strikes on aircraft is concentrated at lower levels. As a result, pilots are advised to approach airfields as steeply as possible.

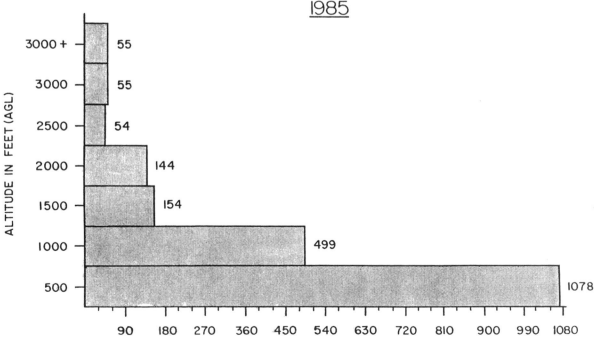

annually. A study conducted by the Federal Aviation Adminstration during 1983 and 1984 showed that **gulls** (*Laridae*) and the **black kite** (*Milvus migrans*) were the species most commonly involved.

In Britain the Royal Air Force has estimated losses at 'millions of pounds' annually, though no special cost analysis is thought justifiable. The Ministry of Defence reports that **gulls** are involved in most birdstrikes to military aircraft and this has been the case for many years in much of Europe. An analysis of military aircraft birdstrikes for several European countries 1978–84 revealed that **gulls** were involved in 28.6% of incidents, **pigeons** (*Columbidae*) 10.2%, **swallows, swifts** and **martins** (*Hirundinidae* and *Apodidae*) 14.5% and the **lapwing** (*Vanellus vanellus*) 9.2%.

The UK Civil Aviation Authority found that, in 1983, of the 405 cases (76% of incidents) where identification of bird remains was possible, gulls were involved on 40% of occasions, similar to the average for the previous five years. The **black-headed gull** (*Larus ribundus*) was the gull most frequently struck (15%), but more involved than any species was the **lapwing** (19%). The rate for birdstrikes was 5.2 per 10,000 aircraft movements, the same as in 1982, and 65% of all strikes were at or near aerodromes.

For the period 1976–80 the CAA reported damage to over 330 engines and the loss of a Boeing 737 and a Learjet. The engineering costs were estimated to be about $17 million plus $4.5 million for the Boeing and $1.5 million for replacement of the Learjet.

The worst aircraft birdstrike involving loss of human life was on 4 October 1960, when a Lockheed LI88 Electra took off from Boston Airport, USA and a flock of starlings was ingested by the engines. Of the 72 people on board, 62 were killed and nine seriously injured.

On 23 November 1962 a 6 kg (13 lb) **whistling swan** (*Cygnus columbianus*) in a flock shattered the tailplane of a Vicker's Viscount flying at 2,000 m (6,000 ft) above Maryland, USA. The aircraft went into an uncontrolled dive and all 17 occupants were killed.

A more unusual strike occurred on 26 February 1973 when a Lear 24 ingested **cowbirds** (*Molothus ater*) into its engines at Atlanta, USA and all seven occupants were killed and a bystander seriously injured. A man was killed when a **vulture** struck the windscreen of a Douglas DC3 at Lahore on 15 July 1962 and another on 7 April 1981 when a **loon** (*Gavia immer*) hit the windscreen of a Lear 23 over Lunken, Cincinnati, USA.

AGRICULTURE'S WORST BIRD PEST
THE RED-BILLED QUELEA

Although the **red-billed quelea** (*Quelea quelea*) is said to be Africa's, and probably the world's, most significant bird pest in agriculture, with a continent-wide damage level of some US $22 million per annum, the loss amounts to less than 1% of Africa's cereal production. But damage caused can be so devastating that it frequently spells disaster for many subsistence farmers who lose an entire year's food supply. The main crops affected are sorghum, millet, rice and wheat.

The red-billed quelea is the world's most abundant bird and an individual eats about 3 g (0.1 oz) of food per day and dislodges about 7 g (0.25 oz) so that its total destructive power is about 10 g (0.35 oz) per day. This can be higher if an unripe crop is attacked. Damage is very concentrated as the species feeds, breeds and roosts gregariously. It is a tropical and sub-tropical weaver-bird related to the finches and ranges over much of central and southern Africa.

The bulk of the quelea's diet is of smaller wild grass seeds, and even in years of severe damage only 20% of quelea food intake is of cultivated cereals. The trouble starts at the end of the dry seasons when shortage of their natural food forces the vast quelea flocks into the river valleys favoured for agricultural crops. At the onset of the rains any remaining seeds rapidly germinate and the quelea faces starvation. Then the already large flocks merge and wander over vast areas in search of places where earlier rains have already replenished seed stocks, both wild and cultivated.

Killing has been the main method in attempting to solve the quelea problem, but infliction of heavy mortality has failed to achieve an overall population reduction, especially as the bird often breeds in areas completely inaccessible to control units. Flame-throwers, dynamite bombs and aerial spraying of poisons and detergents have brought about an estimated annual slaughter of 1,000 million birds, but these methods are inappropriate for use in urban areas, irrespective of their inhumaneness and impact on other wildlife.

More traditional methods of quelea control include the use of native boys to guard strategic points and frighten off intruders with drums, rattles and flashing tins. A boy is usually positioned in some high vantage point with strings leading to noise-making devices in the fields. It is recognized that the quelea will eventually settle and cause damage somewhere so the aim is to ensure that no one person suffers disproportionately.

OTHER SERIOUS BIRD PESTS
RED-WINGED BLACKBIRD, STARLING and WOODPIGEON
The only other species which might rival the red-billed quelea as the world's greatest bird pest in farming and growing are the **red-winged blackbird** (*Agelaius phoeniceus*) of North and central America and the widely introduced **European starling** (*Sturnus vulgaris*). Surveys conducted in 1970 and 1971 showed nationwide USA losses of ripening corn to blackbirds of $15–20 million. But losses to emerging corn by **common grackles** (*Quiscalus quiscula*) and **ring-necked pheasants** (*Phasianus colchicus*) could

be even more important at up to $49 million in 1971. The blackbird is also responsible for great damage to rice, for example causing a loss of $4.2 million in 1963 in Arkansas alone.

In 1976 Canadian agricultural losses, primarily of wheat, to seed-eating birds amounted to $86 million in ten provinces and $33 million in four provinces to waterfowl.

The **starling** eats large amounts of soft fruits – for example, German grapes and cherries worth US $2.5 million annually in the 1960s. Its huge roosts cause physical damage to trees through the sheer weight of birds breaking branches, but this is insignificant compared with the chemical action of accumulated droppings which either kill the trees or inhibit growth. Under some British roosts the droppings are over 30 cm (12 in) thick and will kill the trees via the root system. In just one British forest of 7,500 ha (18,532 acres) of pine and spruce some 40 ha (100 acres) was expected to be totally lost to starling damage, thus writing off £360,000 potential income. More generally, the result is a reduction in timber value of about 60%.

Starling roosts also cause great damage to buildings through the chemical action of their droppings. In London, the City of Westminster employed a man to clean the starling droppings from Leicester Square each morning at a cost of £5,600 per annum in 1985, and the City Cleansing Department spent a further £29,330 annually cleaning up after starlings.

In addition, the starling causes a lot of damage to germinating winter cereals. But the most serious economic loss it causes in Britain is through consumption of cattle food. Figures are not available nationally, but it is known that the starling can eat up to 10% of barley put out for cattle.

Britain's most serious agricultural bird pest is the **woodpigeon** (*Columba palumbus*), which is known to cause millions of pounds worth of damage annually. Originally it was a woodland bird, relying on staple foods such as acorns and beech-mast, which might fail completely in some years. Stand-by foods such as ivy berries and weed seeds were never abundant or nutritious enough to see a large population through the winter. But the arrival of crops such as kale, turnips, clover and brassicae, which stood through the winter, allowed the woodpigeon's numbers to multiply rapidly. The situation became so serious after the last war the Ministry of Agriculture provided a cartridge subsidy to shoot pigeons, but after a while the futility of this was appreciated and now the reliance is on sport shooting. The breeding stock is put at 3–5 million pairs, but the population at the end of July probably doubles by the end of September and natural winter mortality is countered by an influx of migrants.

After a period of some stability, woodpigeon numbers again grew rapidly when oilseed rape became very popular, from the early 1970s. Now the woodpigeon has adopted the unusual position in being the most serious pest of this crop, even above insects. Many farmers have claimed that this is the reason why they have given up growing oilseed rape.

THE MOST HUNTED AND EATEN WILD BIRDS

The flesh of most birds is probably palatable, and even highly palatable, to man, but this century the development of most countries has done away with the need for subsistence hunting of wild species. Yet some large crops are still taken. For example, about 500,000 **short-tailed shearwaters** ('mutton birds') (*Puffinus tenuirostris*) are taken annually in Australia.

In economically and socially advanced countries such as the USA and Britain hunting for the pot now revolves around sport and concentrates on a small number of common species, particularly in the pheasant, partridge, grouse, duck, goose, wader and pigeon families.

For example, in the USA the most harvested bird is the **mourning dove** (*Zenaida macroura*), with an average annual harvest of 50 million out of an estimated total fall population of 500 million. In Britain the most hunted birds are the **pheasant** (*Phasianus colchicus*) and the **wood-pigeon** (*Columba palumbus*). Some 12–15 million pheasants are shot each year, but at least that number are released specifically for sporting purposes. The **woodpigeon** bag consists entirely of wild birds and is considerably more difficult to monitor, but is thought to be in the region of 12–16 million. Despite such a bag the woodpigeon appears to be increasing in numbers and remains Britain's most significant bird pest for farmers.

Bags of migratory species such as ducks and geese are very difficult to assess unless individual records are compulsory. According to the 1980 *Survey of Hunting, Fishing and Wildlife-Associated Recreation* prepared by the US Department of the Interior Fish and Wildlife Service, approximately 5.3 million Americans hunted migratory birds in 1980. As well as waterfowl, migratory species include doves and pigeons, cranes, woodcock and some gamebirds. In 1985 the most commonly shot ducks in the USA were **mallard** (*Anas platyrhynchos*) – 3,234,800 (3,954,100 in 1984) and **green-winged teal** (*Anas crecca*) – 1,001,500 (1,270,100 in 1984), in a total duck bag of 11,033,200 (15,029,700 in 1984). The most commonly shot **goose** was the **Canada** (*Branta canadensis*) – 1,152,700 (1,160,700 in 1984) in a total goose bag of 1,953,400 (2,141,600 in 1984). In Britain the total number of ducks shot each year is thought to be under 1 million, the most commonly bagged being the widely-reared **mallard** (*Anas platyrhynchos*) followed by the **teal** (*Anas crecca*) and then the **wigeon** (*Anas penelope*).

But wildfowl stock replenishment is good in Britan and the USA, the latter having an excellent national refuge system. In the USSR over 30 million ducks, geese and other species such as coots are shot each year and in Sweden sport hunters shoot more than 70% of each year's mallard crop.

However, in many countries there is an irresponsible and indiscriminate bag of non-game and sometimes protected species shot chiefly for the pot. It is estimated that the 25 million or so migratory birds killed around the Mediterranean each year, largely for food, represent 10–15% of available stocks. In Malta, where one in eight men is a licensed hunter, some 1½ million birds are trapped each year and there are now only 13 breeding species on the island. Cyprus is even worse, with up to 10 million birds shot, netted or limed annually – between a half and three-quarters of all migrants, including thrushes, warblers, buntings and other small songbirds – for the pot. In the Lebanon 15–20 million birds of all sorts are killed each year and in Greece the huge toll includes birds such as the **golden oriole** (*Oriolus oriolus*) and the **red-footed falcon** (*Falco vespertinus*).

WORLD CHAMPION BIRD SPOTTERS

With the explosion of interest in birdwatching and much greater mobility of enthusiasts in recent decades, the sport of bird listing, or 'twitching', has really taken off. Served by their own American Birding Association, USA listers in particular have travelled the globe in search of new species – 'ticks'. Now they have a whole host of categories too. As well as the basic life, year and day lists, birders often compile two-day, backyard, hometown, county, state, month, breeding-bird, season and early-spring lists.

At first, listers had a bad name as a bunch of fanatics who rode roughshod over coast and countryside, often gathering in large numbers to harass rarities for the sake of just another sighting – a rather eccentric form of one-upmanship which went against the spirit of true birdwat-

ching. The reality is that most of these enthusiasts are very responsible people who employ great skill, along with a little help from the 'bush telegraph', to see wide varieties of birds which more lethargic watchers can only dream of.

The USA alone has over 11 million birdwatchers, many of whom are serious listers. The 600 Club is an elite organization open only to those birders who have seen 600 or more species in North America in accordance with geographical and ethical guidelines laid down by the ABA. As only about 650 species breed in North America, membership of the 600 Club is achieved only by the dedicated few. Britain has no equivalent to the 600 Club, nor even an equivalent of the ABA, though there is talk of an organization being established to regulate the present system. In all countries, acceptance of new sightings depends on the observer's word as a gentleman, though records of extreme rarities and vagrants are more likely to be accepted among fellow enthusiasts and ratified by the rare-bird committees when the person reporting is known to be reliable and experienced.

Today birding has been taken to such extremes that becoming the record holder of a major list, such as the national year list, will involve great sacrifice of time and money, not to mention flexibility in taking time off work and skill in organizing travel link-ups.

THE WORLD LIFE LIST RECORD HOLDER

STUART STOKES with 7,128 species
Establishing which bird spotter has seen the most species in a lifetime is not easy as some seek no publicity at all and do not submit entries for the few published lists. Such a man is British businessman Stuart Stokes, who now spends most of the year based in Florida. In October 1981 the American Birding Association reported (Supplement to *Birding* Vol 13, p. 193) that Stuart had seen 6,150 species by 31.12.80.

One of the world's most successful bird spotters, Canada's Norman Chesterfield. In 1986, at the age of 73, he had listed 6,220 species.

But recently a reliable source reported that Stuart has now seen at least 7,128 species.

Champion among those who submit their records for publication is Ontario mink rancher **Norman Chesterfield** who, by September 1986, at the age of 73, had listed 6,220 species, yet he did not even buy his first pair of binoculars till he was aged 42, in 1955. Now looking back over a very full life, he says 'I'd like to have started about 20 years sooner and I believe I would have been able to reach the 7000 mark, but at my age it is not a realistic goal. My last mountain to climb is 500 species for Canada. As of now I have 495. Most of my additions at this point are first records for Canada so they are becoming rather slow'.

In tracking down so many species, Norman has visited over 130 countries, his most recent trip being to Indonesia for a month in March and April, 1986 when he was delighted to see the crowned pigeon *Coura* after missing it in 1983. But the sighting which has given him the most enjoyment so far was the hyacinth macaw *Anodorhynchus hyacinthinus*, the world's largest parrot which, after many years hunting, he saw on the Araguia River – a tributary of the Amazon in central Brazil. Since then a reliable nesting spot has been found and the bird is no longer difficult to see.

Once in Mexico Norman ran into a local uprising and soldiers fired at his car. In Peru he experienced a severe earthquake and in Venezuela he was held for 12 hours, along with another unfortunate lister, by over-zealous soldiers looking for drug smugglers.

In the USA the world list requires sight identification, so Norman carries a small tape recorder to flush out skulking species from the undergrowth. He records a promising call and immediately plays it back, when the chances are that the hiding bird will charge out to take on the invading stranger. But now having seen some 70% of the world's birds, Norman is running out of places to go and quarry to track down.

The North American life list record is 765 **species** seen by **Benton Basham** of **Ooltewah**, Tennessee.

Another American, **Peter G. Kaestner** of Washington, is the **first person known to have seen a representative of all the world's 159 bird families**. He achieved his goal on 1 October 1986 when he saw a rufous gnateater (*Conopophaga lineata*) at Iguassu Falls in South America.

BRITAIN'S LIFE LIST RECORD HOLDER

RON JOHNS with 462 species

The person who has seen the most species in Britain during a lifetime is **Ron Johns** of **Slough, Berkshire, England**, with about **462** at the end of 1986, well ahead of his nearest rival, **Chris Heard**, on **449**. A British Gas higher management officer, Johns stresses that 462 is an approximate figure as there are always a few awaiting ratification.

Johns says that he did not set out to become a record holder and has become so only fortuitously, through his own enthusiasm. He started birding in 1952 at the age of 11 and still has his first notes, made on 3 September that year. Since then he has always been so busy in the field that he trusts most things to memory and writes it all up on returning home each evening.

One of about 1,000 hard-core British birders, Ron has been to most parts of the British Isles in search of birds, travelling some 30–40,000 miles in a year, frequently by specially chartered planes and helicopters. One favourite haunt of birders is the Scilly Isles, where Ron has been at least 50 times. He spends about 30 weekends a year based at his Norfolk cottage, a great birding county, and in 1985 he was found at home on only two weekends. Fortunately for him, Mrs Johns is also an enthusiastic birder.

A member of the Rarities Committee for eight years, Johns stresses how important it is to establish a reputation, even though 'there is a remarkable degree of trust and fabrication of records is very rare'. Both he and his wife use Leitz 8 × 40 binoculars and Nikon ED telescopes. Some rarities he has seen alone, but more often he first hears of a potential tick through a telephone call late one evening. Then he must drop everything to dash off and see the bird next day before it has moved on. This 'grapevine' reporting is extremely effective and has resulted in up to 3,000 people travelling specially to see one bird. Birding now adds signifi-

Two British champion bird spotters: Ron Johns (right) is life list record holder and Bryan Bland is day list record holder. (R.K. Coles)

cantly to the tourist trade of the Scilly Isles and the holiday season there has been specially extended into November, though some landowners have cashed in and will charge a fee to see special birds.

Johns' latest was a **red-necked stint** (*Calidris ruficollis*) (a first for GB) seen at Blacktoft Sands, Humberside.

THE WORLD YEAR LIST RECORD HOLDER
JAMES VARDAMAN of Jackson USA with 2,800

The most species seen in one calendar year by one man is **2,800** by **James Vardaman** of **Jackson, Mississippi, USA**. The wealthy president of James Vardaman & Co, Inc, forest management specialists, Mr Vardaman spent $50,000 in achieving this record in 1984. He says: 'I hope to break my own record in 1988 or later. If a man could spend a whole year birding, he should be able to see 4,500 species without spending a fortune or losing his wife or business.'

Britain's Stuart Stokes (now based in Florida for most of the year) is said to have seen at least 2,500 species in some years.

The North American year list record is **710** species seen by **Benton Basham** of **Ooltewah**, Tennessee.

BRITAIN'S YEAR LIST RECORD HOLDER
LEE EVANS with 340 species

In 1985 Vauxhall Motors design student **Lee Evans** (then aged 25), of **Luton, Bedfordshire**, set a new British year list record in spotting **340** species. He has been taking part in the year list stakes since 1977 and has held the record on four occasions. But he finds it 'a very strenuous and tense pastime, involving travelling the length and breadth of the country each weekend, often in vain search'. In an average year he clocks up 60,000 miles. His farthest twitch has been to see the black-browed albatross on Hermaness in the Shetlands, where he goes every year, as well as to the Outer Hebrides and the Scilly Isles.

Evans' most memorable twitch was a wallcreeper living in a small quarry in Cheddar Gorge. He was so taken by its beauty he spent six hours watching it. At the end of 1986 his life list for Britain stood at **432**, placing him 14th nationally.

Only a handful of twitchers have seen over 300 species in Britain in a single year. It is not too difficult to see 200, but many of the extra 100 or so are irregular visitors or very rare vagrants. Many of these often inconspicuous birds appear briefly at unpredictable and out-of-the-way places. Most are very common abroad and have been blown way off course on migration. Seeing them depends on the twitchers' grapevine and the ability to travel quickly. When computer consultant **Steve Webb** held the British year list record of **330** in 1980 he had to travel over 50,000 miles, spend £4,000 and take two months off work to achieve it.

THE WORLD DAY LIST RECORD
342 species

The most species ever seen in 24 hours were the **342** spotted by **Terry Stevenson, Andy Roberts** and **John Fanshawe** on 30 November 1986 in Kenya. The three Kenyans (two originating from England) had entered a sponsored birdwatch in aid of charity, in competition with other three-man teams to break the world 48-hour record. But they had a transport failure on day one and opted to go for the 24-hour record on day two.

During the event a new 48-hour record was established – **494** species seen by **Don Turner** and **David Pearson** of Kenya, with famous wildlife cameraman **Alan Root** as their recorder. The event raised 1 million Kenyan shillings for a local children's hospital.

The previous day record was probably more remarkable as Americans **Ted Parker** and **Scott Robinson** saw all their **328** species on foot (and briefly in a canoe) within an area of only about one square kilometre in Peru in September 1982. Mr Parker's Peru list is just over **1,600** species – possibly the longest single country list in the world. He works as a staff research associate for Louisiana State University and spends about 6–7 months of each year on expedition to remote parts of the Andes and upper Amazon basin.

The North American day list record is **242** seen by **Greg Lasley** of Austin, Texas.

BRITAIN'S DAY LIST RECORD HOLDER
BRYAN BLAND with 158 species.
The record number of species seen on one day in Britain is **158** spotted by **Bryan Bland** of **Norfolk**, accompanied by **Mark Beaman**, who saw **156**, and American **James Vardaman**, who saw **155**, on 11 May 1982. The team played strictly by ABA rules (the only ones then in existence), which state that a team must not accept any assistance on the day and all species must be discovered and identified by a team member.

The team began the day by covering Norfolk in Bryan Bland's minibus, before taking a jet from Norwich airport to Inverness. They got the pilot to fly low over Bempton Cliffs to spot gannets. Then they progressed to Dornoch and John O'Groats via helicopters and cars.

Pursuit of personal day list records is probably the most popular form of birding in Britain. But record numbers are mostly achieved on highly-organized and well-planned 'big days' for teams who compete to raise money for various charities. In such events the rules are more relaxed than those in the USA and verbal communication plus back-up teams are usually allowed, including scouting territory beforehand. The result is a lot of fun, though the birding is still taken very seriously by skilled spotters.

The record for an English 24-hour sponsored birdwatch is **155** species seen by **Peter Smith, Bill Urwin, Jeremy Sorenson** and **David Tomlinson** on 14 May 1983.

BRITISH REGIONAL RECORDS
London – In 1985 30-year-old London Natural History Society recorder **Rupert Hastings** established a new year list record for the area within a 20-mile radius of St Paul's Cathedral. When he saw a barn owl (*Tyto alba*) near Tilbury on 28 December it took his total to a surprising **200**.

County year list – The record is held by **Tommy Corcoran**, who saw **259** species in Norfolk in 1985. Also in Norfolk that year, **Bryan Bland** saw **254** and **Richard Millington 250**.

County day list – The highest total for any county is **150** seen by **Bryan Bland** in Norfolk on 15 May 1982. He was accompanied by **Peter Milford, Nigel Mears** and **Dave Holman**, who saw **148** or **149**. Next comes Kent, where **David Tomlinson, Don Taylor, Andrew Henderson** and **Bob Bland** saw **143** species on 11 May 1986.

Glossary

AFROTROPICAL REGION One of the six major zoogeographical regions, consisting of Africa south of the Sahara, excluding Madagascar and the Comoro Islands but including the islands of Zanzibar, Mafia, Pemba and the Gulf of Guinea.

AUSTRALASIAN REGION One of the six major zoogeographical regions, consisting of Australia, Tasmania, New Guinea, New Zealand and all island dependencies.

AVES Latin for the class of animals known as birds.

AVICULTURE The keeping and breeding of non-domesticated birds in captivity.

AVIFAUNA The birdlife of an area.

BIOMASS The total weight of organisms per unit area of land or the total weight of organisms of a particular kind (e.g. birds).

BIPEDAL Two-footed, not using the forelimbs for walking.

BIRD-OF-PREY Generally, a species that hunts and kills others for food, but particularly the vultures, ospreys, hawks, eagles, secretary bird, falcons, caracaras and, usually, the owls.

BIRD STRIKE A collision between birds and aircraft.

BROOD The young hatched from a single clutch of eggs (collectively).

CARPAL Of the 'wrist', the carpal joint forming the forward-pointing prominence of the wing.

CLASS A primary grouping or classification of animals, birds forming the class Aves.

CLUTCH The complete set of eggs laid by one female.

CONTOUR FEATHERS The main body feathers, with vanes, which are at least partly firm and flat.

COSMOPOLITAN Distribu-
tional term applied to a species, genus or family generally found in all the main zoogeographical regions, and certainly in both the Old and New Worlds.

COVERT Small feathers covering bird's main wing or tail feathers.

ECHOLOCATION Detecting the presence of nearby objects by emitting sounds and analyzing the echoes which return to the ears.

ECOLOGY The study of plants and animals in relation to their environment.

ETHOLOGY The study of behaviour.

EYRIE The nest of a bird-of-prey, especially an eagle.

FAMILY Grouping of birds with common characteristics (not always obvious and sometimes open to disagreement among biologists) or origins, being a sub-division of an order and a grouping of genera, and thus of species.

FLEDGLING A young bird which has just left the nest and acquired its first true feathers.

GENUS A single species or a grouping of species with common characteristics or origins, being a narrower classification than family.

HALLUX The first toe, usually pointing backwards and much reduced in birds.

HOLARCTIC REGION The Palearctic and Nearctic regions combined.

INVASION Sudden range expansion into new area.

JIZZ Combination of characters which identify a bird or other animal in the field, but which may not be distinguished individually.

METABOLISM The process of biochemical breakdown and synthesis of nutrients within
the cells of all body tissues.

NEARCTIC REGION One of the six major zoogeographical regions, consisting of North America north of the tropics, the southern boundary usually being drawn through Mexico.

NEOTROPICAL REGION One of the six major zoogeographical regions, consisting of tropical America and the non-tropical parts of South America, together with the West Indies and other islands near South America.

NICHE A loose term applied to the full range of environmental conditions within which a species can survive, or its ecological role within a community.

NICTITATING MEMBRANE The transparent fold of skin which can be drawn across a bird's eye to form a third eyelid.

NIDICOLOUS Young birds that remain in the nest after hatching.

NIDIFUGOUS Young birds that leave the nest immediately or soon after hatching.

OLFACTORY BULBS Parts of the forebrain concerned with the sense of smell.

OMNIVOROUS Having a varied and unspecialized diet.

OOLOGY The study of birds' eggs.

ORIENTAL REGION One of the six major zoogeographical regions, centred on India, the southern Himalayas, much of China and Malaysia.

PALEARCTIC REGION One of the six major zoogeographical regions, comprising the whole of Europe, Africa north of the Sahara, and arctic, boreal and temperate Asia north of the Himalayas.

PASSAGE MIGRANT Bird that passes through on migration,

mostly in autumn and spring, and does not remain for most of the winter or summer.

PASSERINE Bird belonging to the order Passeriformes, often referred to as the 'perching birds' and including the Oscines or 'songbirds'.

PELAGIC Of the open sea.

PELECANIFORMES The order including the pelicans, frigate-birds, darters, cormorants, gannets and tropicbirds.

pH Expression of the hydrogen ion concentration of a solution, giving an indication of alkalinity or acidity.

POLYANDROUS Referring to females of certain species which regularly mate with two or more males during a breeding season.

PRECOCIAL Active immediately after hatching.

PRIMARIES The 'flight' or longer wing feathers, generally numbered from the carpal joint outwards.

RACE Sub-species, indicating geographical variation within a species.

RAPTOR Bird-of-prey.

RATITE Species with a flat, raft-like sternum (i.e. without a 'keeled' breastbone), especially characteristic of the large, flightless, running birds such as the ostrich.

RESIDENT Species remaining throughout the year in a specified area.

RICTAL Of the gape, or sides of the mouth, generally referring to bristles in that area.

SECONDARIES The shorter, main flight feathers on the 'forearm' or inner wing, generally numbered inwards from the carpal joint.

SEDENTARY Describing a species which is non-migratory.

SPECIES A 'kind' or type of bird, comprising groups of interbreeding natural populations which are reproductively isolated from other such groups.

STOOP Steep descent of bird-of-prey on its quarry from a greater height, or 'dive-bombing' attack of any bird.

SUB-SPECIES see RACE

TIERCEL Male falcon.

TORPIDITY Dormant state with lowered body temperature and reduced metabolism, which enables a species to conserve energy, for periods varying from a single night to several months in a state akin to the hibernation of mammals.

VAGRANT A wanderer outside the normal migration range, usually blown off course by adverse winds.

ZOOGEOGRAPHY Zoology dealing with local distribution of animals or birds.

Acknowledgements

A very large number of people have helped me with provision of information for this book, a considerable amount of which has not been published before. In particular I would like to thank the following: the American Birding Association; the American Racing Pigeon Union; J. A. Bartle, National Museum of New Zealand; Professor Julian Baumel, Creighton University, Nebraska, USA; K. Becker, Food and Agricultural Organization, United Nations; Dr B. C. Bertram, Zoological Society of London; Dr T. R. Birkhead, University of Sheffield; Brian Bell, New Zealand Wildlife Service; Sue Butcher, British Ornithologists' Union; Bryan Bland; staff of the British Library; Professor W. A. Calder III, University of Arizona, USA; Dr Kenneth Campbell, Natural History Museum of Los Angeles County, USA; Richard Cassels, Manawatu Museum, New Zealand; *Cage & Aviary Birds* magazine; Francis Carline, Radcliff Science Library, Oxford; Dr Sankar Chatterjee, Texas Tech University, USA; Professor Charles Collins; Norman Chesterfield, Ontario, Canada; G. S. Cowles, British Museum (Natural History); Alan Crook, The Budgerigar Society; J. P. Croxall, British Antarctic Survey; J. C. Daniel, Bombay Natural History Society, India; S. Day, MAFF; Ian Dawson, librarian, RSPB; Joe Dowhan, Condor Research Center, California, USA; Megan Durham, US Fish and Wildlife Service, Washington, USA; Dr Clive Elliott, FAO; Lee Evans; Dr C. J. Feare, MAFF; Jim Flegg; Professor Alan Feduccia, University of North Carolina; staff of the Game Conservancy, Fordingbridge, Hants; Steve Gantlett; L. W. Goodman, Nitrovit Ltd; Dr John Harradine, British Association for Shooting and Conservation; Michael Harrison, US Federal Aviation Administration; C. M. Hann, MAFF; The Venerable Peter Hartley; Kenneth Hince, booksellers, Australia; Mrs Anne Hollowell, Bristol Museum and Art Gallery; Keith Howman, World Pheasant Association; Robert Hudson, British Trust for Ornithology; the International Council for Bird Preservation; Frances

James, president, American Ornithologists' Union; Dr James Jensen, Brigham Young University, Utah, USA; Dr Peter Jones, Dept of Forestry and Natural Resources, University of Edinburgh; Johnny Karlsson, Sweden; J. Kennett, MAFF; Dr V. M. Konstantinov and H. Aksyonova, Zoology Dept, Moscow State Pedagogical Institute, USSR; Lloyd Kiff, Western Foundation of Vertebrate Zoology, Los Angeles, USA; Dr Roxie Laybourne, Division of Law Enforcement, Fish and Wildlife Service, Washington, USA; Marianne Law, Christie's of London; Dr Kim Lowe, Australian Bird and Bat Banding Scheme; I. H. J. Lyster, Royal Museum of Scotland; Dr Larry Martin, University of Kansas, USA; Dr Graham Martin, Birmingham University; Dr Yvon le Maho, Centre National de la Recherche Scientifique, France; Dr Calum Mackenzie, Tristan da Cunha; B. A. Mayle, Forestry Commission; Stephen Marchant, Moruya, Australia; Professor Miles Markus, University of the Witwatersrand, Johannesburg, South Africa; Martin McNicholl, Long Point Bird Observatory, Ontario, Canada; Chris Mead, British Trust for Ornithology; P. Mongelard, MAFF; Dr Norman Moore; Marvin Moriarty, Office of Endangered Species, US Fish and Wildlife Service; Guy Mountfort; the National Trust; National Audubon Society, New York, USA; National Wildlife Federation, Washington; C. J. Nixon, Forestry Commission; Norfolk Naturalists' Trust; P. J. Olney, Zoological Society of London; Felix Ons, Federation Colombiphile Internationale, Brussels, Belgium; Dr Raymond O'Connor, British Trust for Ornithology; A. W. Owadally, Conservator of Forests, Mauritius; Rick Osman, editor, *The Racing Pigeon;* Ted Parker, Louisiana State University; Dr C. M. Perrins, Edward Grey Institute, Oxford; Dr G. R. Potts, the Game Conservancy; *Poultry World;* John Prior, National Council of Aviculture; Richard Porter, RSPB; Thane Pratt, US Fish and Wildlife Service, Hawaii, USA; Jerry Raffats, US Dept of Agriculture; John F. Reynolds, Rastrick Grammar School; Dr Pat Rich, Monash University, Victoria, Australia; Dr William B. Robertson, Everglades National Park, Florida, USA; Peter Robinson, RSPB; E.V. Rogers, Forestry Commission; Sotheby's of London; Dr J. T. R. Sharrock, Managing Editor, *British Birds;* Dr Lester Short, American Museum of Natural History; Ann Scott, RSPB; Koichiro Sonobe, Wild Bird Society of Japan; William Shake, US Fish and Wildlife Service, Oregon, USA; Robert Spencer, Rare Birds Breeding Panel; Sue Steptoe, RSPB; H. K. Swann, Wheldon & Wesley Ltd; John Thorpe, Civil Aviation Authority; Dr Eduardo Tonni, Facultad de Ciencias Naturales y Museo La Plata, Argentina; David Tomlinson, *Country Life;* Sq Ldr C. J. Turner, Ministry of Defence, London; Dr Steve Tullett, West of Scotland Agricultural College; James Vardaman, USA; Dr John Warham, University of Canterbury, Christchurch, New Zealand; Dr Cyril Walker, British Museum (Natural History); Michael Walters, British Museum (Natural History); Steve Webb; Dr H. Weimerskirch, Centre National de la Recherche Scientifique, France; Timothy Will, BASH team, United States Air Force; P. Wood, Forestry Commission; Professor D. G. M. Wood-Gush, Edinburgh School of Agriculture; R. Wright, National Pigeon Association; Dr V. C. Wynne-Edwards, University of Aberdeen.

In addition my very special thanks go to Miss Honor Head, editor, Guinness Books, and to my family and office colleagues for putting up with my preoccupation while work was underway.

Index
Page numbers in italics refer to illustrations. C equals a photograph in the colour section.

Abundant species, the most 63–67
Acid rain 135–136
Aepyornis maximus 10–11, 14–16, 178
Aerial, most 116–118
Agricultural pests, the worst 180–182
Aircraft loss/damage to birds 179–180, *179*
Albatrosses 97–98, 150, 152, 157–158
  black-browed *46–47*
  grey-headed 46
  laysan 130
  royal 128–130, *129*, 153, 157, 158
  sooty 111
  wandering 80, *82*, 82–83, 130, 152–153. 157, *158*, 158
  yellow-nosed 130
American Birding Association 183
American Museum of Natural History 176
Anis 149, 153
Antarctic, the 22
Appetites, greatest 163–164
Archaeopteryx 6, 6–8
Argentavis magnificens *13*, 12–14, 79
Aristotle 170
Assemblies, the largest 76
Audubon, J. J. L. 16, 172–173, 174
Audubon Society 175
Auk, great 86, *177*, 178; little 64
Auklet, rhinoceros 142
Avifauna, the poorest 22; the richest 22
Avium Praecipuarum Historia 170
Avocet 87

Basham, Benton 184, 186
Beaman, Mark 187
Bee-eaters 88
Bellbirds 94
Bills *90*; longest 89–90; shortest 90; sideways-curving 90
Bird-of-prey, rarest 35, 56–59
Bird, most expensive 169
Bird-protection organizations, largest 176
Birds, characteristics of 77
Birds of Great Britain 173–174
Birds, total number of 19–22
Birdwatchers 45
Bird-spotters, champion 183–187
Bittern, Eurasian 132–133
Bittern, sun 127
Blackbird 20, 66, *67*, 130, 150
Blackbird, red-winged 65, 76, 130, 181
Blakeney Point 175
Bland, Bob 187
Bland, Bryan *185*, 187
Blood-drinking *c* 161
Boobies 115, 125, 126
Booby, masked, blue-faced or white 115, 119, 151, 161
Book of Faulconrie or Hawking 171
Books on birds, earliest 170–171; most expensive C, 172–174
Brambling *50*, 51, 76
Brazil 22
Breeding maturity, fastest to 158; slowest to 158
Breeding, most northerly 75–76; most southerly 75
Breeding species, county with most 22
Brent geese 23
Breydon Water 175
British Museum of Natural History 176
British sighting, longest period

without 46–47
Brush turkeys 138
Buch der Natur 170
Budgerigar C, 76, 125, 167, 169
Bunting, cirl 157
  corn *157*, 157
  Lapland 51–52, *52*
  snow 76, 125
  yellow 157
Bushtits 153
Bustards 98, 171
  great 45, *78*, *79*, 78–79, 80
  kori 79
Buzzard, rough-legged 102

Cachalote, brown 142
  white-throated 142
Cage and aviary birds 165–169; largest 166; most abundant 167–168; most expensive 169; most talkative 168–169
Cahow 27
Canadian Wildlife Federation 176
Canaries 167
Cape Canaveral 29
Cape Sable 175
Caracaras 69; common 131
Carib, purple-throated 123
Cassowaries 92
Chaffinch 51, 66
Chesterfield, Norman *184*, 184
Cheyne Court 175
Chicken, domestic 147, 166–167
  prairie 136
Chough, alpine or yellow-billed 107
Cley Marshes 175
Clutches, largest 148–150; most in a year 150–151
Cockatiels 168
Cockatoos 168
Cockatoo, greater sulphur-crested *131*, 131
Cold, greatest survivors of 119–122
Collisions with building and wires 135
Colombia 22
Colonies, largest 76
Common Bird Census 22
Condors 102
  Andean 40, 83–84, *84*, 131
  California 37–40, *38*, *39*, 136
Coot 136
Corcoran, Tommy 187
Cormorants 67, 115, 125, 152, 163
County lists, record 187
Courser, Jerdon's or double-banded 32–34, *33*
Cowbirds 153, 180
  brown-headed 34, 152
  bay-winged 152
  screaming 152
Crake, spotted 53–54, *54*
Cranes 98
  sandhill 136
  Siberian white 132
Crossbills 122
  parrot 48–50, 161
  Scottish 50, 161–162, *161*
  white-winged 161
Crows 67, 127, 159, 163, 179
Crow, carrion 179
Cuckoos 149, 151, 153
  black-billed 155
  European 92, 132, 151, 152
  'the first' 132
Curlew, bristle-thighed 112
  eskimo 31–32
  Eurasian 89–90
  long-billed 90

Day list record holders 186–187
De Animalibus 170
De Arta Venandi Cum Avibus 171

Deaths, bird, chief causes of 133–136
  sooty 69
De Sermonum Proprietate Seu De Universo 170
Destruction of birds, natural and unnatural, greatest 133–136
Dialogue de Avibus 171
Diatryma steini 12
Diet, largest items swallowed 163; most specialized 159; most wide-ranging 163; most extraordinary 77–78
Dikkop or water thick-knee 143
Dinornis maximus 10, *11*
Dipper 136
Diver, great northern 115
Divers (loons) 113
Dives, deepest 113–116; longest 113–115
DNA-hybridization 24
Dodo 35
Domesticated birds 165–167, 169; largest 166; longest-lived 166; most abundant 166; earliest 165–166
Dotterel 107
Doves 151
  collared *71*, 71–73, 132
  mourning 126, 182
  rock 165–166
Dromornis stirtoni 8–10, *9*
Drought and bird deaths 136
Ducks 136, 149, 154, 182
  canvasback 135
  eider 100, 130, *134*, 164
  long-tailed 134
  muscovy 150
  oldsquaw 115
Ducks Unlimited 176
Dungeness 175

Eagles 163
  African crowned 158
  bald 84, 94, 128, *137*, 137–138
  fish 84
  golden 58–59, *59*, 84, 128, 130, 138, 178
  harpy 128
  Madagascar fish 37
  Madagascar serpent 37
  Pallas's sea 128
  Steller's sea 128
  Verreaux's 142
  wedge-tailed 93
  white-bellied sea 138
  white-tailed sea 45, 59–60, 84, 128, 154
Earliest birds 6–8
Eaten birds, most 182–183
Eastwood 175
Egg and specimen collections, largest 176–177
Egg colour 152
Egg-laying, fastest and slowest 151
Eggs, the largest 14–16, *15*, 145–147, *145*; most expensive 178; most laid in a year 150–151, 167; most variably coloured 151–152; smallest 147–148
Egret, cattle 72–73, 73
Elephant bird 10–11, 14–16
Elopteryx 96
Emu 92, 147
Enaliornis 8
Endemism 22–23
Evans, Lee 186
Everglades National Park 175
Eyesight, keenest 92–94
Expensive bird, most 169

Falcons 67, 69
  peregrine 67, 99–101, *100*, 119, 130
  Philippine 69
  pygmy 140

red-footed 183
  sooty 69
Family, the largest 26
Fanshawe, John 186
Farmland 23
Farne Islands 175
Fast, the longest 164
Fastest-flying 99–101
Fastest-running 107–109
Fastest-swimming 113
Feared birds, most 179
Feathers, longest 91; the least 94; the most 94
Feeding 159–164; most bizarre 161; most remarkable 162–163; most specialized 159–162
Fieldfare 51
Finch, sharp-beaked ground C, 161
Finches 122, 156
  purple 122
  gouldian 133
  woodpecker 127
  zebra 150
Firecrest 85–86
Firewood gatherer 142
Fishing and bird deaths 135
Flamingos 96
  greater 87
  lesser C, 76
Fledging, quickest 156–157; slowest 157–158
Fledglings, most in a year 150–151
Flicker, common 150
Flightless bird, smallest 14, 86
Flycatchers 93
  fork-tailed 92
  pied 164
  tyrant 26
Flying birds, heaviest 12–14; largest 78–81
Forests, tropical 22
Fossil birds 5
Frederick II, Emperor 171
Frigate-birds 96
Frost and bird deaths 136
Fulmar, Antarctic 22

Gallornis 96
Gamebirds 149, 154
Gannet, northern 74, 76, 115, 126, *135*, 154
Gastornis klaasseni 12
Gätke, Heinrich 175
Geese 151, 166, *171*, 182
G force, greatest 118–119
Gigantornis eaglesomei 14
Goldcrest C 85–86, *86*, 130, 144, 148
Goldfinch 122
Goose, African pygmy 142
  bar-headed 105–106
  bean 136
  brent 136
  Canada 136, 182
  Egyptian or Nile 142, 165
  greylag 136, 165
  pink-footed 136
Gould, John 173–174
Grackle, common 181
  great-tailed 152
Grasswren, black 27
  carpentarian 27
  Eyrean 27
  gray 27
  white-throated 27
Grebes 67, 97, 136
  giant 26
  great crested *74*, 74
  western 116
Grosbeak, black-headed 161
Grouse 136
  blue or dusky 112
  red 112
  ruffed 163

Guillemot, Brünnich's 135, 152
  common C, 115, 151–152
Gulls 20, 127, 153, 163, 180
  black-headed 56, 73, 180
  herring 73, 103, 132
  ivory *75*, 75–76
  lesser black-backed 73
  Mediterranean 55–56, *56*
  Ross's 179
Gyrfalcon 47–48, *49*, 69

Habitats, the richest 22–24
Harriers 67
  Montagu's *57*, 56–58
Hastings, Rupert 187
Hatching, adaptations for 155–156; fastest and slowest 155–156
Hawaii 5, 71
Hawfinch 155, 162, *163*
Hawks 93, 136
Heard, Chris 185
Hearing, most sensitive 94–96
Heat, greatest endurance of 125–126
Heaviest birds 8–11, 77–81
Heligoland 175
Henderson, Andrew 187
Herons 67, 171
  green or striated C, 126–127
Hesperornis 115
Hibernation, most remarkable 122–123
Highest-flying birds 103–107
Highest-living 107
Hillstars 143
Historia Animalium 170
Hoatzin C, 96
Holman, Dave 187
Hondecoeter, Melchior 174
Honeyeaters 30–31
Honeyguides 98
  black-throated 98
  scaly-throated 98
Hornbills 89
Hummingbirds 85, 92, *102*, 102–103, 122–123, 147–148, 164
  Anna's 85
  bee 84–85, 143, 147–148
  Costa's 148
  giant 85
  hermit 143
  ruby-throated C, 94, 102, 112
  rufous 102
  sword-billed C, 89
  vervain 143, 148
Hunted birds, most 182–183

Ibis, Japanese crested *43*, 43–44
Incubation, longest 152–155; shortest 155
Incredibilis 12
Intelligence, greatest 126–127
Introduced species, the most widespread 69–71; country with the most 71

Jacanas 88
  African C, *89*
  northern 88
  pheasant-tailed 88
  smaller 88
Jackdaw 168
Jay 168
Johns, Ron 185–186, *185*
Jungle fowls 165

Kaestner, Peter G. 184
Kakapo 44
Kauai O-o-aa 30
Keeping warm, world champion at 119–122
Kent 187
Kestrel, American 93
  common 35, 69, 102, 159
  grey 142
  Mauritius 35–37, *36*, 69
  Seychelles 37

Kingfishers 88, 171
  common 113
  lesser pied 127
  mangrove 113
Kinglets 143
Kite, black 180
  Everglade (snail) 159–160
  letter-winged 127
  red 62, 62–63, 92
Kiwis 84, 92, 97, 97–98
  brown 147, 152–153
  little spotted 147
Knot III

Lammergeier 160, 160–161
Lancebills 143
Landbird family, most
  widespread 69
Lapwing 105, 180
Larks 125
  gray's 125
  Mongolian 167
Lasley, Greg 187
Lead poisoning 39, 135
Legs, the longest 87–88; the
  shortest 88
Leicestershire 23
Lifelist record holders 183–186
Listers, champion 183–187
London 187
Longest-lived birds 128–132
Loons 113, 180
Lothura haitinensis 26
Lovebirds 168
Lowest-living 107

Macaws 168
  blue-headed 168
  blue and yellow 166
  hyacinth 166*, 168, 169
  military 166
  red-fronted 168
  scarlet 166, 168
Mallard III, 130, 135, 136, 150,
  165, 182
Mallee fowl 138–140, 139
Magnus, Albertus 170
Magpies 20, 92, 179
Maurus, Rabanus 170
Martins 76, 180
Mears, Nigel 187
Megapodes 138–140, 152–153,
  156
Megenburg, C. von 170
Merritt, Lake 175
Metal-tails 143
Migration, longest 110–112;
  shortest 112–113
Milford, Peter 187
Millington, Richard 187
Mimic, greatest 132
Moas 163
Moorhen 151, 173
Mousebirds 92, 122
Mudflats 23
Murrelet, Kittlitz's 143
  marbled 143
Mynahs 142
  Bali 168
  hill or talking 168

National Trust 175
National Wildlife Federation 176
Neotropical Region 22
Nest burrow, longest 142
Nests, highest in trees 143;
  largest 137–142; smallest
  143–144; most valuable
  144–145
Nest-sites, strangest 143
New Zealand 71
Nightjars 67, 90, 98, 122–123,
  164
  pennant-winged 91–92, 92
  red-necked 47
Noddies 117
Norfolk 187
North Kent Marshes 23
North-South range, greatest
  74–75
Nuclear threat 135
Numerous bird, most 16–18,
  63–64

Observatories, earliest 174
Oilbird 94, 98
Oil pollution 134–135
Oldest birds 128–132
Onagadori 91
O-o-aa, Kauai C, 30
Oo, Bishop's 31
Order, the largest 24
Organizations for bird
  protection, largest 176
Oriole, black-headed 161
  golden 183
Ornithology of Francis Willughby,
  171
Osprey 61, 61–62, 67, 130, 138
Ostrich 77–78, 107–108, 108,
  108–109, 126, 145, 145–146,
  147, 149–150, 163, 166
Ovenbirds 142, 142
Owls 93, 96, 151, 179
  barn 67, 95, 101, 142, 187
  great grey 95
  long-eared 95, 130
  snowy C, 60–61
Oystercatcher, 130, 162–163
  Chatham Island 42

Paintings of birds, earliest
  171–172; most expensive
  174
Palaeolodus 96
Paleopteryx thomsoni 7–8
Parakeet, Carolina C, 35
  echo C, 34–35
  monk 140
Parascaniornis 96
Parker, Ted 186–187
Parrots 127, 168
  Amazona 168
  golden-shouldered 168
  grey 168
  hispaniolan 35
  Puerto Rican 35
  rarest 34–35
  owl 44
Partridge, grey 130, 148, 149, 150
  redlegged 150, 151
Passeriformes 24–25
Passerines 155; most widespread
  67–68
Peafowl, green 91
  Indian 91
Pearson, David 186
Pelican, 125, 152, 163
  Australian C, 89
Pelican Island 175
Penguins 12, 96, 113
  adélie C, 22, 76, 114
  chinstrap 22
  emperor C, 22, 113–115,
  119–122, 120, 147, 153, 164
Perching birds 24–25
Peru 186–187
Pesticides 134
Pests, greatest 179–182
Petrels 97–98, 154–155
  Antarctic 22, 75
  Bermuda 27
  black-capped 27, 46–47
  fulmar 64, 73, 130, 154
  Jamaica 47
  Leach's 98
  magenta 42
  pintado 22
  snow C, 22, 75
  southern giant 22
  Wilson's storm 22, 65
Pheasant, common or ring-
  necked 92, 109, 181, 182
  crested argus 91
  Reeves' 91
Phoenix fowl 91
Pigeons 67, 98, 142, 151, 180
  cape 22
  Chatham Island 42
  imperial 163
  passenger 17, 16–18
  pink 40–41
  plain 41
  racing 101, 168, 169
Pigeon, rarest 40–41; feral 150;

most expensive 169
Pipits 67
Plover, American or lesser
  golden 112
  Kentish 67
  wrybill 90
Plotopterids 12
Pochard 111
Poorwill 122–123, 164
Potoos 94
Primitive, the most 96–97
Prion, Antarctic 22
Protoavis 7–8
Ptarmigan C, 76, 112, 123–125,
  124, 157
Puffins 116
Pygmy-tyrant, short-tailed 26

Quails 158
  bobwhite 148, 150
  common 158
Quelea, red-billed 63–64, 64–65,
  76, 180–181
Quetzal, resplendent 92

Race, the rarest 27–29
Rails 67
  Guam 42
  Inaccessible Island 86
Range extensions, most
  dynamic 71–74
Rarest birds in the world 26–44
Rarest birds in Britain 44–63
Raven 179
Ray, John 171
Razorbill 115, 135, 155
Redhead 149
Redpoll 125, 155
Rediscovery, longest interval to
  27
Redwing 51
Reserves, earliest 174–175
Rheas 92
Road deaths 133–134
Roadrunner, greater 108–109,
  109
Roberts, Andy 186
Robin, American 95
  Chatham Island 41, 42
  European 66, 130, 153
Robinson, Scott 186–187
Rook 103, 130
Roosts, the largest 76
Root, Alan 186
Rosefinch, scarlet 50–51
Rositten 175
Royal Society for the Protection
  of Birds 175, 176
Ruff 111
Running, fastest 107–109
Rutland Water 23

Sandgrouse, namaqua 125
Sandpiper, purple 51
  wood 51
Sapsuckers 161
Scolt Head 175
Scrub 23
Scrub fowl, common 138
Seabirds 135
Seabird, Britain's rarest 55–56
Secretary bird 88
Serin 53, 53, 167
Shearwaters 97–98, 135, 153
  manx 112, 131, 154
  short-tailed 111, 182
Sheathbill, black-faced 22
  snowy 22
Shorelark 52, 69
Shrike, red-backed 54, 54–55
  San Clemente loggerhead 43
Siskin, pine 122
Skimmer, African 125
Skokholm 175
Skua, Antarctic 22
  McCormick's or south polar
  74–75
Skylark 68, 68–69
Slowest-flying 101–102
Smallest birds 84–86
Smell, most acute sense of 97–98
Smith, Peter 187

Social breeding 140
Song, most far-carrying 132–133;
  most remarkable 133
Songbirds 151
Songster, most energetic 133
Sorenson, Jeremy 187
South America 22
Sparrow, Scott's seaside 29
  dusky seaside 27–29, 28
  house 64, 66, 69–70, 70, 94,
  107, 130, 150
Spatuletail, marvellous 92
Species, number of 5, 19; rarest
  29–44
Spinetail, rufous-breasted 142
Starling, common C, 64, 66,
  70–71, 76, 105, 130, 181
  Rothschild's 168
Stephen's Island wren 14, 15
Stevenson, Terry 186
Stilt, black-winged 87, 87
Stint, red-necked 186
  Temminck's 52, 53
Stodmarsh 23
Stokes, Stuart 183–184, 186
Storks 89
  hammerhead (hammerkop)
  140–142, 141
  marabou 83–84
  wood 89
Storm petrels 153
Stuffed bird, most expensive 178
Swallow, European or barn
  67–68, 76, 92, 123, 180
Swans 79
  Bewick's 81, 131
  mute 79–81, 80, 81, 84, 130,
  146, 158
  trumpeter 79
  whistling 94, 94, 180
  whooper 81, 105, 106, 107, 133
Swifts 88, 90
  African palm 144
  alpine 99
  Asian palm 144
  European or common 99,
  117–118, 122–123, 130, 180
  pygmy palm 144
  white-throated, spine-tailed
  99
Swiftlet, cave C, 94, 144–145
  edible-nest 144
  glossy 90
  grey-rumped 144
Swimming, largest 12
  fastest 113

Taiko, Chatham Island 27, 42
Tail feathers, longest and largest
  91–92
Takahe C, 27
Talkative, most 168–169
Tallest birds, 10, 77–78
Tanzania 23
Taylor, Don 187
Teal, green-winged 182
Temperatures, low, survival of
  119–125
Terns 130, 153
  arctic 110, 110–111, 130
  common 11
  fairy 126, 143
  sooty C, 76, 116, 116–117
Thick-knee, water (dikkop) 143
Thorburn, Archibald 174
Thornbird, rufous-throated 142
Thrasher, brown 133
  pearly-eyed 35
Thrushes 67
Thrush, laughing 167
  song 66
Tits 127, 152, 159, 164
  bearded 157
  blue 66, 148
  great 164
  long-tailed 92, 144, 148
Tody-tyrant, cinnamon-breasted
  26
Toes, longest 88–89
Toki 43–44
Tomlinson, David 187

Toucans 89
Torotix 96
Torpidity 122–123
Tragopan, Cabot's 156
  satyr 156
  Temminck's 156
Travellers, remarkable 111–112
Trogons 94
  violaceous 143
Tropicbird, white-tailed 27
Turbevile, George 171
Turkeys 79–80, 109, 151, 166,
  167; heaviest and most
  expensive 169–170
Turner, Don 186
Turner, William 170–171
Turnstone 111
Twitchers, champion 183–187

Urwin, Bill 187

'Vampire finch' 161
Vardaman, James 186, 187
Vireo, red-eyed 133
Vultures 102, 103, 180
  Egyptian 127, 146
  griffon 171
  lappet-faced 105
  Rüppell's griffon 103–105, 104
  turkey 98, 126
  white-headed 105

Waders 130
  rarest 31
Wagtail, grey 92
Warblers 11, 156
  Aldabran brush 34
  Bachman's 34
  Kirtland's 34
  marsh 132, 133
  rarest 34
  reed 133
  willow 34, 67
Waterton, Charles 175
Waxbills 153
Waxwing 164
Webbe, Steve 186
Weather and bird deaths 136
Weavers 142
Weaver, sociable 140, 141
Weights, greatest carried
  127–128
Western Foundation of
  Vertebrate Zoology
  176–177
Whitethroat, lesser 155
Wheatears 125
Wicken Fen 175
Widespread species, most 67–71
Wigeon 23, 182
Wingbeats, fastest and slowest
  102–103
Wingspan, greatest 13, 12–14,
  79, 82–84
Willughby, Francis 171
Wilson, Alexander 16
Woodcock, American 101–102
Woodland, deciduous 23
Woodpeckers 118
  acorn 153
  black 119
  great-spotted 155
  imperial 30
  ivory-billed C, 29–30
  Lewis's 143
  pileated 30
  red-headed C, 118
Woodpigeon 101, 103, 130,
  181–182
Woodstar, amethyst 102
World Wildlife Fund 176
Wren, common or winter 65–66,
  85, 130, 133, 144, 164
  St Kilda 26
Wryneck 55, 55, 150
Wyleyia, valdenis 8

Year list record holders 186
Yellowstone National Park 175

Zoogeographical regions 20–21